I0887511

THEATER
IN THE
AMERICAS

A Series from
Southern
Illinois
University
Press
ROBERT A.
SCHANKE
Series Editor

CUBA INSIDE OUT

REVOLUTION AND CONTEMPORARY THEATRE

YAEL PRIZANT

Southern Illinois University Press / *Carbondale*

Copyright © 2014 by the Board of Trustees,
Southern Illinois University
All rights reserved
Printed in the United States of America

17 16 15 14 4 3 2 1

Library of Congress Cataloging-in-Publication Data
Prizant, Yael.
Cuba inside out : revolution and contemporary theatre / Yael Prizant.
pages cm. — (Theater in the Americas)
Includes bibliographical references and index.
ISBN 978-0-8093-3308-0 (paperback)
ISBN 0-8093-3308-2 (paperback)
ISBN 978-0-8093-3309-7 (ebook)
1. Theater—Cuba—History—20th century. 2. Theater—Cuba—History—21st century. I. Title.
PN2401.P75 2014
792.097291—dc23 2013016142

Printed on recycled paper. ♻
The paper used in this publication meets the minimum requirements of American National Standard for Information Sciences—Permanence of Paper for Printed Library Materials, ANSI Z39.48-1992. ∞

To my grandparents
my parents
and my siblings

with enduring love

Contents

Acknowledgments

When I began this journey over ten years ago, I could never have imagined just how many minds and hearts would influence this book.

Most recently, I am grateful for the support I have received from the University of Notre Dame. The Kellogg Institute for International Studies generously funded my research and documentation in Cuba, and the Institute for Latino Studies continually supported my work on campus. Agustin Fuentes, Thomas Merluzzi, Kenneth Garcia, and Patricia Base at the Institute for Scholarship in the Liberal Arts, College of Arts and Letters, University of Notre Dame, kindly funded conferences, exhibitions, and community projects related to this study. They are wholly responsible for the inclusion of the stunning photographs by Christopher Stackowicz that appear in this book, a gift I am extremely fortunate to share. Special thanks are also due to Benedict Giamo and Robin Rhodes for their mentorship and publication recommendations. My unending gratitude goes to Jill Godmilow, Harry Karahalios, Lara Arielle Phillips, and Jason Ruiz for their honesty, advice, and devoted friendship throughout this process. I am also fortunate to have the camaraderie of my colleagues in the Department of Film, Television, and Theatre. It is a pleasure working with you and learning from you.

Before heading to the Midwest, I was warmly mentored in Southern California and Massachusetts. I received indefatigable encouragement and vital dissertation input from S. I. Salamensky (UCLA) and Leo Cabranes Grant (UCSB), who nurtured me, and this project, at every turn. Generous, timely grants came from Maddie Katz, Elaine Krown Klein, and the UCLA affiliates. I must also thank Gary Gardner, Michael Hackett, and Patricia Harter for their personal involvement in my success. I would be remiss if I did not recognize the great care taken by Harley Erdman, Ellen Kaplan, William Davies King, and Virginia Scott to inspire me and embolden me to further this research. I also owe an unending debt of gratitude to two other mentors, the late Robert Egan and the late Bert States, whose inspiration I will never forget.

This project would not have existed without the aid of many benevolent Cubans. Cuban theatre scholar Rosa Ileana Boudet had a major impact on this book. I am eternally grateful for her loving acceptance, stellar advice, and the considerable time she spent with me reflecting on Cuba and its theatre. Her continued assistance, warmth, and honesty kept this work nimble and achievable. My visits to the island were made exceedingly joyous, comfortable, and productive because of the affectionate care of friends like Sinecio Diaz, Rusbelt Rosales Fajardo, Lillian Manzor, Rosario Mora, and Andres Antonio Jimenez Rodriguez and his family. No one has earned more of my respect and love than *mi tio*, Alfredo Rodriguez. He and everyone connected to his household—Andrea, Mayrelis, Nelson, Caridad, Vivian, and Nena—fueled my passion for this work every day. Thank you all for your indispensable support and for making Calle 25 my extraordinary home on the island.

I am also incredibly grateful for theatre artists Flora Lauten, Raquel Carrió, Miguel Terry, Nilo Cruz, and Julio Cesar Ramirez, whose work I have had the pleasure of examining. Rogelio Martinez was particularly obliging as well, meeting with me in New York and engaging in lengthy email discussions. I am eternally indebted to Nara Mansur for initially inspiring this project and for entrusting me with her friendship and her work, both of which made a great portion of this book possible.

On a more personal note, I owe the completion of this book to my collaborator, Christopher Stackowicz. This publication would not have existed without his vision when I had lost my way. I deeply appreciate his understanding, creativity, patience, and friendship. Special thanks to my loving sister, Ayelet Prizant, whose diligent editorial eye and generosity of spirit made this text shine. Many thanks to my closest friends, like Karl Anderson, Josh Diamond, Rayna Hickman, Deb Kaplan Jacoby, James Kerby, and Emily Sandock, who brought me joy and companionship when I needed it most. I'd also like to extend my deepest gratitude to Natalija Nogulich and Anne García-Romero for their attentive input and genuine encouragement throughout this entire process. Everyone at my artistic home, Langlab South Bend, has earned my esteem for arousing my creativity, for giving me opportunities, and for making me look good—you feed the fire. I especially want to acknowledge Rami Sadek for his loyal comradeship, perpetual positivity, good humor, timely reassurances, and gentle care. I must also thank my fellow *peregrinos* Matthew Grattidge and Maurizio Cortesi for always walking beside me, and my immeasurably beloved Thiago Formolo Dalla Vecchia for expanding my view of the world so that I could imagine this book.

1
Overture

Cuba and the Evolution of Revolution

In 1968, celebrated Cuban playwright Antón Arrufat won the José Antonio Ramos prize—the country's top award for drama—for his play *Siete contra Tebas* (Seven against Thebes). Highly lauded by UNEAC, the Unión Nacional de Escritores y Artistas en Cuba (Cuban National Union of Writers and Artists), Arrufat's adaptation of Aeschylus's drama garnered substantial literary acclaim. UNEAC published the text, as was customary for that organization. Yet before the play could be staged, it was effectively censored—so harshly that nearly forty years passed before it was performed on the island. Several voting members of UNEAC claimed the depictions in the play were "too alienated for the aims of our revolution"[1] and insisted the play's contradictory ideas were overlooked when it was selected to receive the award. A preface was added to the publication, condemning the play as counterrevolutionary, and its circulation was banned.[2] Arrufat and his work were blacklisted; he would not resurface in theatre and literary circles again until the 1980s.

Siete contra Tebas is a dialogue-based (rather than action-based) play that describes the fratricidal fight for power between Eteocles and Polynices, cursed sons of Oedipus. The characters explain that, although Eteocles agreed to share power with his brother Polynices by ruling in alternate years, he refuses to step down after his year at the helm. Hence, Polynices has raised an army, with Argive captains prepared to attack the city from each of its seven gates. When Polynices reveals that he will act as commander before the seventh gate, Eteocles resolves to face his brother there to fight him in person. Eteocles and Polynices kill one another in battle, as the brutal conflict decimates both armies and destroys their beloved Thebes.

Arrufat's version could have been interpreted as a dangerous political critique due to the nature of the play's conflicts—between individuals and the state (capitalism and communism), between outsiders and insiders (exiles and nationals), and between two disagreeing brothers intent on governing (Fidel and Raúl Castro).[3] Finally republished on the island in 2001, the play

Most documentation in this book is contained in endnotes, but where some works are discussed or quoted extensively, page numbers from the source are given in parentheses.

featured a new foreword emphasizing the controversy around the original edition. When theatre director Alberto Sarraín and the Mefisto theatre company finally mounted *Siete contra Tebas* in Havana in the fall of 2007, Cuban newspaper *Juventud Rebelde* noted that the production of the mythic text settled "an old debt."[4]

Arrufat suffered terribly for misinterpreting his moment, for misconstruing the "aims" of the Cuban Revolution and how Cuban artists might work to support them. Fidel Castro iterated Cuba's policy for the arts in 1961: "Within the Revolution, everything; against the Revolution, nothing."[5] This vague, evolving dictate raises key questions about the definition of *revolution* and its boundaries: Is political revolution implied? Social? Artistic? All of these? Is revolution a single event or ongoing? Local and/or global? Could its transformations be destructive as well as constructive? And, half a century after the previous government, what might the term "revolución" signify in Cuba now, in a post-Soviet world, for artists there and abroad? Is the idea applied as it was in other countries, such as France, Russia or Mexico, for instance? What about in other disciplines, such as science or industry? Is the idea still applied as it was in Cuba in 1959? In 1975? In 2000? In modern-day Tunisia or Egypt?

Neither Cuba nor revolution was my topic of study when I began my research in 1999. I was interested in playwrights who had written under censorship, specifically in the former Soviet bloc countries of Romania, Bulgaria, and Poland. I wanted to know how playwrights said what they wanted to say without actually saying it and how they used theatre to convey the messages in their texts. Sadly, my limited capacity with Eastern European languages was an insurmountable disadvantage, so I began looking for other contexts in which my ideas could apply.

Around this time, I started reading plays written by Cubans since the Revolution of 1959. The works were dynamic, startling, and complex. What I found was that I had to entirely reimagine my notions of how both revolution and state censorship function. On my first trip to Cuba in 2003, I was forced to reconsider much of what I had learned about the island; it is a highly nuanced and complicated place, where the obvious is muddled and change is constant. I have met and interviewed playwrights and directors, attended shows and rehearsals over the last ten years, been a guest for several international theatre festivals in Havana, and written for the *Havana Times*. Yet Cuba frequently defies explanation, even for me. Cuba's mythologized past, precarious present, and unclear future have always inspired more questions than answers, leading me to travel there at least every two years, often staying for months at a time.

Cuba and its theatre were intensely affected by the previously inconceivable collapse of the Soviet Union in 1989. Nearly overnight, the island lost the majority of its trade capacity. To combat this "acute recessive economic crisis,"[6] Cubans made enormous daily sacrifices, reduced product and fuel use wherever they could, and were forced to adhere to strict governmental usage limitations as vehemently as possible. Theatre artists had never faced such dire circumstances. Food and consumer goods were scarce, transportation had ground to a halt due to fuel shortages, and electricity was intermittent at best. Nevertheless, Cuba's playwrights were still writing new plays. This study focuses on courageous, innovative pieces created since Cuba's greatest economic disaster. In spite of tremendous hardships and often at personal peril, artists like Nara Mansur, Teatro Buendia, and Miguel Terry continued creating challenging, thoughtful theatre. Meanwhile, Cuban American playwrights such as Rogelio Martinez and Nilo Cruz reacted to the country's situation by depicting Cuba and its quandaries on stages in the United States. Cuban novelist and playwright Reinaldo Arenas dared to question his country's uncertain future, far beyond this major economic decline.

At its core, every one of these plays reconsiders the Cuban Revolution, which has profoundly affected people living on and off the island. The plays included here, all written or staged since 1986, illustrate just how much the meaning of the Revolution has continually evolved over the last five decades. In order to contextualize how Cuban artists and their society function today, we must study the *concept* of revolution in general, which has its own particular history, significance, and legacy, as well as specifically within Cuba. The second chapter of this book, "Staging Revolutions," investigates two plays that engage revolution directly. "Revolution under Siege," the third chapter, examines plays that depict the hardships of the Special Period as it is happening, while "Revolution from Afar" (chapter 4) discusses Cuban American plays that contemplate the meaning of revolution from beyond the island. The final chapter, "*Para Siempre*: Staging the Future," speculates about the future of Cuba and the continuation of its revolutionary ideals. All of the theatrical depictions of Cuba reflect the country's vast, complicated transformations within its revolution, at present and over time. The photo gallery is included to firmly locate the references made within the plays to contextualize the living conditions in urban Cuba that few tourists (and even fewer Americans) get to see. These photographs are not documentation of the plays or productions. Instead, they are intended to provide readers with information about the cultural milieu in Cuba's largest cities and depict some of the allusions made within the plays.

Heralding Revolution

The particular history of the island nation of Cuba incorporates many reasons for its revolution. With military aid from the United States, Cuba formally gained its independence from Spain in 1898, in what later became (revealingly) known as the "Spanish-American War," a conflict in which Cuba is no longer mentioned. After this third devastating war for independence, Cuba essentially substituted its ties to colonial Spain for a neocolonial relationship with the United States. At the conclusion of the war, the U.S. military occupied Cuba, with American forces remaining on the island until 1902. Despite Cuba's own substantial military contributions and the vast physical destruction the island endured while defeating Spain, Cuba was not allowed to have a representative at the Paris Conference that ended the conflict, "as its part in its own liberation was rendered invisible."[7]

The Platt Amendment, establishing the United States' ongoing right to intervene in Cuba to maintain a stable government, was drafted along with the Treaty of 1903. (It also granted the United States its now infamous military base at Guantanamo Bay.) The sheer scope of the North American presence on the island contributed greatly to the national construction of independent Cuba. Spanish colonial class structures (in which social mobility was hereditary) disintegrated and were replaced by American principles of mobility, based on acquiring wealth and power.

The economic ties between the United States and Cuba were as significant as the political ones. As historian Louis A. Pérez explains, "By 1909, more than 50 percent of Cuban imports originated from the United States,"[8] creating an ongoing relationship that hurled Cuba into modernity. Although factional struggles dominated the political scene on the island throughout the early 1900s, the financial relationships between Cuba and the United States were continually strengthened. One key example: by the 1930s, Cuban sugar accounted for 42 percent of the sugar imported by the United States.[9]

As in most of Latin America in the early twentieth century, volatile social protests were increasing in Cuba against poor working conditions and a lack of services. These protests were met with increasingly repressive measures by the postcolonial government of Gerardo Machado, dictator of Cuba in the early 1930s. Student leader Antonio Mella and the Communist Party he directed enjoyed a considerable following but were marginalized because they refused to merge with other anti-Machado forces. As historian Geraldine Lievesley notes, "Originally, Mella adopted a political programme which called for a broad, multi-class anti-imperialist struggle, but he subsequently moved to a Marxist perspective which stressed the importance of building a worker-peasant alliance which would focus upon destroying capitalism and building socialism."[10] This perspective laid the groundwork for midcentury Cuban politics. Though Mella was assassinated in Mexico in 1929, his socialist message had penetrated the Cuban psyche.

In 1933, a group of Cuban civil servants led by Fulgencio Batista seized power, and Ramón Grau San Martín was made president of the island. Although the Platt Amendment was abrogated in 1934, little changed in the daily interactions between Cubans and Americans. Grau San Martín's government lacked U.S. support and therefore could not survive Batista's coup that same year. Batista became the power behind the next several puppet presidents and, by 1940, he had won the presidency himself, securing nearly 60 percent of the popular vote and the backing of the United States.[11]

Corruption and struggles between political factions created intense governmental instability in Cuba throughout the 1940s. Eduardo Chibás and his ethically minded Partido Ortodoxo (Orthodox Party) won intensifying support under the administration of President Prío Socarras (1948–52) and it appeared certain that Chibás would win the next election. But he could not produce evidence to support his vehement campaign against governmental corruption, and immediately after a 1952 radio broadcast, Chibás committed suicide. His emotional repudiations of dishonesty swelled the nation's support for the Partido Ortodoxo in the upcoming election.

That election never came. Backed by the United States, Batista staged a military coup and again assumed the presidency in March 1952. Fidel Castro, a young lawyer influenced by both Chibás and Cuban poet and independence leader José Martí, petitioned against Batista's coup in Cuba's constitutional court. Castro's case was unsuccessful, but he remained actively anti-Batista, masterminding an attack on the Moncada army barracks at Santiago de Cuba on 26 July 1953. The disorganized Moncada operation failed, and those rebels who were not tortured and killed by Batista's soldiers were taken prisoner. However, this violent breach of existing law rallied Cuban peasants because it proved the rebels were serious. In a speech entitled "History Will Absolve Me," Castro defended himself in court by making bold accusations against the Batista government, leading to his imprisonment. Like the storming of the Bastille during the French Revolution, the 26 July Moncada rebellion took on far greater significance than its outcome. It named the movement (El movimiento 26 de julio) and became a powerful revolutionary symbol of defiance and courage.

Because Batista was well-connected, ran unopposed, and had the support of the United States, he was effortlessly reelected in 1954. Governmental repression by Batista's cohorts led to a period of ostensible calm on the island, a tranquility bolstered by U.S. investments and tourism. Casinos, nightclubs, hotels, and other tourist attractions flourished (according to Pérez, over one million U.S. citizens visited Batista's Cuba in the 1950s), but the gap between rich and poor Cubans grew exponentially. Moreover, brutal responses to general strikes, the exclusion of alternative political factions, and close ties to organized crime had tarnished Batista's support from Washington. In the hopes of repairing his reputation, Batista offered amnesty to the Moncada rebels in 1955. Fidel and Raúl Castro were released from prison and took refuge in Mexico.

The Theatrical Precedent

Cuba's dense political history is paralleled by its rich theatrical history. Before Spanish colonization of the island began in the last decade of the fifteenth century, the country's indigenous Taino population traditionally produced *areitos*, highly theatricalized rituals involving songs, dances, and mime. Due to the liminal elements within these pieces, the Spanish viewed them as subversive and prohibited them after 1512. Closely following models of Spanish dramaturgy, the first recorded Cuban plays were published in Spain in the 1730s.[12] Playwright Francisco Covarrubias, often called the father of Cuban theatre, courageously introduced nationalistic themes to the Cuban stage by the end of the century. His work established the character of the *negrito* (a foolish black boy played by a white man in blackface), who would appear onstage in various incantations for decades to come. Covarrubias also significantly influenced the romantic period of the early 1800s in Cuban theatre, during which playwrights like Heredia, Milanes, and Gomez de Avellaneda produced works that attempted to reconcile Spanish neoclassicism with individual rebellion while intentionally straying from the formulaic Spanish musical comedies (known as *zarzuelas*) that were popular at the time.[13]

Joaquin Lorenzo Luaces (1826–67)[14] penned the first Cuban plays that outwardly criticized colonialism and advocated a national identity, doing so by attacking foreign fashions, ideas, and norms. (In the Castro period, Luaces's work has often been revived and admired for its nationalistic and anti-imperialistic themes.) Satirical comedies known as *bufos habaneros* became popular in the 1860s because they used recognizable situations from everyday Cuban life to deride Spanish melodramas and zarzuelas. As Cuba became immersed in its struggle for independence, plays that supported national sovereignty grew ever popular, including several by José Martí himself. By the late 1880s, the buffoon-like *negrito* had evolved into a racialized dramatic hero who reaffirmed Cuban social identity and was a conscious alternative to white, slave-oriented traditions. *Diablitos* (little devils) appeared during this period as well; as generalized, allegorical representations of the many African cultures on the island, their performances were part of spiritual processionals, ceremonies, religious rituals, and initiations. These diablitos have remained part of Cuban folklore and are often performed at modern-day carnivals and festivals.[15]

By the time Cuba gained its independence from Spain in 1902, the Alhambra Theatre in Havana was the center of popular and high culture. The Alhambra cemented Cuba's popular music theatre tradition throughout the 1920s and 1930s, presenting works by artists like Lecuona, Roig, and Grenet. Owing to the Alhambra's popularity, proscenium theatres became exceedingly common throughout Havana and in other major urban centers on the island. However, when a combination of economic decline, neocolonial decay, and struggles under the Machado dictatorship plagued the republic in 1935, the Alhambra was closed. With this closure, the music theatre tradition in Cuba waned.

The increasing political turmoil on the island in the late 1930s was reflected in many other state-supported, but short-lived, theatrical ventures. The Teatro Cubano de Selección (Cuban Select Theatre) was created in 1938 as a vehicle for producing modern, prize-winning national plays. The group produced dramas with strong social messages while promoting theatrical experimentation. Recent exiles from Spain and Nazi-occupied Europe added their expertise to this burgeoning new Cuban theatre. In 1944, the Teatro Popular was formed under the direction of Paco Alfonso. Associated with the socialist workers' movement, the group performed socially committed dramas in public factories and open-air plazas, as well as in formal theatres. Funded by workers' unions, the collective published socialist pamphlets and magazines and staged the first Soviet plays produced in Cuba. Nonetheless, its existence was brief: anticommunist repression forced the group to shut down in 1945.[16]

The state's utter indifference to or unsympathetic view of the arts during the postwar years made small, individual theatrical ventures indispensable. By the mid-1950s, *salitas* (pocket theatres) were drawing attention in Havana. These extremely popular, small theatres (with fewer than 150 seats) were typically embedded within residential neighborhoods and often presented experimental or avant-garde works. It was also during this period, in 1958, that Vicente Revuelta founded Teatro Estudio (Studio Theatre), a fully professional theatre focused on plays with Marxist ideals, including works by Bertolt Brecht. This highly unique experimental company—which was very supportive of the Cuban Revolution in 1959—toured internationally and often hosted foreign theatrical companies.[17]

Conditions for Change

On the eve of the Cuban Revolution, conditions on the island were distressing at best. According to Fidel Castro's 1960 address at the United Nations General Assembly, roughly 12 percent of the population of six million Cubans were unemployed in 1958 (even more were underemployed, depending on the season), while rising urban rents consumed a third of family incomes. Because conditions in urban centers were better than those in rural areas, Cuba's cities experienced heavy migration—more than one-sixth of the nation's population lived in the city of Havana alone. The majority of the rural population lived in huts or slums without proper sanitation or electricity, 37.5 percent were illiterate, and 70 percent of rural areas lacked teachers. Outside of urban centers, there were roughly four hospital beds per thousand inhabitants, and the infant mortality rate in the countryside was far greater than the 6 percent national average.[18] Though parasites and tuberculosis were widespread in rural areas, half of Cubans with medical degrees practiced only in Havana.

Still, these conditions were far superior to those in most Latin American countries because Cuba had become what Julio García Luis calls an "economic colony" of the United States.[19] By the late 1950s, the island's economy was wholly dependent on foreign trade, the historical result of a single crop system (sugar) with a slave/plantation model fully ensconced by 1800. Tourism, particularly by pleasure-seeking Americans, became a vital sector of the Cuban economy after World War II. U.S. consumerism became the model for upwardly mobile Cubans; American shops, appliances, services, and technology saturated Cuban markets. Cuba "ranked fourth in Latin America in per capita gross national product and first and second in the possession of televisions and radios per person," Lievesley notes.[20] Cubans saw and heard from the entire world; however, the country's largest public services (electricity and telephone) belonged to U.S. monopolies.

Most significantly, by the 1950s, more than 46 percent of the arable land in Cuba was controlled by less than 2 percent of the landowners, the majority of whom were U.S. citizens. North American organized crime relocated many of their rackets, casinos, and nightclubs to the island, where Batista's officials tolerated their activities in return for access and payoffs. With governmental help, Cuba became the most popular money laundering site in the world. As Pérez explains, "In the 1950s gambling receipts exceeded $500,000 monthly."[21] Yet, even with money readily flowing to the island, Batista depleted over $400 million from the Cuban treasury between 1953 and the Revolution.[22] His government's blatant sponsorship of and participation in privileged social and economic relationships brought about its demise.

While Castro was exiled in Mexico, Cuba's workers responded to deteriorating wages and working conditions by staging general strikes in the cities. These slowdowns helped pave the way for greater upheaval, engendering the Cuban Revolution. Because his legal attempts to thwart Batista had been unsuccessful, Castro began enlisting and training a guerilla force to act against the Cuban government. The rebels trained outside Mexico City, where Castro met an idealistic Argentine named Ernesto "Che" Guevara. On 24 November 1956, the *barbudos* ("bearded ones," Castro's rebel army) boarded the *Granma* (Spanglish slang for "grandma"), an overburdened cruiser bound for the coast of Cuba. They aimed to invade the island and then join already mobilized land forces to begin a series of guerilla actions against the Batista government.

The mission did not go as planned. After a harrowing journey at sea, the *Granma* arrived two days late, making it impossible to link up with rebels on land. In addition, Batista's army had discovered the plan, forcing the rebels to disperse once they arrived. Roughly twenty men avoided capture, making their way into the Sierra Maestra mountains. While hiding there, the rebels organized their forces with the aid of broadcasts from their radio station Radio Rebelde and support from local peasants. Because this fighting group was small and contained, Fidel Castro was able to quickly assume all decision-making power.[23] Within months, two thousand armed rebel volunteers were prepared to fight against thirty thousand demoralized government soldiers.

The Cuban Revolution was fought as a guerilla war, involving small units of combatants operating as rebels against/within their own country. The press bolstered the rebels' efforts both in Cuba and abroad, cementing the macho guerilla myth and further tarnishing Batista's disintegrating reputation. Urban underground guerillas in the cities (known as *llanos*) served as an indispensable part of Castro's success—their distractions drew Batista's troops away from the rebels in the Sierra Maestra. Coupled with rebel successes on several fronts (e.g., in Sierra Cristal and other mountains in addition to the Sierra Maestra), the fractured unity of the armed forces hastened Batista's downfall.

By the time the United States suspended military aid to Batista in March of 1958, government army deserters and agricultural recruits had begun joining Castro and his group en masse. The United States refused to support the obviously compromised presidential elections of November 1958 and advised Batista to flee the country for his own safety. In the early hours of 1 January 1959, Batista and his accomplices escaped by plane to the Dominican Republic. Guided by Che Guevara and Camilo Cienfuegos, troops entered Havana the next day and were met with a hero's welcome. Fidel Castro soon followed.[24]

Now What? Constructing and Sustaining a Revolutionary Society

As Prime Minister of the Revolutionary Government of Cuba (the title he assumed in May 1959), Castro continually emphasized the people's ownership of the Revolution and urged the masses to keep it strong. Cuba immediately embarked on what Lievesley calls "a programme of structural changes [that] sought to transform the lives of its people."[25] The goal was to establish a governmental system that would utilize the country's resources to attain autonomy and counter threats from more advanced nations, especially the United States.

The First Agrarian Reform Law established Cuba's socialist composition by expropriating land for distribution to landless agricultural workers and farmers. Processes of nationalization continued, as the revolutionary government seized dozens of industries and businesses regardless of their owners' nationalities. Article 3 of the Agrarian Reform Law even included the redistribution of "land belonging to the Government, provinces and municipalities,"[26] over and above foreign-owned property. These changes created broad sectors of the Cuban economy that were now owned "by the people" and centrally managed on a socialist basis (although not yet publicly acknowledged as such). In addition, the Cuban state would assure the people's financial stability by controlling the market.

In his first year, Castro signed major trade agreements with the Soviet Union ensuring that Cuba would receive oil, wheat, steel, and manufacturing equipment in exchange for sugar and other agricultural products. When the United States objected to this coalition by refusing to refine Soviet oil in its refineries on the island, Cuba responded by nationalizing all of its U.S.-owned oil-processing plants. In response, the United States immediately decreased its Cuban sugar quota. The external presence and actions of Cuba's northern neighbor had a direct effect on the island's major industries. Castro's socialist model for development became Cuba's attempt not only to rectify unequal distribution but to free itself from financial reliance on the United States

Although Castro had not yet directly aligned the Revolution with Marxist communism, his public acceptance of Soviet military support signaled his movement in that direction. Yet Lievesley asserts that Eisenhower had begun creating an invasion force "before Cuba had entered into any commitments with the Soviet Union and also before it had proclaimed itself socialist." She continues, "It can be argued that the U.S. response was much more the product of the desire to reassert hegemonic control than of fear of a yet unknown ideological challenge."[27] Cuba's anticapitalism could therefore be viewed as a reaction to U.S. aggression. It was not until 1961 (during his speech at the funeral for seven Cubans who died resisting U.S. air attacks) that Castro called the Cuban Revolution "the socialist and democratic revolution of the humble, by the humble, and for the humble."[28] In this speech, Castro's rhetoric clearly linked the working class with socialism and socialism with a "free" Cuba.

When militants from the United States attacked Cuba at Playa Giron (Bay of Pigs), Cuba's revolutionary forces destroyed the convoy from the United States in less than seventy-two hours. This embarrassment made it clear that the United States had never considered the idea that the Cuban people actually viewed Castro's government as legitimate. This strategic defeat for the U.S. government emboldened the Revolution exponentially; Castro reinforced the anti-imperialist nature of the victory, remarking, "This is what [the United States] can't forgive, the fact that we are still here, right under their very noses, and that we have brought about a socialist revolution."[29] Nonetheless, Castro differentiated the people of the United States from their government, an important distinction for future interactions.

The U.S. government's inability to unseat Fidel Castro led the Organization of American States (OAS) to denounce the threat of "Castroism" (read "Marxist-Leninism") in Latin America and to expel Cuba from its membership. According to Lievesley, the United States "defined 'communist' in a highly elastic manner as anyone who was challenging the conservative political status quo, endangering their economic investments, or championing the interests of the poor."[30] The OAS, an inter-American council controlled by the United States, argued that it could not permit any competing system of government because that would "destroy hemispheric unity and solidarity."[31]

As with other industries, theatre in Cuba was radically transformed by its new system of government. The theatre was quickly decentralized and expanded beyond Havana, with state-funded companies being formed in each provincial capital. Socially committed plays by Cuban playwrights began receiving especially strong governmental support. Theatre was considered an expression of national culture and, as such, theatrical jobs were legitimized—actors, for example, were paid as professionals and eligible for government retirement benefits. This distinction altogether invigorated the once tentative relationship between actors and spectators; like all other Cubans, theatre practitioners were made professionals and employed by the state.

By 1960, the Teatro Nacional de Cuba was created with five separate divisions—theatre, dance, folklore, music, and cultural dissemination/education. Casa de Las Americas, the nation's largest cultural organization, soon produced Cuba's first international festival of Latin American theatre and created a prestigious annual prize for playwriting. Expensive and ambitious stagings were again undertaken (the likes of which had not been seen since the 1930s and 1940s), and major playwrights who previously could not afford to publish their works (Virgilio Piñera and Hector Quintero, for example) had the state printing their plays and paying them copyright fees. For the first time in Cuban history, the state paid royalties when plays were produced, triggering an explosion of playwriting activity. Absurdism, existentialism, farce, and Artaudian forms became familiar on the Cuban stage. Piñera's work, for instance, analyzed the frustrations of Cuban society by employing local customs in critical ways. Nationalism and support for the Revolution were expected, however, so extreme experimentation was limited. A new sense of Cuban cultural identity was emerging, yet the Revolution was not thus far included within it; the Revolution itself did not appear on stage until years later. Instead, the plays produced in the early 1960s focused mainly on the evils and corruption of the capitalist era. Cuba was a new society attempting to reconcile its demons, and the theatre became a platform for interrogating the past.[32]

In 1961, the Consejo Nacional de Cultura (National Council for Culture) was established to support artistic and cultural institutions, research centers, arts schools, publications, cultural festivals, and (often international) arts forums. The group made it financially possible for Cuban companies to participate in global festivals in the Americas, Europe, and Africa. Because of its funding ability, the organization had a direct effect on which Cuban theatre projects would actually be produced across the island and/or exported through tours. The organization adhered closely to the arts policy Castro had announced in 1961: "Within the Revolution, everything; against the Revolution, nothing."[33] Although the Cuban Constitution of 1940 guaranteed freedom of creation and the revolutionary government actively promoted arts education, the economic reality was that Cuban artists found it virtually impossible to acquire adequate funds to stage work outside of the state-supported system.

Definitions and Reactions

In February 1962, the United States inaugurated a total blockade against Cuba. President John F. Kennedy's Executive Order 3447, an economic and psychological effort to overthrow Castro, has remained intact for more than half a century. Lievesley supports T. G. Paterson's contention that "the error made by the United States, born out of its huge arrogance, was to believe that 'every Cuban leader had his price and any Cuban government that wished to survive had to respect the United States and its interests.'"[34] Unprecedented in international law, the economic embargo to this day restricts all goods exported from or through Cuba and halts all exports (except certain foods and medicines) from the United States to Cuba. The original aim of Kennedy's legislation was to isolate the revolutionary government of Cuba in order to provoke regime change and to diminish the risk posed by Cuba's solidarity with other communist powers.

Santa Camila de La Habana Vieja (St. Camille of Old Havana), by José Ramón Brene (1927–90), was the Revolution's first popular theatrical triumph, also in 1962. The often humorous but intensely dramatic piece reflected the new social reality on the island, while promoting the eradication of class distinctions. Set in 1959, the prorevolutionary play depicted familial conflict enhanced by the inherent contradictions within any revolution—the clash of new social structures with old ways of thinking. In the play, an underprivileged Cuban couple, Nico and Camila, sees their relationship tested by the changes sweeping the nation. Nico, a social parasite who lives off women, is reinvigorated by the Revolution and decides to become a self-sufficient and productive worker. Devoted to Changó, the patron saint of Santería, Camila struggles to hold on to the status quo and its traditions. Ultimately, she chooses her love for Nico and her country over her desire to preserve what once was. She chooses the future over the past, a major tenet of the Revolution.

Santa Camila was highly popular because it incorporated common Cuban idioms and characters, modern music, and Afro-Cuban beliefs. Like Brene, Cuban playwright Abelardo Estorino and members of the Teatro Estudio were also creating pieces that dealt with social issues. Their work experimented with traditional dramatic structures and elements of time. Both Brene's play and Teatro Estudio's work played well to "new" audiences in Cuba, now comprised of more workers, farmers, students, and children than wealthy aristocrats. Plays created for these audiences were heavily subsidized by the state, and although each theatre group chose its own repertoire and style (there was no "official" canon or method imposed), the state was closely involved in the general planning of theatrical events.

The early years of the uncompromising blockade, along with escalating animosity between Cuba and the United States, compelled Cuba to mobilize its military rather than apply its resources toward economic development. Because the Soviets purchased nearly 75 percent of Cuba's exports after 1962, Castro firmly allied his government with the Soviet communist system. Following the loss of its primary trading partner, the United States, Cuba's economic regeneration took considerable time. When ration cards were instituted in March 1962 to offset shortages of food and industrial products, the practice became an expression of the shared responsibility for equal distribution on the island, an active manifestation of Cuba's Marxist-Leninist principles. Sacrifice became part of the Revolution.

Controlled redistribution required more centralized administration than Cuba had, demanding further consolidation of the power of the Cuban state. If Cuba had adhered to Marx's idea that "the emancipation of the working class can only be achieved by the working class itself,"[35] such a powerful centralized state could not have emerged. If the emancipation of man *from* the state (rather than the deliverance of man *by* the state) is an essential goal of Marxism, the centralizing Cuban government could not fairly identify itself as Marxist. Cuba was trying to reconcile its nationalization of production (the divide between labor and its products) but was replicating this division in the form of the state. Cuba's economic isolation due to the U.S. embargo altered the Marxist-Leninist construction of the revolutionary state entirely. The needs of the Revolution changed, its responsibilities shifted, and its priorities were often derailed by harsh economic realities.

The Revolution in Crisis

The situation in Cuba would worsen before it improved. García Luis suggests that the Missile Crisis of October 1962 was caused by the U.S. government's persistent plans to carry out subversive actions against Castro and the Cuban nation (e.g., assassination attempts, exploiting psychological vulnerabilities, intelligence collecting, acts of economic sabotage, etc.). Although it may have been reasonable for Castro to request protection from the Soviets, there is little historical evidence to support that he did so. According to Arthur Schlesinger's biography of (then Attorney General) Robert Kennedy, "Castro's aim was to deter American aggression by convincing Washington that an attack on Cuba would be the same as an attack on the Soviet Union."[36] Cuba was now a part of the Cold War; its acceptance of missiles from Soviet Premier Nikita Khrushchev effectively transformed the island into a Soviet military base only ninety miles from the shores of the United States.

Because the missiles on Cuban soil belonged to (and were controlled by) the Soviet Union, Khrushchev negotiated directly with Kennedy; the two leaders agreed that the United States would not attack Cuba if the Soviet missiles were safely returned to the U.S.S.R. Castro was powerless over his country's fate—he was not consulted by either country during negotiations and was only informed, via radio broadcast, *after* the agreement had been brokered. Lievesley explains, "The 'hollowness of Soviet protection' had been revealed and Cuba had to come to terms with the fact that it was just a pawn in the Great Power game."[37] Yet Castro did not waiver in his alliance with the Soviet Union, at least not publicly. In his speech on 1 November 1962, he remarked, "above all, we are Marxist-Leninists; we are friends of the Soviet Union."[38] The Missile Crisis, however, set a guarded tone for the nearly thirty years of contact that followed between Cuba and the Soviet Union.

Trade agreements with the Soviets almost single-handedly kept the Cuban economy afloat for the remainder of the 1960s. Though Marx insisted that the laws of state could not make a revolution,[39] the Cuban state, and its power, grew. In 1965, The Communist Party of Cuba was officially formed with what Castro had previously defined as the task of orientation: "[The Communist Party] orients on all levels, it does not govern on all levels. It fosters the revolutionary consciousness of the masses. . . . It spreads the ideas of revolution. It supervises, controls, guards, informs. It discusses what has to be discussed."[40] Castro claimed that the party had emerged from the people and was to maintain close ties with them because they were responsible for its status, authority, and potency.

The initial rhetoric of the Cuban Communist Party was linked to the aspirations of Cuba's freedom fighters (such as Martí, Mella, and the *mambís*—mostly black soldiers who had defeated the Spaniards in the War of Independence) and a broad, hand-picked combination of Marxist and Leninist ideas, including dialectics. Cuba's transformation into a country for the masses was woven into its revolutionary character. García Luis argues, "Fidel Castro resolutely divorced himself from dogmas that resulted from a narrow reading of Marxism and Leninism and helped to define the Cuban essence of the revolution—and, especially, Cuba's determination to think for itself."[41] The state became the *core* of revolutionary action, as Lenin had suggested.

Cuba was attempting to create a new society of new men, transforming social relations through an egalitarian, selfless consciousness rather than becoming a society "established by things."[42] The government encouraged volunteer participation in the sugar harvest, literacy drives, national health campaigns, artistic ventures, and infrastructure development projects in order to inspire unity beyond distinctions such as gender, ethnicity, class, or race. These new communal/social relationships—along with assumed loyalty to the Revolution—were ingrained in the education provided to all Cubans. Thousands of teachers were trained to meet the demand precipitated by the building of primary schools all over the country. Significant investment in secondary education, universities, polytechnic, and vocational schools was evident as well,[43] though most programs lacked a component of critical thinking or any platform for thorough debate. (However, to date, the Cuban educational system remains the gold standard for underdeveloped countries and has sustained impressive accomplishments.) Many Cubans believed that if they worked together for the good of the nation, a cohesive, integrated Cuba would emerge.

In addition, local resources were sorely needed on the island, and sugar was Cuba's strongest industry. Sugar had become Cuba's primary source of income between 1965 and 1970, as the nation's industrial capacity was considerably increased by state investment after the Revolution. In 1970, likely because "Castro had always been identified as privileging action over ideas,"[44] the Cuban government set the imposing goal of a ten million ton sugarcane harvest. Though the goal was not met, a record 8.5 million tons of sugar were harvested, "the highest sugar production figure in the history of Cuba and the greatest production figure for cane sugar in the history of the world."[45] Still, this burgeoning Marxist society, based on the redistribution of the means of production, faced a failure directly related to its capacity for production. The failure to meet the harvest goals challenged the basic principles of the system.

The disappointing sugar harvest shifted the Castro administration's focus to more realistic, effective means of bolstering the Cuban economy, through areas such as tourism and education. The incident reflected Cuba's tendency to imitate Soviet models that often did not account for Cuba's specific circumstances or were already obsolete by 1970. Soviet hegemony pervaded Cuban sovereignty. As García Luis claims, the Cuban government ignored "Martí's warning that the government in each new republic should reflect the nature of the country; and Mariátegui's foresight in saying that, in Latin America, socialism couldn't be a copy but must rather be a heroic creation."[46] Cuba was becoming aware that—in order to survive—it must diversify its Revolution and create its own brand of socialism.

The ideological struggles taking place in Cuba finally appeared on stage in the late 1960s and early 1970s. Cuban artists attempted to use the forms that were growing popular all over Latin America (such as absurdism, happenings, and theatre of cruelty) to represent the Cuban reality. Although some productions imitated U.S. or other Western models, the theatre of the period was isolated because, for financial and ideological reasons, few Cuban companies went abroad and even fewer foreign companies visited Cuba. The last of the *salitas* were nationalized in 1967 so that, by 1970, all theatrical productions on the island were financed by the state.

In addition, a congressional resolution against homosexuality in the early 1970s forced many Cuban artists and intellectuals from their jobs. The government compiled official lists of forbidden plays and authors and cracked down on anything it deemed subversive or antirevolutionary by closing theatres, censoring plays, creating blacklists, and arresting "subversive" artists and writers. Several theatre companies disbanded, while others were created that abided by the new censorship policies. For instance, the Teatro Politico Bertolt Brecht, formed in 1973, took a socialist approach to all of its material and was known for producing the work of many Soviet authors. Co-productions with directors and/or theatre companies from Russia and the Eastern Bloc were typical fare. These external models were often unfamiliar, inaccessible to many Cubans who did not connect with the more stoic formalism of Soviet theatre.[47] As in other fields—such as architecture, painting, and modern dance—imposed Soviet models did not mesh well with the internal development of Cuban culture. These forms did not reflect Cuba's particular colonial history, cultural developments, climate, race relations, use of language, religious influences, or way of life.

Organizing Power

The First Congress of the Communist Party of Cuba was held in December 1975, nearly sixteen years after the fall of Batista. It was convened to construct a new Constitution of the Republic as well as to create administrative divisions (such as voting districts and systems for economic management) for the country. Adopted in 1976, the Socialist Constitution confirmed that the Marxist-Leninist Communist Party of Cuba was the guiding force of Cuban society and government, with its power derived directly from the people. The terms *socialism* and *communism* are used interchangeably in the document, which guarantees all Cubans access to jobs, education, medical treatments, culture, and "comfortable housing."

Article 12 of the Cuban Constitution guarantees "the principles of equal rights" and "free determination by the peoples," but does not define those terms. And because the people are expected to live by the Party's decrees, any act of self-determination on the part of the masses may be viewed as counter-revolutionary. This is just one of many contradictions in Cuban doctrine. Collective ownership of the means of production and the suppression of exploitation are secured, as is the distribution of goods "from each according to his capacity, to each according to his work."

The Socialist Constitution of Cuba also called for the creation of what's known as Poder Popular, or the National Assembly of People's Power, a democratic governing body of elected delegates with constitutional and legislative authority. In his address to the first delegates of Poder Popular, Raúl Castro blamed the "shortage of material means"[48] for the lengthy delay in creating this element of proletarian rule. The revolutionary government had existed for nearly seventeen years without citizen representation, yet it was called democratic, Marxist, and socialist. Although its creation resulted in more government, Raúl Castro imagined that the Poder Popular would "eliminate the bureaucratic centralism that still exist[ed] in many parts of [the] government apparatus, replacing it with democratic centralism," which he insisted was "Marxist-Leninist."[49] Cuba stands alone in its particular understanding and implementation of communist ideals. It is undeniable that "as the heroic period of the Revolution ended," asserts Lievesley,

> the Cuban political system and Cuban society became more institutionalized and, in many ways, more resistant to innovation and debate. In adopting a state socialist model in the 1960s, the Cubans were able to make great advances . . . , but these successes were tempered by an inability . . . to avoid the centralization of decision-making. (99)

Living with(in) the System

The 1970s and early 1980s saw the rise of what is known as Teatro Nuevo[50] (New Theatre) as Cuban theatre began to recuperate. This period was focused on collective theatre that dealt with the country's ongoing transformations, centralization, and localized concerns. Theatre became a means for actively engaging the social process, and government officials believed it expressed a uniquely Cuban, and collective, revolutionary spirit. Hence, Teatro Nuevo and its many regional theatre companies received unparalleled state support.

Teatro Escambray, the nation's most famous theatre collective (and several companies modeled after it) identified social problems by doing research within communities across the island. Led by director and actor Sergio Corrieri, the group, founded in 1968, made direct contact with audiences; it used Brechtian aesthetics and techniques and allowed local residents to partake in creating theatrical material developed by, from, and for their own communities. Presentations took place in nontraditional, mostly outdoor venues, and the group's highly visual approach to urgent local concerns was enthusiastically received. Innumerable new plays were produced, and eager new audiences were forged. Teatro Escambray applied a sharp critical lens in its productions, where working-class characters were central. Its pieces were community-based, dialectical, and accessible. Through its dedication to tackling specific regional problems (past and present) from a contemporary perspective, this adaptable company helped establish a distinctly Cuban alternative to traditional dramaturgy.[51]

Several festivals of Latin American theatre (such as those in Camagüey) brought renowned international theatre artists to Cuba throughout the decade. By 1980, many Cuban artists who had been expelled from the stage returned to practicing their crafts, as repression eased. Overcoming redundancies, routines, and state control, a new generation of actors, playwrights, and critics attempted to emerge. Yet fears of political repercussions meant that complex themes and critical approaches were rare on the Cuban stage; many theatrical endeavors were flat and formulaic. This period's greatest achievement, however, was that the individual reappeared onstage; the monologue was revitalized. This was a key development for a collective society that had overwhelmingly privileged the masses over the self for more than twenty years. As audiences migrated toward films and television, the theatrical community was striving for a definitive, decidedly Cuban aesthetic that might reengage Cuban audiences.

Cuba's artistic, social, and economic climate reflected the government's commitment to provide resources for formerly underserved rural sectors, but doing so contributed to the deterioration of urban conditions. In Havana, for instance, the demand for housing outpaced building projects by the early 1980s, and existing structures were increasingly dilapidated. Slums sprouted around cities, and fuel shortages exacerbated the burgeoning gap between rural and urban environments. The island's trade deficit also grew, as the prices of Cuban exports struggled to keep pace with Soviet imports. The Soviets extended price subsidies and low-interest loans to Cuba, both of which increased Cuba's dependency and led to persistent tensions between Cuba and the Eastern bloc. However, argues Lievesley, "it was not the case that Cuba had no choice but to slavishly copy the Soviet model, but rather that the options open to it were severely circumscribed."[52]

No matter what, Cuba was not producing enough consumer goods to fund its own interests, and those it did produce were often substandard due to a lack of materials and equipment. Less food was available on the island than before the Revolution, and although Cuba's dedication to health standards did not waver, difficulties in procuring basic goods led to the growth of the black market. As of 1979, Cuba permitted visits from Cubans living in the United States These visitors brought needed income to the island but also highlighted the ideological gaps between Cuba and its northern neighbor. Cubans could not have survived the decade without substantial Soviet support.

Three years after Cuba ratified its socialist constitution, the United States began awarding entrance visas to ordinary Cubans who committed violent acts against the Revolution. On 28 March 1980, a group of Cubans in a bus stormed the gates of the Peruvian Embassy, killing a Cuban guard. Swayed by U.S. influence, the Peruvians allowed the Cubans to take refuge in the building. Cuban security guards abandoned the mansion, and thousands more asylum-seekers overwhelmed the grounds. The Peruvian government helped groups of Cubans emigrate to Lima or to Costa Rica, but could not secure visas to the United States In response, the Cuban government began allowing those who wished to emigrate to the United States to do so legally and directly by boat from Mariel, a port on Cuba's northern coast.

This instigated what García Luis calls "the largest migratory bridge in the history of the conflict between the United States and Cuba."[53] In a span of only five weeks, roughly 125,000 Cubans whom Castro dubbed "criminal or lumpen elements" left the island for Florida. Lievesley claims that 41 percent of those who left from Mariel were under twenty-seven years old,[54] an alarming statistic that the Cuban government has never acknowledged. Castro directly challenged U.S. president Jimmy Carter in a *Granma* editorial: "For our part, we aren't breaking any laws: entries in and departures from the port [of Mariel] are free. If the United States wants to impose its jurisdiction, it should do so in Florida; it can't do anything in Mariel."[55] Despite hundreds of Coast Guard rescues and substantial Cuban casualties on the rough seas, the response from the United States was muddled. Lievesley explains:

> The Carter administration's initial pragmatic response was to attempt to restrict the exodus but it backed down for fear of alienating Cuban-Americans. It then pledged to accept all arrivals but later backtracked, arguing that all boats should be sent back and their occupants and future emigrants be screened by Cuban authorities.

Lievesley duly adds that, "The behavior of both sides during the Mariel crisis has been criticized."[56] Neither country was blameless. The political implications of the four-month crisis would taint Cuba/U.S. relations for years to come.

The tension between Havana and Washington was palpable in the early 1980s. President Ronald Reagan promoted an extreme anticommunist stance and viewed Cuba as a satellite of the Soviet Union. However, Soviet General Secretary Leonid Brezhnev's position was clear—the Soviet Union would trade with Cuba but would not fight in Cuba. The Revolutionary Armed Forces of Cuba had to become self-sufficient by developing military reserves, modernizing equipment, and acquiring survival supplies. The Cuban military wanted the ability to independently feed, clothe, arm, and supply the entire Cuban population, although Raúl Castro admitted it would also rely heavily on its moral superiority if the island were attacked.[57] Military self-sufficiency and economic rectification were vital to the country's corrective processes, as it reconsidered its version of a system it had modeled on the Soviet Union.

Bureaucratic reform on the island was imperative, and the state had to battle bureaucracy and corruption without undermining its own authority. "Aware that it must be seen as responding to a climate of insecurity and dissatisfaction," Lievesley suggests, "the government responded by loosening various social controls. Thus, there was a relative relaxation of press censorship and political leaders, academics and intellectuals entered into a public although restricted debate about the perceived shortcomings of recent years" (123). Although continuing Soviet support was still assumed, tenacious efforts to seek what Castro called "new solutions for old problems"[58] would inadvertently enliven the arts and also help Cuba prepare for the staggering difficulties it would face over the next two decades.

The demise of the Soviet Union by 1991 led to Cuba's use of the "special period in time of peace," an all-purpose strategy for withstanding any exceptionally severe situation.[59] Since 1992, the term has been associated with the loss of the Soviets as Cuba's economic buffer against the effects of the U.S. blockade. Its purchasing power having sharply declined, the island could no longer afford imports. Hence, the state enacted a series of measures in order to restore the economy. These included partially legalizing the dollar (until 2004), expanding the tourist sector, encouraging foreign investments, and permitting various forms of self-employment. In essence, the Cuban government had to make "some concessions to capitalist formulas"[60] in order to ensure that the Revolution would survive. However, Castro was sure to emphasize that, rather than embracing a neoliberal free market, Cuba was merely "relinking into the world system but under strict state control."[61] Lenin's idea of "capital as economics or as an object rather than a social relation; as an area separated and completely differentiated from politics"[62] had become an impossible ideal to uphold.

The Special Period required Cuba to conceive of a revolutionary struggle *against* power rather than for possession of it, and to move toward attaining power rather than seizing it. Along with self-sufficiency, this struggle would entrench socialism as an ongoing process, Lenin's primary goal when he examined the *practice* of revolution in *What Is to Be Done?*, a "how to" of change. Here, Lenin strays from conventional Marxism when he proposes that revolutionaries be professionals rather than amateurs. Lenin advocated "highly skilled workers" engaging in strategic revolutionary efforts such as secrecy or sabotage. Fidel Castro and Che Guevara were educated intellectuals, "highly skilled workers" (a lawyer and a doctor) who were not part of the masses. Both were privileged, had mingled with elites, and had traveled outside of their homelands. They understood the delicate coupling of class-conscious dialogue with the need for secrecy. Sergio Tischler takes this notion of professionalism one step further, noting that the Party and its leaders "create[d] class consciousness among the working classes, who could not otherwise produce conscious revolutionary action."[63] Yet when the Soviet Union was dismantled, the severity of the Special Period challenged any and all class consciousness in Cuba. Even highly educated Cubans had to acquire money, food, goods, and services by inventive means such as bartering, contact with tourists, the black market, and so on. Daily survival, by whatever means necessary, usurped class.

In a televised speech, Carlos Lage, then Cuban secretary of the Executive Committee of the Council of Ministers, explained that there was "no branch of the economy where there [wasn't] a significant proportion of technology from the socialist bloc, and once the economic relations were interrupted, technical assistance and [Cuba's] chances of obtaining spare parts for the functioning of this machinery were also cut off."[64] Just when they most needed national production, Cuban factories struggled to maintain/operate the equipment they had. This only increased the severity of Cuba's circumstances, as technological shortfalls and fuel shortages tangibly inhibited the country's output.

The Special Period brought significant modifications to the Cuban economy, but the state did not sell off property to foreign investors or devalue its currency as had other Latin American countries. Cuba entered into substantial joint ventures so that it could maintain control of its land and resources while enabling its state expenditures. The country fought to preserve its social achievements while participating in global financial markets that did not support socialism.

The institution of a dual peso/dollar economy (now the "convertible" economy) may have saved Cuba's currency from sharp decline. However, it also had significant social implications for Cubans. Apart from the effects on the Cuban psyche of adopting U.S. currency without direct access to the United States, the choice created an undeniable schism between Cubans with access to *pesos convertibles*[65] (from remittances or the tourist sector) and those without it. The consumer capacity of those with *pesos convertibles* was substantially greater than those with *pesos cubanos*, fueling a growing black market and an increase in private production. The government urged Cubans to restore relations with their family members abroad in order to secure remittances and encourage lucrative visits, even if these interactions might incite discontent on the island.

Racial divisions in Cuba also became much more prevalent with the two-tiered economic system because far fewer Afro-Cubans had family in other countries than "white" Cubans did—the egalitarianism established by the Revolution was now at stake. Life became exceedingly difficult for Cubans earning only *pesos cubanos*/MN, as basic government services and supplies rapidly deteriorated, forcing purchases in convertible pesos/CUC. Coupled with the absence of consumer goods, cuts in electricity and water created extensive, daily hardships. As reliable transportation waned, this nation striving to modernize was suddenly reliant on bicycles and animals for mobility, reverting rather than advancing.[66]

The desperation during this period led to pessimism about the future at a time when the Revolution needed determined, unwavering support. Those who risked their lives to leave the island on rafts (known as *balseros*) in the early 1990s revealed the overwhelming despondency some Cubans were experiencing. Yet despite these difficulties, the Cuban government continued to provide primary health care and educational opportunities that, although diminished, still rivaled many wealthier countries. Social services that ensured housing (even if substandard) and equitable food rations for Cubans also remained. Most Cubans lost weight, but they did not die of starvation, even during the harshest moments of the Special Period. Sustained even under the most strenuous conditions, these considerable social achievements mark definitive ongoing triumphs of the Revolution.

"The question facing Cuba during the Special Period was whether the socialist character of its political and social system would be subsumed by its insertion into the world economy," Lievesley asserts. The Revolution often evaded the social abuses, widespread crime, illness, and crippling poverty that decimated the countries of the former Soviet Union by allowing what Lievesley calls "entrepreneurial socialism" to become the heart of its market transition. She explains: "The government was adamant that, whilst it needed to respond to changing circumstances and probably make compromises, the essentials of its ideological commitment were not negotiable."[67]

The Impact

In the last twenty years, the economic deterioration of Cuba and communism's global retreat have often eclipsed the Revolution and its accomplishments. Although it and its fearless leaders have certainly begun to show their age, the Cuban Revolution has had a profound impact on change in Latin America and on the entire idea of revolution. While its continued existence may be something of an anomaly, facets of the Cuban experience are echoed throughout Latin American history. Much of the region has experienced revolutionary movements, often (at least initially) modeled on Cuba's success. Cuba blazed a trail for others to follow and gave its support to dozens of uprisings around the world. During the 1980s, however, most of Latin America's return to civilian rule dampened its revolutionary impetuses. Economic difficulties such as recessions and enormous foreign debts drew increasing political attention, as both the extreme left and the far right significantly declined in the southern hemisphere.

The decline in Cuba since the collapse of the Soviet bloc proved to some that Cuba had not really achieved sovereignty by escaping U.S. dominance, but instead had exchanged one master for another. Cuba's experience with complete autonomy since the early 1990s has not been entirely successful, yet the Revolution could never have survived the Special Period without popular endorsement for what C. Peter Ripley calls "a struggle of renewal and affirmation, involving more than just holding the line against decay and decline."[68]

Just how Cuba's socialist character would be altered, subsumed, developed, or reinvented by globalization and its foray into the world economy became a key concern during the Special Period. While foreign capital has been the means of the island's sustenance for the past two decades, its long-term effects on the country's ideology remain unclear. Cuba's recently strengthened alliances with leftists in Venezuela, Bolivia, Ecuador, Brazil, and Chile also alter this picture. Despite Cuba's hemispheric impact over the past half-century, the most important issues facing its people today concern their own future—their own economic survival, as well as their ideological and political status beyond the Castro brothers. They wonder how long Cuba's situation might be considered a "revolution" and how that complex designation may continue to shape their lives.

Revolutionary Transgressions

In spite of a resurgence of the arts and the slackening of some governmental controls (due to funding shortfalls) since 1995, Cuban artists still must make tactical choices in order to persevere. Controversial discourse on the island is framed through a process that articulates a definitive rhetoric of resistance, as James C. Scott argues in his book *Domination and the Arts of Resistance*. Although his work does not mention Cuba directly, Scott's ideas are highly applicable to an evolving but tightly regulated, postcapitalist society such as the one Cuba became after the 1960s.

Scott explains that, under systems of weighty censorship, a "hidden transcript" is produced. Comprised of speech acts as well as a whole range of other expressive practices, this hidden transcript is produced under the constraints of power but includes various layers of meaning intended for a subcultural audience. Scott argues that the hidden transcript is "the privileged site for non-hegemonic, contrapuntal, dissident, subversive discourse"[69] even within state-supported artistic ventures. Because working from within the system means Cuban theatre artists "prudently avoid, with few exceptions, any irrevocable acts of public defiance" as Scott insists, "their politics too might make use of disguise, deception and indirection while maintaining an outward impression, in power-laden situations, of willing, even enthusiastic consent."[70]

In Cuba, the hidden transcript has become a necessary part of the artistic sponsorship game, not simply a reaction to it. Subsumed and variable meanings are a vital part of the aesthetics of postrevolutionary arts in Cuba. The performances included in this study take place in public view, many with international audiences, but are often designed with double meanings that make it difficult to censor the work. These plays avoid censorship and endure *within* the structure of authority because, to date, they do not have what Scott calls the "luxury of direct confrontation"[71] without severe consequences. Little on Cuban stages is entirely straightforward—theatre artists employ metaphors, euphemisms, hearsay, slang, folklore, specific gestures, sarcasm, or a unique mixture of these techniques to veil their criticisms. What Homi Bhabha calls the "untranslatable residue" within the opacity of language and action creates space for these playwrights' assessments of their living conditions. It is also the opacity and concealed layers of meaning in many contemporary Cuban plays that protect theatre artists from repercussions—their intentions can be denied if directly challenged because there is space for both innocuous and subversive interpretations of their works.

The fact that there are active, contemporary theatre companies in Cuba at all is a great achievement, considering the island's economic difficulties over the last quarter century. Scott's contention that "this is not to imply that the realm of cultural practices is unaffected by the dominant culture; only that it is less effectively patrolled than, say, the realm of production"[72] is accurate with regard to Cuba's theatre. Stringent governmental efforts to control theatres would only reinforce their position as significant sites for coordinating and communicating controversial viewpoints. Even today, under the strenuous economic conditions that have closed many other artistic venues in Cuba, theatre still thrives all over the island.

The plays included here explore the potentially transgressive acts[73] beneath the apparent consent on the island and the imaginative futures these acts suggest. In a space where, after five decades of Revolution, there are few opportunities to gain alternative knowledge, it is captivating that many Cuban artists do not view their destiny as inevitable. Although the consequences for doing so may be severe, artists in Cuba dare to transgress, to question, and to reconstitute their experiences in ways that often diverge from the official versions promulgated by the state.

Scott asserts that "the creation of disguises depends on an agile, firm grasp of codes of meaning being manipulated. It is impossible to overestimate the subtlety of this manipulation."[74] These manipulations do more than encode meaning—they define a tension on the island. Theatre is not merely a substitute for activity but serves as opposition when direct offensives are impossible. The plays and playwrights included here are momentous, effectual, and constructive because they note objections to *both* state control and global capitalism. They question the past and the future, interrogating many economic and social models. They express the intellectual and emotional burden of half a century of continued revolutionary rhetoric on a people and they ask what can be done to ease it. These pieces create a forum in which Cubans may see a portrait of themselves as caught between history, ideology, and reality, a space where their daily achievements, doubts, poise, fears, humor, pain, and frustration are revealed and acknowledged.

2

Staging Revolutions

Past and Present Conversations

> Without reducing [the Cuban] Revolution to a spectacle, it is important to notice that its spectacular components . . . captured worldwide attention; they rallied their followers and admirers by ennobling the revolutionaries and giving them an identity. . . . a new world was being created before one's eyes. . . .
>
> —Diana Taylor, "Framing the Revolution: Triana's *La noche de los asesinos* and *Ceremonial de guerra*

The Cuban Revolution of 1959 was undoubtedly spectacular: it was a rare and extraordinary series of events that played out in a public display of impressive scale. Events like the guerilla army proudly streaming into Havana on New Year's Day or the sight of a white dove landing on Castro's shoulder as he spoke to crowds left their imprints on Cubans. Half a century later, however, conditions in Cuba call for repositioning the vestiges of revolutionary spectacle. Crucial questions remain about how revolution—and its impact on contemporary problems—is defined, represented, and understood.

(Re)Defining Revolution

Webster's dictionary defines *revolution* as

> 1. a complete and forcible overthrow of an established government or political system, 2. a radical and pervasive change in society and the social structure, esp. one made suddenly and often accompanied by violence, 3. a complete or marked change in something, 4. a procedure or course as if in a circuit, as back to a starting point in time, 5. a single turn of this kind.[1]

The LaRousse Spanish dictionary defines *revolución* as an "abrupt or violent change in the social or political structure of a state" or as "a total and radical change"[2] (translation mine). These definitions are dense and multifaceted (several others—relating to astronomy, mechanics, rotation, and geology—have been omitted here). However, these definitions suggest two intriguing ideas for exploration here: that of revolution as a significant shift in social structures due to political transformation, and as a motion that returns something to its original position.

Although today the word *revolution* refers to many different transformative actions (e.g., the feminist revolution, the digital revolution, etc.), residue of the cyclical idea within the concept—of something that revolves and returns to its beginning—remains embedded within the term. The extent of revolutionary change determines the use of the term; if only limited aspects of society were altered, that action might be classified as a shift or reform rather than a revolution. A revolution tends to include drastic modifications to, or the replacement of, existing social, economic, or political institutions.

Modern uses of the term *revolution* share three basic elements: they are intended to signal a new era in history, they imply violence, disorder, or disruption that leads to (or is part of) upheaval and its consequences, and they often have greater than national relevance. Tracing usage of the word *revolution* may help to better refine its elaborate meanings and applications. The Latin word *revolutio*, meaning "moving a thing from one place to another," was not widely used in the rhetoric of the classical world. However, thinkers as early as Aristotle noted a universal desire for equality as the chief cause of the revolutionary impulse. Throughout much of the ancient world, various systems of astrology encouraged the belief that the movement of constellations was mirrored on earth in political and social events. Copernicus later used the term to describe the movement of stars. Due to the pervasive belief in astrology during the sixteenth century, people believed that political and social events on earth mirrored the movements of the constellations. The ensuing dominance of science and Judeo/Christian thought, in addition to the amassing of wealth and the growth of military might, rendered classical assumptions about the stability of social order obsolete. By the medieval period, it was evident that rulers fell, dynasties disappeared, and empires evolved. The term *revolution* embraced growing skepticism about power and implied important variations in government. It became fashionable to speak of "revolution" in the late 1500s because it allowed for reintroducing the cyclical thought (movement that returns to a point of origin) that had pervaded classical ideas about government.[3] Concepts within the term *revolution* were malleable, associated with many images and schools of thought, and therefore useful to philosophers attempting to explain political and social change.

By the late eighteenth century, philosophers such as Voltaire envisioned profound change and therefore built upon the flexibility of the term. Belief in progress and in the contributions of their own age became necessary elements of revolution for thinkers such as Rousseau and Robespierre.

Although fear was associated with political and social crises, the Enlightenment signaled a shift in beliefs from superstitions and blood feuds to defendable logic and wisdom. It was apparent that substantial transformations could arise from innovative intellectual insights rather than from fate.

The use of the term *revolution* to describe widespread changes in economic and social developments, such as the "industrial revolution," extended the word's meaning even further. The concept of industrial revolution was reflective of the *history* of industry as well as its present state. This use profoundly influenced other labels that incorporated historical achievements, such as "scientific revolution." Though limited to their specific fields, these revolutions were interrelated—together they indicated the rise of capitalism between the sixteenth and nineteenth centuries. The industrial and scientific revolutions were direct responses to changing social and political conditions.

Scientific historian Thomas Kuhn observes that both political and scientific revolutions are generated by a growing sense that existing frameworks no longer sufficiently engage contemporary problems. He suggests that these failures lead to crises in both politics and science. The scientific revolution indicated a modern outlook by *incorporating*, rather than disregarding, ideas from the past. Kuhn defines a *scientific revolution* as transforming "the scientific imagination in ways that we shall ultimately describe as a transformation of the world within which the scientific work [is] done."[4] Changes and the controversies that accompany them are the defining characteristics of scientific (and other) revolutions. Kuhn astutely notes that "during revolutions scientists see new and different things when looking with familiar instruments in places they have looked before" (111).

Kuhn's emphasis on immediacy coupled with history and revision, on development-by-accumulation *and* reconsideration, illustrates science's desire to understand the historical integrity of its own advances. If any accepted scientific paradigm is "an object for further articulation and specification under new or more stringent conditions" (23), as Kuhn suggests, then altering or abandoning a paradigm becomes crucial for any scientific revolution to transpire. Hence, Kuhn explains that the inventors of new paradigms are almost always young or are very new to their fields, a feature also crucial in political and social revolutions. The process of discovering new phenomena as a direct response to crises is exceedingly complex: it involves faith, recognition, and the development of new vocabulary and concepts, initiatives more readily accepted by younger, more idealistic generations. Rookie scientists may be less likely to dismiss anomalies without thoroughly investigating them, thus discovering new phenomena.

Yet once a scientific theory has become paradigmatic, Kuhn insists it can only be discarded when a viable alternative is available to replace it. "To reject one paradigm without simultaneously substituting another is to reject science itself" (79), an act Kuhn claims reflects more on humans than on science. Is this also true for social and political movements? Does rejecting one system automatically mean "accepting" another? If "each group uses its own paradigm to argue in that paradigm's defense" as Kuhn insists (94), does that necessarily ensure the triumph of one model over another or are compromises possible? A new paradigm can resolve a recognized problem in a way no other option can, yet it is expected to preserve, challenge, and advance the achievements of its predecessors. These transformations are at least cumulative and, at most, evolutionary.

Kuhn proposes that, "The more precise and far reaching [the] paradigm is, the more sensitive an indicator . . . of an occasion for paradigm change, . . . [until] the initially anomalous has become the anticipated" (65). In order to induce a crisis then, an anomaly must be more than merely an exception. Certain anomalies inspire serious scrutiny because those that create paradigm change affect existing knowledge at its core. The stakes are incredibly high.

Political revolutions bring about change in ways prohibited under the systems they oppose. The idea that even a seemingly localized, single incongruity within a field can evoke profound change far beyond the local (or national) level is particularly important when considering a small country like Cuba within Latin America. The global assimilation of new, international circumstances or ideas may create crises *outside* the community that initially experienced the changes. "The Cuban Revolution has had a profound and enduring influence upon world politics," writes Geraldine Lievesley, "an influence which belies its status as a small, poor Third World country."[5] In other words, revolutions have reach.

Intellectual transformations predictably generate regular, passionate debate within the sciences. This is because paradigm shifts do not merely add to the scope and precision of science, but *reshape what is possible*, thus modifying (often essentially) our world view. Just as envisioning the world as round instead of flat altered all possibilities, the Cuban Revolution illustrated that a modern, successful revolution with minimal collateral damage was feasible in Latin America—a major shift in paradigm. Lievesley argues that the Cuban Revolution was actually responsible for inaugurating "an age of revolutionary optimism."[6] Like a scientific revolution, the Cuban Revolution incorporated history, transition, controversy, reevaluation, and the future in its scope.

The scientific use of the term also clarifies revolution as an extended process, reviewed over time and impossible to date, that alters one's perception of the world. As do social upheavals, scientific revolutions play a vital role in the evolution of institutions and their daily practices. Old manipulations become irrelevant or are employed differently once transformed. After a revolution, the scientist and/or the civilian responds to an altered environment to which he or she must be reoriented. A revolution is successful, according to Kuhn, in terms of the "evolution [of] the community's state of knowledge at any given time."[7] So despite conceptual changes, what is revolutionary today may well be considered mainstream tomorrow.

Two recent Cuban plays, *Carlotta Corday* by Nara Mansur and *Charenton* by Raquel Carrió and Flora Lauten (of Teatro Buendia), incisively trace the contradictions within revolutions in complex and paradoxical ways. Both plays use the French Revolution as a model for offering revisions of Cuba's revolutionary history based on the present state of contemporary Cuba. Building on their theatrical predecessors, these pieces are transgressive, postmodern, transitory, and hyper-imaginative. They reveal how recent obstacles, from the absence of materials to recurring power outages, have engendered thoughtful ingenuity and unique dramatic irony on stages in Havana. *Carlotta Corday* and *Charenton* indeed create new worlds before the eyes of their audiences—worlds that include a dialogue between reality and history, between spectacle and lived experience.

Revolution and Its Elsewheres

Cuban playwrights Nara Mansur and Raquel Carrió wrote plays using the historical frame of the French Revolution to encode their discourses about their country and revolution. They employed the example of the French Revolution because it clarified that, more often than not, revolutions do not bring about stability but, instead, inspire greater flux. The French Revolution firmly entrenched the idea of revolution as an ongoing political construct in the late eighteenth century. While internal conflicts had certainly affected other European states, no previous struggle against oppression was as recognized or as complex as the French Revolution. The incursion shaped the very construction of the French nation—it caused changes in the social relations between classes, it ensured citizens greater involvement in public affairs, it canonized the use of brutal force, and it altered the country's view of government. Its goals were constantly redeveloped, reformed, and refocused while being furthered by urban and rural violence. The expansiveness of the French Revolution was viewed as a threat to the security of other European governments, as foreign politicians feared that their own populations might covet similar empowerment. The French had refashioned the idea of revolution into "the combining in one concept of two notions which had previously existed side by side: that of revolutions as changes in government; and that of revolution as ushering in a new social order and a new stage in world history."[8] The French Revolution demonstrated that governments were not permanent or divine, that leaders were fallible, and that no single party had all the answers. It was at once evolutionary—a response to the crisis of ensuing modernity—and also chaotic, violent, and erratic. Its goals continually shifted and its reach was immeasurable. Therefore, the French Revolution serves as a useful stage metaphor, as an allegory for Cuba's own historical experience.

Dozens of political, economic, and social factors led the French people to take revolutionary measures in the late 1700s. The rise of the intellectual movement that came to be known as the Enlightenment during the period made the divine right and absolute power asserted by King Louis XVI increasingly untenable. The French treasury was depleted not only by the French army's involvement in nearly forty years of wars in Europe and America but also by the extravagance and corruption of the nation's royalty. The profound psychological effects of this constant warlike volatility took a toll on the French public, many of whom suffered daily under oppressive feudal conditions that were compounded by France's divisive class system. Since 1774, Louis XVI and Marie-Antoinette had served as brash symbols of excess and corruption. Nobility and clergy did not pay taxes because of their elite, usually inherited, titles. Commoners had no input in the decisions made by their government, though they contributed nearly all of its tax revenue. There was no prevailing national law; taxation was France's only means of raising money. Although the peasantry had valid grievances—mistreatment by the aristocracy, skyrocketing food prices, unfair feudal contracts—the wealthy commoners and the bourgeoisie were the first objectors to the societal inequalities of their nation. These were educated French citizens with stable occupations who embraced Enlightenment thinking, leading them to become the catalyst for a revolution, which soon inspired support from the peasant classes.

The bourgeois reached their threshold of tolerance for the French political system in May 1789 when France's legislative body, the Estates-General, convened to rescue the country from financial ruin. No matter how severe the circumstances, the upper classes were not willing to relinquish their privileges for the welfare of the country. They refused to pay taxes that could immediately make France financially solvent. What began as an attempt to level the tax burden and increase participation grew into a revolutionary battle for equality, incorporating more extensive aims than merely rectifying France's economic instability. The outcomes of the revolution reflect its social aims far more than its financial ones.

German playwright Peter Weiss (1916–1982), whose work inspired both Mansur and Teatro Buendia, put the aftermath of the French Revolution on stage precisely to explore the instability and disillusionment that revolution could engender. Born near Berlin, Weiss was of Austrian, Hungarian, and Jewish descent. His education was interrupted by the Nazi regime, and his family became exiles in England in 1934 and then moved to Sweden in 1939.

Weiss took an interest in surrealist art, particularly the work of Max Ernst, Salvador Dalí, and André Breton. He later studied psychoanalysis, out of which he grew fascinated by the conflict between the artistry in the subconscious and the need for postwar artists to work in an overtly conscious manner. In his notebooks, Weiss commented that:

> Art . . . only conveys activity, it communicates qualities which we have to detect in ourselves. We are the ones who, upon closing in on a work of art, liberate the powers confined within. Without our ability to ingest, our own ability to think, the work remains powerless. However, with our attentiveness we transpose the latent vision into real, perceptible deeds.[9]

After working on several films, Weiss began writing *The Persecution and Assassination of Jean-Paul Marat as Performed by the Inmates of the Asylum of Charenton under the Direction of the Marquis de Sade* (a.k.a. *Marat/Sade*) in 1963. Significantly more political than Weiss's previous work, *Marat/Sade* interrogated the idea of revolution and reflected the start of his open affiliation with socialism and his desire for theatre as political action.

Marat/Sade is a play within a play that intertwines historical facts with theatrical imagination; it is set in the French asylum of Charenton, where the Marquis de Sade (1740–1814) was confined in 1801 for his morally challenging, sexually explicit writings and behavior. While interned, Sade often wrote plays, though he never actually created one about the French Revolution. The asylum director in Weiss's play decides it may be therapeutic for the patients to perform a piece that Sade will write and direct. Sade chooses to depict the murder of French Revolutionary leader Jean-Paul Marat (1743–1793) by young Girondist Charlotte Corday (1768–1793). The entire action of the play occurs within the confines of the hospital and Sade assigns the roles of various French Revolutionary figures to the impulsive, often volatile asylum inmates. Because Marat's history is well known (thanks in part to Jacques-Louis David's 1793 painting of the invalid Marat dead in his bathtub), the play is not about narrative action (*what* happens), but instead relies on more thought-provoking theatrical techniques (Brechtian and Artaudian, for instance) to impart *how* the events unfold and what they might mean. The play presents the bleak world after the French Revolution, where madness and cynicism compound key questions about the differences between the aristocracy and the lower classes. The death of Marat is central, but Corday must come to his home three times before assassinating him. Therefore, much of the dialogue between Sade and Marat is rhetorical and didactic. The mania of the inmates as they attempt to play their roles—complete with songs, excesses, fits, and fury—infuses the philosophical arguments at hand.

Weiss's *Marat/Sade* uses the story of Marat to simultaneously critique the postrevolutionary Napoleonic regime of 1808, the rise of Nazism in the 1930s, and the politics of the 1960s. While clearly a product of a postwar/post-Holocaust Europe, the play is also a commentary on its own cultural moment in the 1960s; it represents Weiss's view of the complicated ideological position of artists, particularly Germans, at this point in European history. In *Marat/Sade*, the passionately sought-after revolution has already happened and great changes in the French government have transpired, but momentous inequities of power, access, and privilege remain. Weiss's work unequivocally examines whether or not daily life has improved enough to have warranted the death and destruction within the revolution. The meta-narrative character of Marat is conscious of ideology, particularly the immediate need for social and political change. The Marquis de Sade emerges as the intellectual and sexual individualist in the play, a detached nihilist seeking the revolution of the academic and the personal, supposedly with little interest in practical politics. Through these historical figures and the institutionalized people who play them, Weiss's work gives voice to a discordant clash of seemingly incompatible polemic positions.

The concept behind Weiss's play is itself revolutionary—residents of the asylum (locked away from society because they did not fit the values of the Enlightenment) perform the roles of influential revolutionaries, while their own revolution materializes before our eyes. The actors play inmates playing historical figures. These performers are not satisfied with the historical events as they occurred, nor with their aftermath; their performances become their protest against their own institutionalized existence. Their involvement makes the audience question just who, and what, is revolutionary and how sanity is defined. The layered roles of actors as inmates submerged within inmates as characters effectively deconstruct Enlightenment thinking in a play cleverly set at its conclusion. The piece directly critiques norms of representation and theatre itself while simultaneously exploring the boundaries of sanity. In Cuba, the piece was accepted as a vital part of the Marxist, pro-revolutionary international theatrical canon and was widely studied. Nara Mansur, Flora Lauten, and Raquel Carrió have each created new plays that actively interrogate historical and artistic texts, anchored by Weiss's *Marat/Sade*, highlighting them for reinterpretation.

Carlotta Corday

Born in Havana in 1969, playwright Nara Mansur grew up in revolutionary Cuba, (though she moved to Argentina in 2007) where she studied theatre from around the globe. A graduate of the Instituto Superior del Arte with theatre as her specialty, Mansur is also a published poet, essayist and former editor for the theatre area of the state-run Casa de Las Americas. Her "dramatic poem/monologue" *Carlotta Corday* was a finalist for first prize at Casa de Las Americas' Festival Escena Contemporànea de Dramaturgia Innovadora (Contemporary Stage Festival of Innovative Dramaturgy) and was originally published in the Cuban performance magazine *Tablas* in 2001.

Because the Cuban government interpreted Peter Weiss's groundbreaking play *Marat/Sade* as highly antiaristocratic and pro-Marxist, Cuban theatre scholars have been permitted to study it, according to theatre critic Rosa Ileana Boudet. During a personal interview I conducted with Boudet in Los Angeles in 2004, she explained that the play and Peter Brook's 1968 film version of it were often studied in universities in Cuba until the rapid economic decline of 1989, when luxuries like videotapes became increasingly scarce. Mansur told me she first read *Marat/Sade* while studying at the University of Havana. She begins her play *Carlotta Corday* with an extended quote directly from Weiss's script. In an exceedingly complex manner, *Carlotta Corday* reiterates Weiss's play-within-a-play model (at least for educated theatre audiences who recognize it) by directly referencing *Marat/Sade* and blending the past with the present. *Carlotta Corday* represents not only our historical knowledge but also our theatrical knowledge of the French heroine and her country's revolution.

Mansur's play is written as a poem, without a named speaker identified, and it works as a didactic conversation. It could be staged as a monologue or performed by many actors. The prologue immediately acknowledges its debt to Peter Weiss by incorporating his description of Charlotte Corday. The character speaks initially in third person, and then switching to first person singular, acknowledges the presence of the audience. She, presumably Corday, explains her preparation to kill Marat, ruminates on the nature of revolution, and struggles to define her identity. Questions about death, exile, and wish-fulfillment plague her. Then Marat speaks, posturing, daring others to take action, praising nationalism, and instilling a sense of urgency for political action. Corday returns and takes action—she kills Marat. She ponders whether or not future happiness is achievable, whether or not her action will "cure" any ills. The piece ends with a jarring, modern mix of snippets of politically charged global rap and salsa, thumping rhythms that distance the audience from any sense of genuine emotion. The final moments blend past and future actions, insisting that the labors of liberation (and self-liberation) remain ongoing, as the character comments, "Hasta la victoria siempre" (Toward victory, forever).

Carlotta Corday uses Charlotte Corday's history to comment on the construction of revolutions and their effects on contemporary, globalized citizens. Although Corday's story is a well-known part of French revolutionary history, her narrative is distanced, refracted, reconstructed, and re-represented by Mansur, generating substantial meaning far beyond its national and historical origins. It is highly significant that the historical Corday did not oppose the revolution, but was a committed revolutionary Girondist who did not like what the French Revolution had become. Soon after 1789, the radical Jacobin faction—of which Jean-Paul Marat was an outspoken member—initiated mass atrocities and beheadings known as the Reign of Terror. Robespierre instigated ruthless, unchecked executions with abandon. When Marat altered the course of the revolution by calling for dozens of Girondists to be guillotined, Corday began plotting to kill him.

Although the Cuban Revolution has been widely historicized and mythologized over the last fifty years, it, like the French Revolution, has often changed courses and has been highly contested for doing so. While many promises of the Revolution have been realized, sustaining the movement for such an extended period has required incredible malleability. Despite changes, Fidel Castro remains a national icon and a global symbol of socialism and defiance. Cubans often remark, "Fidel is the Revolution and the Revolution is Fidel." And, like Marat, Castro and Che Guevara's propensity for violence has often been obscured by their legendary status. They are intensely politicized and their historical personas, like those of Marat and Corday, continue to shape contemporary politics.

Carlotta Corday asserts that by killing Jean-Paul Marat, Corday paradoxically gave his supporters an excuse to execute even more dissenters. The outcome was exactly contrary to what Corday had hoped for, yet she has been immortalized in history for altering the French Revolution. Mansur's play acknowledges the "story" element of history, insistent that the moment history happens, it becomes myth—a key idea for the study of contemporary Cuba.

Mansur's play *Carlotta Corday* overtly cites Weiss's *Marat/Sade*, expressly stating, "Our show will be that of Jean-Paul Marat and his agony which we all know took place in his bathtub beneath the vigilant eye of Charlotte Corday,"[10] but the French revolutionary narrative primarily functions as an analogy and an allegory in Mansur's piece. The sole character in *Carlotta Corday* is unidentified and purposely elusive, constructed around what performance scholar Ann Pelligrini might describe as, "Less a matter of arriving at a fixed and final destination as it is of stopping off at points along the way to a somewhere and a someone else."[11] Often directly or nearly quoting Weiss's work, Mansur creates a complex pastiche of art and history that uses Corday to analyze revolution while presenting her in a way that is revolutionary itself. Just as *Marat/Sade* sharply alluded to Nazi Germany but also to its present moment, Mansur carefully envelops her criticism of the Cuban Revolution in French history in order to create space for her own articulations within the present epoch. Akin to the Marquis de Sade's play-within-a-play, *Carlotta Corday* is explicitly crafted to challenge political, social, and cultural boundaries *without* openly alarming the state. The French Revolution and Weiss's intervention become tropes Mansur uses to investigate decisive moments of Cuban history as well as the island's present. If, as literary scholar Sidney Parham has argued, "The similarity of the actual histories is less important than the similarity of the ways in which they are perceived,"[12] it is clear that this theatrical production heavily relies on the *perception* of associations between the French Revolution and that of Cuba.

"History says that [Corday] is a myth, a stranger who became the most famous assassin of any politician,"[13] asserts Mansur in the prologue of her dramatic poem. If we view transgression as that which exceeds established boundaries or limits, Corday was surely transgressive. However, in his book *Transgression*, author Chris Jenks states unequivocally that crimes and transgressions are not necessarily the same thing, and that only certain crimes can be viewed as transgressive acts. Jenks claims that a transgressor often attempts "to maintain control of a situation that verges on total chaos."[14] Corday clearly sees her murder of Marat as a valiant attempt to maintain control of France, to end the irrepressible Reign of Terror. However, the lasting effects of her actions were far more transgressive than the actions themselves. Contrary to Bataille's notion that death is the final limit that shapes humans,[15] Corday's execution did not restrain her expansive legacy of transgression. Corday continues to arouse adoration from those who regard her as a timeless heroine of France, a secular version of Joan of Arc, although she did not directly achieve the goal she set out to accomplish.

Once France was finally secure and its finances organized, Robespierre could no longer justify the slaughter of the Reign of Terror. He was executed in July 1794, but not before his viciousness had altered the definition of a revolutionary. The term would now denote a person not only active in the transformational events themselves, but one who could justify exerting excessive power subsequent to this kind of transformation. Although Napoleon wiped out some of the revolution's democratic advances when he came to power in 1799, the revolution had achieved a number of irrevocable victories. No French leader after 1790 dared rescind the rights and property stipulations gained during the revolution. Under all successive systems of taxation, every French citizen paid according to his or her wealth rather than his or her status. The feudal system was eliminated, freeing peasants from oppressive contracts and servitude. The French people gained considerable influence over their government and would not soon forget the atmosphere of liberation the revolution created, no matter how slowly practical changes came.

A member of an aristocratic but impoverished family, Corday was well-educated and had once vehemently *supported* the revolution through the

Girondist party. Mansur claims, "maybe [Corday] did not know where the circumstances of [Marat's] bloody death would lead. . . . In Marat's slaughter, Corday gave an ironic twist to the circumstances of a revolutionary cause."[16] By killing him, Corday turned Marat into an even greater revolutionary hero. Additionally paradoxical is the fact that Corday died, remorselessly, via the guillotine, the central instrument of the brutal terror she had protested.

Historians Nina Corazzo and Catherine R. Montfort affirm that Corday "brazenly transgressed the basic moral orthodoxies of her time"[17] in her roles as an unmarried woman, an intellectual, a female, and an assassin; all four of these roles were diametrically opposed to the idealized conduct acceptable in the late eighteenth century. Yet rather than being "ostracized from socialized womanhood" for defying societal norms, as Jenks argues,[18] Corday became a model for what Corazzo and Montfort call the "informed and politically engaged woman of the future."[19] For Mansur, that future was in Cuba. Her play comes from the perspective of an individual who has had first-hand experience with and knowledge of the results of a revolution.

The Cuban Revolution is continually contested because it has been transformed considerably since its inception nearly fifty years ago—its initial Marxist/Leninist principles have been altered, its social objectives have often shifted, and its concerns have varied. Like French revolutionaries Danton, Robespierre, and Marat, Castro and Guevara were educated intellectuals (a lawyer and a doctor, respectively) who led an anti-intellectual rebellion of the populace against the elite. They desired to create a country where equality was indispensable, and they attempted to redistribute wealth among the people.

While many of the promises of the Cuban Revolution have been realized, sustaining the movement for nearly five decades despite a hefty U.S. embargo has required increasingly authoritarian governance. Dissidents historically have been and continue to be jailed, exiled, or executed for their disagreements with the Castro administration. The government's sentences for crimes against the state are generally swift and terrible. Guevara's persistent avowal of violence as a means of purporting change is often masked by the mythical reverence he has inspired since his death. Fidel Castro remains a global symbol of socialist defiance against capitalist hegemony. Repetition was his greatest tool—he wore green military fatigues and the same scraggly beard since 1959, he consistently gave public speeches for hours without notes, and he unfailingly reiterated revolutionary slogans year after year. Even with Raúl Castro now in power, it is suspected that Fidel rules the country from behind the scenes. In many ways, he is the embodiment of how Cuba's mythical past is infused throughout its political present.

In *Reading Plays*, performance scholar Una Chaudhuri writes of the politics of interpreting *Marat/Sade*. She explains that in the play, "a 'there and then' is rendered as a 'here and now.'" Although the French Revolution and Sade's play about it supposedly occurred years before, Chaudhuri writes, "Everything occurs in the present tense, before our eyes."[20] Her text is crucial to investigating the Cuban adaptations of Weiss's work, because these adaptations focus on the anachronistic openings in the text, those ideas that are currently transforming and contested rather than merely historically represented. Like Diana Taylor's conception of the "new world" being constructed as Cubans watched, Chaudhuri aptly insists *Marat/Sade* depicts much more than two revolutions, the sociopolitical and the revolution of the body, not as fixed histories but as "in process." Her work reveals the immediacy of *Marat/Sade* as a play in which modern views can actively alter the reception of events from both 1808 and 1793. When Mansur writes of Charlotte Corday and the French Revolution, she uses present-day Cuba to frame the past and the past to frame present-day Cuba, layering and obscuring chronological time and our perceived notions of history.

Carlotta Corday begins in 1990, with a girl attending her grandfather's funeral; Mansur immediately grounds the piece in contemporary times, with Cuba's history as the play's pretext when the speaker remarks, during a blackout, that "the lantern with which my grandfather made the 'Campaña de Alfabetizaciòn'[21] illuminates the tiny shadow of the coffin."[22] The Revolution's recent struggles to keep electricity flowing and the grandfather's participation in its national literacy campaign of the early 1960s are mingled together to create a pastiche of periods and circumstances. Being able to read, to comprehend, and to see (i.e., to have enough light to read) are comingled. The character then mentions a friend who "arrived yesterday" with a photo album of pictures of contemporary Boston, creating a juxtaposition between modern Cuba and the United States. Globalization reigns, as the performer also notes the "bitter agricultural landscape of Afghanistan, and its dead, and more dead, and more death" and her relief that her grandparents died "without any news" (5). Is Mansur referring to the fact that although the last Soviet troops left Afghanistan by 1989, a brutal civil war between the mujahedin and communist Najibullah regime killed thousands of Afghans in 1990? Mansur specifically references a country that experienced a post-Soviet civil war. Her work might imply that Cuba could experience a similar situation. America's brutal incursions in Afghanistan only further complicate this remark. Because Mansur describes Corday as an "intriguing figure of the Worldwide Revolution" (3), this character is undoubtedly linked to dozens of transformative movements around the globe and throughout history; in this manner, Mansur's piece effectively complicates historical space and time.

Mansur's character also admits,

> Before I used to think of the impression of my submerged
> country
> of the peasants, of the streets, of the garbage. . . .
> Before I used to meet revolutionaries in school.
> Before.
> Before. (6)

The idea of submersion is particularly evocative of the strenuous conditions in Cuba by 1990, after the collapse of the Soviet Union. It also posits the demise, or sinking, of the island itself. Mansur's Cuba is floundering. What exactly does "before" signify? Fifty years later, it is difficult to accurately recall or understand how Cuba functioned *before* the Revolution. Mansur's repetition of *before* takes us back even further, possibly to a time when revolution wasn't even a part of Cuban consciousness. Moments later, this character explicitly questions, "And later? / And the past and the present?" (13). The archetypal conflict between history and myth, between the old and the new, slowly emerges as the revolutionary past is blended with a theatrical and historical present.

If *Marat/Sade* introduces "the problematic of our access to the real," as Chaudhuri suggests, *Carlotta Corday* dispenses with *any notion* of the real in order to problematize its very existence within an ever-evolving political reality. And like Sade, who, according to Chaudhuri, "repeatedly enters . . . not as a character but in his own person" in *Marat/Sade*,[23] Mansur creates a postmodern "character." There are no individually delineated "roles" in her dramatic monologue/poem. This speaker could be understood as a present-day Corday, an anonymous woman, or possibly Mansur the poet herself. This restructuring of a traditional narrative expands Weiss's metanarrative concept one step further, outwardly critiquing all categories of theatrical portrayal. Mansur's piece also depicts the "madness" engendered by this blending of identities, especially that of playwright/poet with character.

This amalgamation is Mansur's way of using what Chaudhuri describes in *Marat/Sade* as "a radically nonpsychological coding of human experience in terms not of ideology but of physical symptoms."[24] In *Carlotta Corday*, history and revolution appear on the body itself. For instance, Mansur directly quotes Weiss's description of Corday's arrival in Paris, noting her fatigue and the ways in which the city bombards her senses. The effect is corporeal—noticeably sensual and sexual. Mansur's character sees and smells "perfumes and cosmetics" and is offered "tricks against syphilis/pears, sponges, bottles, condoms."[25] The sound of birds and the scent of flowers intrigue her, but she resists them as she resolutely pursues Marat. The body is inundated with sensations, made conscious and stirred, yet its awakening is disregarded in favor of Corday's ultimate objective. The body is not silenced, however; its reactions persist. The character/performer questions the physical experience of "the lack of breathing" (7) on her journey and implores,

> What can I do with my illness? Should I put sun-lotion on it?
> . . . My crime releases me from the disease that I am suffering,
> an isolation, a criminal desire of desolation. (9)

Mansur also maintains the sexual nuances of *Marat/Sade* throughout *Carlotta Corday*, as her character performs acts such as "preparing the weapon, fitting [her] corset, masturbating with the future sparkle of the blaze" (6). Furthermore, she describes her relationship to Marat like that of a spurned lover. Like Weiss, Mansur creates distinctive, intermingled layers of sexual, physical, and political meaning in her poetic, encoded remarks such as, "Oh no / once more the immense supposed happiness / is delayed"(11). *Carlotta Corday* also blatantly sexualizes the revolution itself, commenting that it "lasts as long as an orgasm, / in a minute lightning falls, consumes, and dazzles" (11). Revolution is equated with a brief sexual climax and an impressive, though fleeting and uncontrollable, weather condition. *Carlotta Corday* physicalizes the weakened state of this über-masculine revolution, associating it with the "diluted virility" of the clipped trees in Havana's public parks.

In Mansur's play, just as in *Marat/Sade*, "Ideas about violence become violent gestures and movements, talk of revolution becomes active rebellion, and a mythologized, dehistoricized past regains a new particularity."[26] The ideas expressed by Mansur's character are revolutionary themselves, and the body is reinserted into the political/historical as this subversion is enacted. The talk, gestures, and actual rebellion all emerge from Mansur's single female character/body, who, "when killing"—destroying one body—is "saving thousands" of other bodies.[27]

In *Reading Plays*, Chaudhuri writes, "Multiplicity is not merely a fact of [*Marat/Sade*'s] stage history . . . or even of its textual history; rather it is a property of the play's meaning, structured into its text in the form of a complex system of historical and psychological layering."[28] It is by subsuming Weiss's work into her own that Mansur manipulates this multiplicity and adds to it another intriguing layer. For instance, the audience may hear echoes of Weiss's insistence that "the highway led over mountains of dead"[29] when Mansur's character repeats lines such as, "The revolution taught us that sometimes the flowers are devastated by the tanks."[30] Yet Mansur's heroine insists on taking it all one step further than Weiss does, indicting revolution itself and outwardly advocating for change. This character clarifies her comment about the tanks when she bravely insists, "I do not say the society, I say the revolution. I say 'the revolution of the revolution of the revolution.'"[31] Moreover, the outspoken speaker in *Carlotta Corday* even audaciously proposes an antinationalistic future, demanding that "the idea of a great army and an Olympic team be erased from our spirit,"[32] in order to integrate into a globalized society.

If, as Parham asserts, "Our interpretation of history is determined by the politics prevailing in our time,"[33] the critique of contemporary Cuba within Mansur's work cannot be overstated. Because a reader produces a play as much as the play itself operates on the reader, a Cuban audience witnessing *Carlotta Corday* must question boundaries when Nara Mansur, an educated female within a revolutionary system, writes about an educated female within a revolution who chooses to murder a revolutionary in the hopes of restoring her country. The play exposes what Corazzo and Montfort argue, that, "On the symbolic level, [Corday's] act was construed as constituting the slaying of the Patriarch and by extension, as life-threatening to the patriarchal structure as a whole."[34] Mansur's piece lyrically declares:

> Oh father. Pater. Pathetic. Pathetic father. Pathetic paternity.
> Unemployed father. Papa. Potato. Pope.
> Mobile—Pope. Pa lo que sea Fidel pa lo que sea. [For what is to be, Fidel]
> Pa pa pa pa pa pa pa pa pa (onomatopoeia of an AK-47 burst)[35]

The play is inevitably contextualized by the audience's awareness of the existing patriarchal system in Cuba (and the possible censorship) under which Mansur wrote. Their "experience is shaped by the power relations around [them]," as Parham suggests.[36] When her character points out that Marat is "too much a father for those who are not his children," Mansur's critique of the Cuban political patriarchy can be inferred. When Mansur's character asks, "What does a bathtub of blood mean in relation to the blood that is still to be shed,"[37] the provisional future of Cuban politics comes to the fore. Will there be bloodshed in the island's future? Much more than the French Revolution is evoked when this character, on stage in a struggling post-Soviet Cuba, poignantly tells the public, "We are the inventors of the revolution but we still don't know how to use it" (7).

In *Carlotta Corday*, Mansur's character deals with the Revolution's effect on personal identity by expressing her own troubled subjectivity. The Cuban Revolution's impact comes rapidly and has an immediate effect on her home life. She recalls, "Early in the morning we were playing in our parents' bed and the revolution appeared, very quickly on the TV set, on the 'hot corner' of 23rd and 12th" (9). These references to the "esquina caliente" (hot corner)—a place where locals hold heated discussions of politics and baseball—and the immediacy of television express an initial view of the Revolution as dialectical and modern, but also dazzling because of its spectacle and rapid inception.

This character attempts to sort through the crisis of identity she soon experiences in the revolution's wake, but she encounters fundamental obstacles to doing so. She painfully admits, "In order to distinguish the false from the fair you have to know yourself. / I do not know myself" (7). Her efforts at identification are illusory, as she asserts,

> I'm an assassin
> But this is not an identity
> As if something were an identity
> In reality, I was born in Latin America
> I ate a lot of magic beans since I was a girl. (8)

Here, philosopher Mikhail Bakhtin's notion that the unfixed, open-ended body creates cultural and political intimations is apropos. These allusions are precisely why this character emerges before the audience's eyes, in the present. She clearly views herself as part of something larger, a globalized Latin America, yet she can only tie herself to those countries through their staple food item, beans. Hence, she acknowledges the slippages within this designation "Latin America" and within the vague unification of many distinct identities.

Unlike Weiss's Corday, who is never fully dimensional because she is led around the stage by others while in a narcoleptic, dreamlike state, Mansur's character is healthy, entirely present, and maintains agency. Like the Revolution, she can never be completed, but she attempts to develop some semblance of an identity within the play. Because Mansur asserts that "history says that [Corday] is a myth" (3), this Corday-like character is unsure of her own identity—she grows increasingly perplexed and even remarks, "I don't know if I am the executioner or the victim / the instrument of torture or the messenger of God." She questions the utility of "self-destruction" but also of "self-exposure," and it is clear that her general "delirium" (12) has the potential to be profoundly detrimental. She is trapped in interstitial space, as she explains that she has "always felt like a stranger" but admits "the exile for me has yet to begin. / I still dream with my country" (10). These dichotomies cause her to doubt her personal discoveries and ultimately create the need for her "to forget and to destroy the illusion or hope so that the illusion does not destroy me" (8). The literal "revolution," an intense spinning, has left subjectivity unclear.

At moments throughout *Carlotta Corday*, the parallels between contemporary Cuba and eighteenth-century France are unambiguous and therefore startlingly subversive. Mansur courageously contends,

> Be convinced of this. To die. His death will return peace to us.
> It will restore democratic behavior

To our citizens
He very slyly still wants to make us believe that the terror will
be brief
But we know what he thinks about the greatness of our nation
Charlotte Corday, suppress this heroism,
Scoff at France and all nations. (10)

Mansur stays just within acceptable limits by consistently framing her comments in French history, by returning to Corday and her task of killing Marat, while still allowing for important slippages in meaning within her work. Marat is the assumed "he," but others can surely be inferred. The text's dynamic relationship to *Marat/Sade* and to Cuba's particular revolutionary history make it possible to read *Carlotta Corday* as much more than simply an impassioned view of the past.

Where, as Chaudhuri notes, "in the final moments of [*Marat/Sade*] the assassinated Marat's spirit has entered . . . to lead a new revolution, in response to a new oppression,"[38] *Carlotta Corday* sarcastically employs identifiable Cuban revolutionary slogans to advocate victory beyond its own "Marat," or rather "the revolution, of the revolution, of the revolution." If, as Parham contends, "all the behavior in the modern world is an equally logical response to a person's experience of that world,"[39] the play's ending is a thinly veiled, impassioned cry for further aggressive change. "At the same time," writes Parham, "we understand that the violence of the Revolution, while liberating to its participants, ultimately brings on the equally oppressive Empire, which has callously co-opted the slogans of the Revolution"[40] Mansur has pinpointed this double bind and does not posit a way out. Her ensnared character remains ensnared, longs "to be free of [her] own gaze . . . to be free of [her] own accusations"[41] as she questions her own part in the entire revolutionary process—she implores, "What does it mean, civil complicity?" (8). Rather than answer this query, she presents a sardonic chef's recipe for "floating islands" that "makes 11 million servings" and notes that the "survivors are floating in the Gulf of Mexico" (14). This remark reinforces Mansur's intense skepticism about the making of a nation after years of globalization and the imposition of uniformity that any process of nation-making entails. She acknowledges that Cuba still seems to float, untethered, and precarious. Eleven million, Cuba's population, are "served" by the state. The "survivors" in the Gulf could be the *balseros*, rafters who have risked their lives to leave the island over the last fifty years.

The performer in *Carlotta Corday* asks "the improvisers / to propose the future happiness / an uncertain song" (18), although she does not suggest what that future might involve. In a song globalized by its "rap" and "salsa rhythm," Mansur's character ties her physical needs and desires to her own psychological needs and the desires of women everywhere, remarking, "I want a dress / I want a destiny / I want a castle" (18). A dress is basic, a destiny is epic, and a castle is fantastical. Her desire for a destiny signals her desire for a future. The piece then bids a fond good-bye to Cuba's specific circumstances, as Mansur writes,

> Farewell to arms
> Farewell to the shipwrecked
> Farewell to the guillotine
> To paredones [execution walls]
> To barbudos [the bearded ones, i.e., the revolutionaries]
> To delinquents. (19)

This dense stanza references the influence of iconic American author Ernest Hemingway (alluding to his home in Cuba and close relationships with Cubans), Cubans and other refugees who leave their homelands in makeshift boats or other vessels, and the killing mechanism of the French Revolution but also the figurative beheading (anti-intellectualizing) of Cuba. The island is intimately connected to people and ideas outside its borders. The "farewell" disappears in the last three lines, perhaps to signify that these things still exist in Cuba.

The character, who has become an assassin herself, looks forward to a moment beyond all of these brutal extremes, and she hopes that Cuban children will "grow up without restrictions" (20). Yet, as a dedicated citizen, she cannot avoid co-opting a revolution, reiterating Guevara's "*hasta la victoria siempre*" as part of her final acceptance of her condition. This ultimate concession, that the sought-after utopia could still be in the future, enables the play to avoid government censorship. Ultimately, the work insists, as Jenks does, that transgression is not necessarily revolutionary or disruptive, but rather an intrinsic component of postmodern aspirations for the future.[42]

Charenton

In late September 2005, Teatro Buendia produced *Charenton*, an adaptation of Peter Weiss's *Marat/Sade*, by Flora Lauten and Raquel Carrió. Teatro Buendia was formed in Havana in 1986 and is mostly comprised of graduates from the Instituto Superior del Arte The group focuses their projects on two parallel goals—(1) creating large, often spectacular productions and (2) investigating the cultural traditions of Latin America and the Caribbean as part of a permanent center known as EITALC, the Escuela Internacional de Teatro para América Latina y el Caribe (International School of Theatre for Latin America and the Caribbean). Lauten and Carrió are theatre professors who also work with the International School of Theatre Anthropology

(ISTA) and at the University of Arts of Havana. In 1998, Teatro Buendia garnered the Ollantay Prize, awarded by CELCIT, the Centro Latinoamericano de Creación e Investigación Teatral (the Latin American Center of Theatrical Creation and Investigation), for their contributions to Caribbean theatre. Two of their most famous productions include *La Otra Tempestad* (created in 1997 and remounted in 2003, using material from Shakespeare's *Tempest*) and *Bacantes* (performed in 2001/2002, an adaptation using material from the Dionysian myth and Euripides' *Bacchae*). Well-known for its expressive acting and innovative reinventions, Teatro Buendia has toured extensively and presented works at the most significant festivals in Latin America, Europe, Asia, Africa, and Australia.

Teatro Buendia made their U.S. debut in July 2010, when their latest production, *La visita de la dama vieja* based on Friedrich Dürrenmatt's *The Visit*, was performed at the Goodman Theatre's Latino Theatre Festival in Chicago. Buendia also remounted *Charenton* for this festival, and both pieces were presented with English supra-titles. (They also gave a single performance of *La visita*, but not *Charenton*, in Miami.) The group's U.S. visit garnered intense national attention. Flora Lauten and Goodman Associate Artistic Director/Festival Curator Henry Godinez were interviewed on a National Public Radio broadcast, 13 July 2010, and Godinez wrote a short piece for *American Theatre* (May/June 2010) about Buendia's impact. Playwright and author Caridad Svich also profiled Buendia's history and development processes in the same issue, in an article entitled *A Flower in Havana*.[43] Both pieces drew large, excited, engaged audiences who, no matter their political views, highly praised the performances.

Lauten and Carrió chose to adapt *Marat/Sade* because they shared Weiss's confusion about his goals as a writer and artist—should a play be a call for socialist action or instead focus on the need for aesthetic revolution? In his review of the piece for the Cuban newspaper *Granma* on 7 April 2005, Amado del Pino wrote that *Charenton* "manages to engage in a dialogue with the Cuban spectator on as decisive subjects as the concept of personal freedom, the utopia, the place of art, the relativity of the historical process, and the diversity of human passions."[44] Buendia's production posits that if Sade and Marat function as the two halves of a dichotomous philosophy, the play could possibly advocate for, and critique, both ideas.

Charenton was first staged at Teatro Buendia's theatrical home in Nuevo Vedado (on the outskirts of central Havana) during the International Theatre Festival of 2005. Their reappointed church's remote location, alone on the fringes of the urban center and difficult to reach by public transportation, contributes to the impression that Buendia is an alternative company. However, the company is certainly not immune to Cuba's current conditions; I attempted to see this performance twice before actually being able to do so.

The first night of the performance, in early September 2005, so many tickets had been promised to those from the foreign press that very few members of the Cuban public were admitted, despite some having waited in ticket lines for hours. On the second night, the performance was cancelled due to an area-wide power outage. On the third night, after I had waited outside in line for several hours to get a ticket, Flora Lauten (the show's director) emerged to apologize to the audience for a delay in that evening's performance. She explained that the electricity had gone out around 5:00 P.M. and although it had recently been restored, the cast and crew now needed time to prepare for the performance. Originally scheduled to begin at 7:00 P.M., the show finally started shortly after 8:15 P.M.

For this production, the theatrical space was arranged intimately, with a three-walled stage and a very tightly packed audience of roughly seventy people on bleacher-style seats. The company's choice of title for their adaptation, the name of the French asylum itself, immediately determined and made pivotal the insular sanctuary of the space. The piece is described in its program as an "Ópera bufa," a popular comic opera with recognizable, lower-class characters and secularized music.[45] The dim, dramatic lighting at the play's inception created a sinister and serious ambience. Skulls and large dolls were used as set dressing, as were tattered velvet curtains. A sheer paneled scrim separated the audience from the performers, subtly indicating the opening and closing doors of Charenton.

As the light slowly brightened, actors were revealed sitting with their backs to the audience but partially visible in the mirrors of vanity/dressing tables, in cells all over the playing area. The actors appeared sickly, wearing white facial makeup and threadbare, flowing cream-colored costumes made of a frail, bandage-like material. Some wore late-eighteenth-century wigs. On the ringing of a bell by director Lauten (who was seated in the center of the first row of the audience), the actors subtly came to life amid strains of Berlioz's "Spectre of the Rose," the orchestrated romantic lament of a plucked rose worn at a fancy ball. This poem-set-to-music expresses the morning after the event, when the fragile rose is dying. The music's arpeggios echo the waltz danced the night before, a fading memory of an unrepeatable moment. The piece transports the audience into a luxurious fantasy world that seems genteel and appealing, but ends forlornly. It could be a reference to both the Napoleonic aristocratic age and its imminent decline, or the wilting aspirations of the beloved Revolution. Lauten's external involvement broke the fourth wall, unified space and time as being within the asylum walls, and made it obvious that these performers and their environment were exceedingly controlled, even within their fantasy world. On a second bell from Lauten, a hanging effigy of Coulmier, the asylum director, was made visible above center stage. Without this censor, the internal means of control had been eradicated and these prisoners, on the lowest rung of the social ladder, might now be given voices within this setting.

Charenton links several revolutionary eras and circumstances in order to capture the indeterminacy inherent in these movements and in the present. The actor playing the Marquis de Sade, dressed in disheveled but accurate period clothing, suggestively remarks, "It's not difficult to transport yourself in time,"[46] yet he cleverly does not suggest whether the audience will be transported to the past or the actors to the present. He immediately blends insular space with historical time; moments later he announces the year "1793" while the cast begins to quietly sing the French national anthem and surround a skeleton at center stage. (The dialogue is generally in Spanish but often fuses the two societies by incorporating French idioms. All translations are mine.)

Directly addressing the public, Sade ironically asks, "Who doesn't remember the bloody actions of the Great Revolution that changed the world,"[47] a remark followed by Marat shouting, "Viva la Revolución," a phrase still widely used in Cuba. Hence, in only these first several moments of the play, a connection between revolutions has already emerged. The play seeks to reveal something from the past that might posit a future. It grapples with how artists within a revolution that, according to José Quiroga, "always looked at the present from the point of view of the future"[48] might represent the past. Sade soon notes that, "Some say that history repeats itself . . . first as tragedy, and after . . . as comedy!"[49] The piece implies that revolutions might be at once repeatable and ridiculous.

A reiteration and revision of Weiss's narrative device, the character of the Herald soon introduces the other characters on stage. In *Charenton*, the characters constantly destabilize the position of a traditional narrator by mixing various personas, plots, and descriptions. These begin with the corpulent Marquis de Sade, who enters dressed in high-heeled period shoes and a purple wig. In cheeky, almost mocking rhyming verse, the cast members describe the physical and creative attributes of this radical writer. A character named Napoleoncito then renames the hospital an "arsenal," but when Antoineta (who thinks she's Marie Antoinette) insists they do not want it to explode, the inmates respond that this is only because of "diazepan" (diazepam, a sedative used to treat anxiety, mania, epilepsy, and addictive withdrawal). This modern reference undeniably removes the audience from the period and firmly situates the action in the pharmaceutically tempered present. This reference might also raise questions particular to Cuba's economic situation and the reach of globalization. Cubans understand what diazepam is, yet if someone on the island were to want or need it, it would be difficult to find and even harder to afford due to the U.S. embargo. References to modern items, like prescription medications, make the parallels between the French and the Cuban Revolutions overt and palpable.

With *Marat/Sade* as the inspiration behind *Charenton*, it follows that layers of iteration are crucial to understanding the latter. Because of speculations about Fidel Castro's mistrust and obsession with security, the fact that the revolutionary leader Marat is written as a "patient that suffers from paranoia"[50] is infused with meaning. The uninhibited inmates decorate Marat's body with yellow paint, depicting the cheese-like effect of his skin disease, while he is drenched in his bathtub by his ominous companion Simone. Much like the mythical Castro, the people create this Marat, literally applying his diseased skin. Yet unlike the virulence once attributed to revolutionary guerillas, Marat is confined to his bath and is diminutive, physically weak and reliant on others for his daily survival. An aging, sickly Castro, who remains powerful although he no longer appears in public, comes to mind. Confined to his tub, Marat assumes the position depicted in David's famous painting, "The Death of Marat." This repetition is crucial; it ties this play to Weiss's (the cover of which was David's painting) and Weiss's play to David's painting. Although Taylor argues that the revolutionary image involves a "rigorous elimination—rather than the traditional accumulation—of signs,"[51] *Charenton* continually amasses and combines recognizable visual representations to highlight the links between movements.

This multivalent layering calls on the audience's historical, artistic, and theatrical knowledge of Marat, even before they have had a chance to form impressions of this particular performance. The piece suggests that modern revolutionary iconographies (famous photos of a young Fidel Castro or statues of Che Guevara, for example) work in conjunction to color impressions of revolution. Add these tiers of comprehension to the actor-as-inmate, then the inmate-as-character matrix, and the theatrical effect is increasingly complex. It's difficult to assess whether the audience is affected by *this* Marat or by their own perceptions of him. The spectacle is familiar.

Power emerges as another central theme of the performance as the Marquis de Sade's mother is presented. She is attractive and dressed in tight clothing that accentuates her shapely figure. While a lullaby plays, the Marquis is forced to his knees and suckles his mother's overtly naked breast, highlighting his unconventional sexuality (Freudian) and the obsession with power relations that arouses him throughout the piece. In another struggle for power, the inmate playing Charlotte Corday firmly resists her role. She fights and screams as she is brought before the audience, although she is described as both "noble and provincial."[52] She is forced to enact this role, although she objects.

Power and its limits are again invoked when the character Toussaint, played by the darkest-skinned actor on stage, is introduced as "the liberator of Haiti" (11). His theme song is played, a lament of plantation slaves that Simone mournfully sings. Toussaint appears gentle and sympathetic;

however, it is unclear just how his inclusion comments on the French Revolution or reflects on Cuba's particular history. The historical freed slave Toussaint L'Ouverture (a moniker that means "the opening," given to him for his battlefield savvy) was inspired by the French Revolution's Enlightenment promise of the Rights of Man. L'Ouverture led a valiant Haitian army against the British and the Spanish in the 1790s in defense of the French Revolution, leading directly to the British withdrawal from Haiti in 1798. L'Ouverture is also credited with freeing the slaves of Santo Domingo. There is no such character in Weiss's play. The fact that Toussaint is included as a character in *Charenton* raises crucial questions about the inclusion of Afro-Cubans in Cuba's history, as well as current racial inequities, slavery, and colonial subjectivity. Issues of power and control are emphasized, along with the impact of courageous dissent in the Caribbean. The far-reaching influence of the human rights sought during the French Revolution is also foregrounded. Here, *Charenton* seems to suggest that the power struggles within all sorts of global revolutions are interrelated, that they somehow breed and certainly influence one another.

Charenton explores how violent historical events, such as L'Ouverture's battlefield victories, Castro's attack on the Moncada barracks, or Marat's murder, generate an immense cache of symbolic meaning within revolutionary contexts. The events are more symbolic than necessary. For example, when the mounting tension between French commoners and the elite morphed into a scramble to amass arms, Assembly supporters raided town hall and later, on 14 July 1789, stormed the sizeable armory of the Paris prison known as the Bastille. While the weapons recovered there were undoubtedly useful, taking over the Bastille conveyed the message that the revolutionaries were a serious force to be reckoned with. The spectacular, mythologized storming of this medieval fortress became the focal event of the French Revolution and is often synonymous with it. This event *was* the violent, rapid breach of law, the "complete and forcible overthrow" (as defined by *Webster's*) that cemented the French Revolution in time and history. The months of secret messages relayed by citizens, the makeshift barricades in the streets, and the French army advancing on its own people are often framed as merely the historical backdrop for the dramatic events on 14 July. The *meaning* of the fall of the Bastille became far more significant than the event itself ever could have been. This invasion defined taking a stand against the aristocracy, against injustice and excessive authority through specific action. The Bastille became a symbol of the triumph of the less powerful over the dominant, of underlings over the privileged. Similar to Fidel's triumphs in the Sierra Maestra, the Bastille became a symbol of revolution itself.

Leadership and responsibility also become essential themes of the play. For instance, when Marat is praised as the friend of the "pueblo" (the people, the nation), inmates cry out, "We're hungry, Marat" and "Marat, we don't have bread!"[53] They sing, "We live imprisoned!" (17). They complain about daily injustices like ridiculously long bread lines, a condition familiar to contemporary Cubans. The inmates' clamoring for bits of bread, shouting that they are hungry, serves as an open analogy for modern Cuba in the Special Period. And when Simone insists, "Marat, the enemies of the people double-cross the revolution" (19), does this reflect the frustration and cynicism of the people, like the inmates' contemptuously imploring the afflicted, restricted Marat to "rise up" and go forward? (20).

The inmates soon grow hostile, insisting that the revolution should have brought them "food" and not "bread!" Their complaint is that a revolution should nourish a population rather than merely feed it. This raises key questions about whether or not the Cuban Revolution has nourished, or cultivated, its people. Several characters tell Marat, "It's incredible not to know where we're going" (21), reflecting their dissatisfaction with increasing uncertainty. Contemporary Cuba is also indeterminate, also unsure of its future. The piece speculates as to whether or not revolutionary leaders are responsible for what comes *after* their revolutions, and, if so, for how long. This crucial query undoubtedly resonates for contemporary Cubans as well.

The Marquis and the sound of the guillotine then enter the fray, mocking what comes after leadership of any kind. Sade snidely insists that Marat writes in "service" of the people while his own writing does the "contrary," because it is not geared toward utility (18). Sade's position is that revolution should inspire the liberation of the individual. If, as Taylor claims, "the [Cuban] revolution encouraged the surrender of the personal to the collective ideal,"[54] then Sade's position is particularly complicated for a Cuban audience. He could represent what has become of the revolution, or act as a counterpoint to it. In Kaja Silverman's estimation, both Marat and Sade may be understood as "dominated by identification and duality."[55] Sade mocks Marat for saddling the entire proletariat with burdens while ignoring the bullying power of the guillotine. When Marat reacts violently to these provocations, Sade claims that Marat's behavior is "characteristic of all tyrants,"[56] an expanded commentary on political power all over the world. These arguments are often posed about Fidel—some believe he has not adequately wielded his power to enforce revolutionary ideals, while others see him as a bully or dictator.

Sade goes on to ironically criticize the role of the arts, particularly his own and Marat's writings, noting that the people "will not have bread . . . but a lot of literature!" (23). He sardonically explains that he is "an aristocrat," but that there are worse things than revolt, such as "not being published." Buendia's complicated position, of providing art at a time when basic necessities are lacking, is thus revealed. Sade scornfully gorges himself on a lavish tray of bread and fruit in front of his hungry countrymen, mocking their longing to merge into a collective because it conflicts with his quest for separation. With his mouth full of food, he sarcastically adds, "And you already know that man cannot live by bread alone" (24).

As Napoleón's theme is played, Napoleoncito enters, dressed in rags that suggest the clothing of the French leader. Sade remarks on the image:

> From the old and from the new regimen. It still lives . . . [Napoleoncito advances, marching to a drum roll] Ah, but you can't imagine what comes after! You don't have the slightest idea of what a little soldier can do, a simple little tiresome soldier . . . [Napoleoncito at center stage gives a military salute with a saber] full of dreams and inventions! (24)

This passage invokes the shock many Cubans experienced years after the revolution, when state controls became increasingly severe. To Cuban dissidents, Fidel Castro, constantly dressed in his military fatigues, has proved reminiscent of Napoleon, a "soldier . . . full of dreams and inventions." The passage also reflects modern-day Cuba's conundrum about what might happen after Fidel Castro is gone; or it may serve as a general critique of the shortsightedness of any action taken without a delineated plan for what to do afterward.

The duration and reach of revolution remain central questions in this play. Sade tells Marat, "Think about it . . . the writings of Rousseau, of Voltaire . . . they led to the Revolution. And the Revolution . . . to Napoleon!" (25). Sade insists that no one can determine what actions an ideology may inspire. When Marat replies, "Napoleón? I don't know him," Sade alters time and explains that Napoleón is part of Marat's political party, the Jacobins, "only after" (25). Marat interrupts Sade, fervently insisting, "There is no after!" (26). Sade parodies Marat, laughing as he reiterates Marat's dictum, "I am the Revolution," after which there is "nothing" (26). The vital question of when a revolution is completed, of how it endures, is invoked by this exchange. If "Fidel is the Cuban Revolution, and the Cuban Revolution is Fidel" as is often noted, what might come after him is entirely unclear.

Roux, a deranged priest in the play, answers that the people are constructing a republic at the "edge of the guillotine" (26). The irony here is that this brutal device was primarily used by the Jacobins, for years, *after* the storming of the Bastille. This symbol of vicious violence continued well into the new France, as did violence by the Church. It was unclear when the revolutionary republic would take hold and its violence subside. Many Cubans fear the possibility of violence in their future, after the Castro brothers, as their country is transformed. These scenes artfully pose questions about when a revolution ends and what happens when it does.

After this revelation, the ambiance changes entirely. La Gran Feria de Paris (The Great Fair of Paris) begins—a vibrant public street celebration much like the opening of the international theatre festival in which *Charenton* was performed. The fair features lively circus music, crashing cymbals, and lavish costumes, and the inmate/actors dance with large puppets on stilts. It could be Cuban carnival. The stage directions read, "It is the representation of the arrival of Charlotte to the city . . . that received her in all its splendor" (38). Bizarre, macabre objects and dissonant sounds that are included help to make theorist Mikel Dufrenne's point about their incompleteness: "the represented world is not truly a world." This circus performance is not, in fact, "self-sufficient," as Dufrenne argues, and it is certainly "indeterminate."[57]

This simulation grows as Charlotte reenters on a wooden cart, as if she were a freak-show performer or an invention being displayed for the public at an exhibition. Both she and L'Ouverture emerge enslaved in chains. Their presence reminds us that women and racialized bodies remain embattled. This moment also ties France with the history of Haiti, situating black-led revolution on a pan-Caribbean stage. Considering the difficult, unstable conditions in modern Haiti, the connection is not positive. If these artists are suggesting that Haiti's fate was Cuba's alternative, this moment is highly politically charged. A visibly shaken L'Ouverture then performs a knife-throwing routine with the terrified, ill-prepared Corday, who catches one knife in her mouth and another between her legs. This Afro-Cuban body assaulting a white body could acknowledge Cuba's fears and racial prejudices, but both inmates seem so uncomfortably forced into these roles that the audience instantly absolves them of any responsibility for their actions. This circus act could suggest that both women and black men are pawns, without substantial agency, in this revolutionary chess game—that only white men in power will benefit. Corday's bound posture and the alluring, sexualized nature of their circus act merge this revolutionary hero and heroine with the sadist imagination. The scene could easily have come from one of Sade's banned novels, with which the inmates are clearly familiar.

As the brash carnival continues to become more and more surreal, Sade presents several "nobles" to the audience. Six large, grotesque puppets are brought onstage. One resembles "La Reina/the Queen," whom Sade calls "whore," and who has only a head and breasts for body parts but carries a pink-feathered fan. Another puppet is Madame Lavado (from the Spanish word meaning washed), an aging female devil, complete with long, dainty gloves. There is a puppet with red curly hair and a moustache as well as a male aristocrat, the Captain, with an enormous phallus that the queen sucks. While the scene mocks the aristocracy and critiques the "puppets" these aristocrats have become, it also suggests an eerie, sexual violence within the upper class. The devil drives the action, mostly centered on gendered body parts and overt sexual behaviors. Excessive, vicious laughter and the unrestrained pleasure of the puppeteers make these absurd moments particularly intimidating and unnerving. Fractured "bodies" seem to be all that is left when the past refuses to disappear. As eerie instrumental music plays and dry ice fog rolls in, the puppets freeze and "there are echoes, shadows, sounds, and deformed figures,"[58] ever-present vestiges and reminders of the past. Images are obscured and fragmented. The lunatics are now agitated and grow monstrous. Sade, "writing the text of the scene," explains, "The dead are staying" (43). This singular comment reflects much revolutionary rhetoric in Cuba, a nation predicated on how the past will construct the future.

Amid sounds of the guillotine's blade dropping and heads rolling, several puppets without heads laugh at Charlotte. She is naked from the waist up and appears above the wretched inmates, viewing, but not recognizing, this bizarre and outrageous scene. Here she mimics Weiss's Charlotte, questioning what city she has entered as she reacts to the stifling, sweltering air (possibly references to Cuba's oppressive heat, pollution, and humidity) tainted with blood and ashes. Charlotte questions, "Why do they dance . . . and laugh . . . and applaud . . . ? This mass of people who hit . . . insult . . . [and] murder!" (44). The stage direction reads that, around the image of Charlotte and the decapitated puppets, "enters the text of Marat in counterpoint with the text and image of Charlotte" (44). Charlotte sees Marat below, preaching liberation; the image suggests that Marat has become the talking head the aristocrats once were, that his revolution has merely replicated power hierarchies.

In a delirious state, Marat screams out, "Who are the real enemies?" and "The country is in danger" (46). He "doesn't know if what he hears is real or if they are visions and hallucinations" (47). Suffering from extreme paranoia, the leader cannot see. Marat calls out to Sade, "The difference between us, Marquis, is that I have a cause. . . . I want to create a new world!" (48). If the cause is the people's liberation, as Marat suggests, the setting within the confines of the asylum (a metaphor for an island?) ironically renders that goal null and void from the outset. Sade tells Marat, "There are no greater truths . . . than the changes experienced daily . . . in which a victim turns into an executioner and the most noble maiden [becomes] . . . a prostitute!" (49). This reference is especially poignant in modern Cuba, where the underprivileged control the black market and various forms of prostitution are rampant. In contrast, Sade speaks in singular terms, referring to the individual rather than to the collective. He insists that the changes brought on by revolution, although notable, have not necessarily been improvements for individuals.

The inmates are proof of Sade's idea. Caught up in the fervor of the fair and the murky haze that has enveloped them, they disdainfully remove Sade's wig, ruffled collar, and coat, leaving him in only white linen long underpants. The act is impulsive and callous, an attempt at fully exposing the Marquis. They also hastily undress Marat, leaving him in the same undergarments. Marat and Sade face one another with naked torsos and flimsy underpants. They appear the same, although one is thin and the other is plump. They appear equal, on the same physical level, although their aims are increasingly different. The stage directions explain that Sade and Marat should appear in their solitude but across from each other, at the same time. "Marat doesn't see anything, only shadows, and Sade has his eyes closed" (50). Neither is a visionary, neither sees as he should. While Sade is pleasurably and ritualistically flogged by Napoleoncito's long hair (as he is in Weiss's text), Charlotte viscerally reacts to each painful stroke. Marat is left out of this sexualized torture, this moment of masochistic release. His exclusion could be understood as a critique of either his inability to physically engage, to fight, or to feel human desire, or of the emotional, sexual, or physical detachment of leaders. For example, little is known about Fidel Castro's personal relationships or sexual encounters. Rather than Marat, it is Charlotte who ties the two revolutions (sexual and political) together, yet the flogging reinforces that she suffers great pains while taking part in each.

Marat excitedly exclaims, "One day the Revolution will be possible" (52), a challenging remark for contemporary Cubans. Is their revolution possible currently, or was it ever? Addressing the National Assembly, Marat reveals, "What does it matter that my eyes cannot see . . . ? We have to unite against the common enemy!" (54). Of course, Marat does not specify exactly who or what this enemy might be. His primary goal is blind unification, an objective of many world leaders. As Arif Dirlik explains, he lacks the understanding that "the revolution must emerge in the course of the struggle . . . the revolutionary, too, must be listening all the time and must not merely impose his abstractions upon the revolutionary process."[59] Instead Marat implores, "We need a politician who comes from the people!"[60] This is his last, desperate attempt to connect with them, to tie the public to their government. Marat comes from the people, a position paradoxically rendering him institutionalized by the masses.

As dissonant, loud music begins, the crowd of gyrating inmates grows disenchanted with Marat. They begin to demand, "Down with Marat! Down with the dictator!" (55), calling Marat a murderer and insisting he change course. Toussaint insists, "Down with the bars and the closed door!" and Juana chimes in, "Open the border and distribute the bread!" (56). These are pointed observations for a modern Cuban audience that is desperate to engage in global exchange while living with closed borders and rationed goods. Both the past and the present are directly invoked, as similar problems remain nearly half a century later.

Inmates themselves, Marat and Corday are only part of the cycle of revolution, a spinning wheel that returns to some point of origination. The piece suggests that history is a wheel, moving but repetitive rather than progressive. Devastated by Marat's impending murder, Simone laments: "But you can't stop this river of people without a history... without a future ... this mountain of men and women that are on this land. A land plagued with hunger... sickness... death. (*She cries.*) A land that could be... the paradise Marat dreamed of" (62). Her reference to "this land" provokes the conflation of revolutionary France and present-day Cuba. The beautiful socialist island is often marketed to tourists as a paradise, "the pearl of the Antilles" with its pristine beaches, mountains and colonial cities—it could be a utopia. When Charlotte asphyxiates Marat on stage, Sade offers her the knife to finish Marat off. Napoleoncito intercepts the weapon and offers it to the audience, enticing us to participate in this murder. Who dares assassinate the utopian ideals of "the revolution"? Sade cynically accuses Marat, "You saw the Revolution as a way to rise to power" (62), an especially audacious remark for Lauten and Carrió to present onstage before their own revolutionary government.

Like *Marat/Sade*, *Charenton* consciously balances on the edge of limits—hence Napoleoncito insists, "This is only a representation" (63). Sade immediately retorts "Of a work that you are going to prohibit," but Napoleoncito replies, "Not me! I don't like your experiment! I prefer the street a thousand times over, the odor of blood... than this lie" (63). Rather than attacking recognizable icons, this spectacle has incorporated these characters who use vivid theatricality (puppets, music, etc.) to raise questions about representation itself. The work is particularly risky when these pronouncements could directly indict the Cuban revolutionary government, Cuban audiences, or both. Disconcertedly emerging from her character, Actress-Juana tells the audience, "We are only actors... a group of comedians that you want to rescue... in this basement!" (64). Somewhere "between history and fiction," Sade indicts the privileged audience, asking "They didn't work for the king? They didn't enjoy the court? They didn't shave while the people in the streets suffer hunger, pain... and humiliations?" (64). No one is innocent as Sade's play ends.

Actor-Napoleoncito then opens a grate at the back wall of the stage, revealing the exterior door of the theatre and perhaps the exit from Charenton itself. In Weiss's play, the inmates enact their own revolution, beating the asylum director and his wife and daughter. In Buendia's version, Napoleoncito boisterously steps out into the Havana night, into "life outside of this representation" (65). The inmate-actors run to the door. With the actual city street visible in the background, Actress-Antonieta remarks, "Someone will arrive, two centuries later, to see the heavens that I didn't see" (66). Two centuries later would be the year 1993, the hardest part of the Special Period in Cuba. While the cast expresses hope for a future leader, Sade eradicates all meaning from this thought. His final observation is that the presentation was “A simple game of representation: din and fury . . . that signifies nothing!” (67). His critique—that revolutions and their accompanying spectacles signify little, that the revolution of the individual entails a profound loss of meaning for the collective—is direct and harsh. The layered, confusing images and contradictory icons in the play induce constant interpolation and analysis, while the play continually asserts that its observations could be entirely irrelevant.

The obscuring scrim is again arranged in front of the audience, as it was at the beginning of the play. The inmate-actors slowly return to their dressing tables, to the mirrors where they must see themselves anew, as they interrogate the stage as mirror. These mirrors, as scholar Jill Dolan argues, are able “to reflect what is now seen as an unstable, non-unified self.”[61] Actor-Toussaint covers Charlotte’s body with a red, white, and blue flag, a message that could be twofold—as signified by the flag, the nation can either protect and swathe its own, or obscure nakedness and reality. The flag’s colors are those of many nations, including France, Cuba and the United States. Actor-L’Ouverture returns to his cell as the lights go out. (Considering recent blackouts, I was not sure if this was intentional at first—then I noticed the streetlamp outside was lit.)

Everything and everyone had been utterly transformed, yet the euphoric and confusing environment remained. The world outside was still visible, the theatrical space extended out into Cuba’s capital and into oblivion. Like the poetic pieces Quiroga describes, *Charenton* became “a text of waiting, but . . . also a text that waits for something that may have already happened.”[62] The piece is a journey that will be repeated, by actors and audiences, again and again. Its unfixed conceptual depth and its insistence on repetition are its intervention, its attempt at regeneration and renewal.

Past and Present

Charenton and *Carlotta Corday* engage the spectacle and violence inherent in revolutions, dismantling them and investigating their extremes. The toll of violence on the individual, as well as its often-ineffectual continuance, is highly scrutinized on the Cuban stage. The extent of change within a revolution, change beyond the spectacle that might emerge from this violence, is explored as well. In *Charenton*, the promise of the greater freedom usually incorporated in revolutionary movements is eradicated from the outset because the piece is enacted by confined asylum inmates. In *Carlotta Corday*, Mansur’s character is imprisoned by her own disidentifications, exiled (rather than freed) by her own experiences. In her home, as in the asylum, self-determination has given way to authoritarianism. Hence, both pieces warn against the institutionalization of revolution, against warping its boundaries, ideas, and goals to force its adherence to a framework.

These plays also question formulations of the nation state as a vital component of revolutionary rhetoric; Teatro Buendia mingles nationalities and encounters with revolutions that do not necessarily bring significant change, while Mansur even suggests the end of nationalism itself. Like one basic definition of revolution, these plays signal, solicit, and demand a new era. These artists indicate that it is now the existing *revolutionary* frameworks that no longer sufficiently engage contemporary problems. The French Revolution did not achieve the majority of its coveted social outcomes—has the Cuban Revolution followed suit? Its defined goals have been considerably altered, and its classes have been newly (re)stratified (especially since the 1990s). The characters in these pieces desire the massive ripple effect that revolutions were previously thought to have globally; they long for the kinds of transformations that entirely reshape what is possible. But just as the island itself is never determinate, *Carlotta Corday* and *Charenton* directly engage the country's paradoxes, presenting revolution as ceaselessly and simultaneously constructive and destructive.

These plays are dialectical and have a profound largess precisely because they span decades, continents, theories, and styles. They pointedly refocus the earlier discourse surrounding rebellion by situating worldwide revolution as a struggle *against* power rather than for possession of it. Lauten, Carrió, and Mansur depict the aftermath of revolution, gazing back at it with a critical perspective, from years beyond its inception. Their reflections on the entire revolutionary process are experientially substantiated and informed. Their reliance on their theatrical predecessor Peter Weiss illustrates both their considerable knowledge of theatrical practices and their formidable ability to creatively cite, interpret, analyze, and expand the existing philosophical and performance discourses. They use reiteration as a launching pad for reimagination and reinvention. Their works successfully investigate a collective chronicle of revolution, both theatrically and historically, while engaging the extended moment of uncertainty in which Cubans live.

3

Revolution under Siege

Theatre, Globalization, and the Special Period

> The Special Period dealt us a bad hand.
> The habit of idealism ran dry.
>
> —Nara Mansur, *Ignacio y Maria*

In August 1990, the Cuban government officially recognized that the nation's economic situation was unsustainable and demanded drastic measures be undertaken during what it called *El periódo especiál* (the Special Period). The previously inconceivable demise of the Soviet Union left Cuba and its inhabitants in financial turmoil, as the country was forced to completely reorganize in order to participate in a now globalized world economy. For decades, extensive bartering agreements with the Soviets were Cuba's economic protection from the immediate effects of the U.S. embargo. The loss of major trading partners throughout Eastern Europe created a catastrophic contraction in Cuba's economy. Many trade shipments that were essential for Cuban industry (such as raw materials and spare parts) ceased altogether. Imported consumer goods declined nearly 75 percent, and favorable markets for Cuba's primary exports—sugar, coffee, and tobacco—vanished. Cuba's access to credit, oil, raw materials, equipment, spare parts, and affordable foodstuffs declined precipitously. These changes had a profound impact on development and living standards across the island. Cubans were expected to make daily concessions wherever they could, reducing their use of fuel and other products and abiding by stringent governmental restrictions. During the Special Period, "Life in Cuba settled into a grim and unremitting cycle of scarcity," writes historian Louis Pérez, "in which shortage begat shortage and where some of the most basic daily needs and wants could be satisfied only by Herculean efforts."[1]

The immediate consequences of ongoing "shortages" and "efforts" are represented by Cuban playwrights Miguel Terry (also known as Miguel Terry Valdespino) and Nara Mansur, who depict the exceptional circumstances faced by Cubans living between fractured modernity and postmodernity. These writers portray how the economics of globalization and the

Special Period affected individual identities and relationships. Terry and Mansur illustrate how Cubans integrated the "costs and ideological risks"[2] implied by market reforms such as self-employment and booming tourism. Their plays theatrically convey the losses and inventiveness, the connectedness and isolation, and the disruptions, fissures, and indeterminacy of the Special Period. Desire, fear, hope, despair, and imagination are common themes of the extraordinary era of evolution wrought by the globalization of Cuba. The complications of the island's solitary social and economic positions affect the daily experiences of the Cuban people, especially their individual identities and intimate relationships.

Néstor García Canclini writes, "the whole crisis of modernity . . . lead to a postmodern problematic (not a phase) in the sense that the modern explodes and is mixed with what is not modern." Recent Cuban theatre claims that this problematic is "affirmed and debated at the same time," as García Canclini does.[3] While many studies have suggested that postmodern political autonomy has declined since the globalization of capitalist production, the specific effects of this decline on people living in a country like Cuba are understudied. Terry, in his early Special Period play entitled *Laberinto de lobos* (Labyrinth of Wolves, published in 1994), questions the very nature of relationships themselves within Cuba's newly skewed, transmodern economy. His Cuban characters have lifelong relationships that are permanently altered by attempts to participate in the global market, with its threats of calamity juxtaposed with its potential for reward. Daily interactions between Cubans are transformed by outsiders in the play, namely tourists and foreigners who have access to wealth. Nara Mansur's play *Ignacio y Maria* (published in 2003) also reveals the tension the Special Period and globalization create within everyday situations on the island, but from much later in the era. Mansur's work is framed by the conflicts over the desire for, acceptance of, resignation to, and defiance toward the economic and social integration of Cuba into the world market. Together, these plays depict the personal consequences of a socialist nation's efforts to negotiate the global hegemony, examining cooperation and resistance in national and global relationships by closely investigating personal ones.

Laberinto de lobos

Afro-Cuban writer Miguel Terry is best known as a respected journalist and novelist. Born in 1963 in Ceiba del Agua, Caimito (Havana Province), Terry studied journalism at the University of Havana, earning his degree in 1989. He has garnered numerous theatre awards, including El Premio La Habana, Teatro, 1991 (Havana Prize for Theatre) for his play *Angeles y cenizas* (Angels and ashes) and the "Pinos Nuevos" prize for his second theatrical work, *Laberinto de lobos,* in 1994. His other acclaimed works include

Páginas finales de la náusea (2008), *La pierda en la boca* (2004), and *Los duros pierden como Humphrey Bogart* (2003), all of which have been published and staged in Cuba. Terry has also won major prizes for his humorous essays and his novels, such as *Caballo de battalla*. Magazines and anthologies in Spain, México, and Brazil have published Terry's plays, stories, and poems, which have also won acclaim in the Dominican Republic and Puerto Rico.

Laberinto de lobos (1993) was produced for the stage by actor Miguel Navarro, who first heard a Cuban radio version of the play. The play's title refers to many encounters with wolves that are part of the Cuban imaginary. The most palpable include a well-known Spanish children's song, "Juguemos en el bosque," that joyfully states, "Juguemos en el bosque, mientras el lobo no esta" (Let's play in the woods while the wolf is away). The words convey the knowledge that the "wolf"—something fearful—is always present, even if he is being avoided momentarily. The wolf is also anthropomorphized in the song, when he responds that he is "dressing," "putting on his pants/vest/hat" or "brushing his teeth/hair." However, the song eventually ends with the wolf eating a person singing the song. Another reference of the title is to Senal Paz's 1991 short story *El lobo, el bosque, y el hombre nuevo* (The wolf, the forest, and the new man), later adapted for the stage and for Tomás Guttierez Alea's 1994 film, *Fresa y chocolate* (Strawberry and chocolate). Paz's critical view of intolerance takes place in 1979, when Diego, a cultivated artist and homosexual, educates and falls in love with David, a young, dogmatic communist who is highly suspicious of culture. Despite their conflicting sexual and political ideologies, they build a friendship that proves human connections can overcome divisive beliefs. Terry may have also intended references to children's fables, such as "crying wolf" (with regard to ongoing rumors about the death of Fidel Castro) or the disguised wolf in the tale of Little Red Riding Hood (*La capuercita*) who attacks her. Journalists have pondered whether Cuba can "invite the wolf to dinner"—that is, open up and allow new freedoms under globalization—without being swallowed whole. Fidel Castro may even be referred to as a wolf—majestic, self-confident, and wise, yet also sly and insatiable. The labyrinth, an elaborate nonbranching maze of Greek mythology with only one path to the center, evokes a confusing journey with only one possible solution. However, Terry's labyrinth could also refer to a series of short stories published by Argentine writer and poet Jorge Luis Borges in 1962 titled *Labyrinths*. Borges's stories allude to many leading intellectual figures and deal with themes such as idealism and immortality.

Terry's play *Laberinto de lobos* confronts the notion of *jineterismo* in Cuba head-on. The word, which means "horseback riding," connotes a range of activities that are part of "riding" the new Cuban tourism economy. Some of the illegal and semi-legal activities that earn *jineteros* convertible pesos, meals, entertainment, or desired products include hustling, prostitution, and selling goods, services, and companionship to tourists. Although most *jineteros* are mixed race or white, the most common stereotype of a *jinetera* is an Afro-Cuban woman soliciting white male tourists in the street. Since the early 1990s *jineterismo* has been viewed as a livelihood tactic in the struggle to meet daily needs, but there is no doubt it overtly challenges all revolutionary narratives about social, racial, and gender equality. It is an unsanctioned practice that yields access to money, goods, and sometimes the option to leave the country by marrying a foreigner.[4]

Laberinto de lobos takes place in Beatriz's small Havana apartment, where a radio announcer comments on the economic crisis and principles of socialism. Beatriz's friend Felipe soon arrives with their old friend Sebastián. Felipe explains they had a party the night before, with imported champagne and food given to them by foreigners. Sebastián, a devout socialist, disapproves. When Beatriz enters, the attraction between her and Sebastián is palpable, even though her face is disfigured. She and Felipe attack each other with accusations of pandering for money by marrying foreigners. Felipe leaves as Sebastián realizes that Beatriz has chosen prostitution rather than working for the state. They drink and coyly insult each other before finally kissing passionately. The second act takes place the next morning, when it is clear that Sebastián has spent the night. Beatriz insists she has no options other than prostitution because she is not desirable as a wife, especially since her Italian boyfriend, Luciano, left her. She gives Sebastián Luciano's clothes to wear, as Sebastián defends the Revolution but admits to frustrations about corruption, all while insisting he is not a hypocrite. Felipe finally returns, indicting all systems for their abuses against common men. The phone rings with news that Luciano is back and wants to see Beatriz; she is thrilled and Sebastián is enraged. When Beatriz leaves the room to get dressed, Sebastián takes off the Italian suit she gave him, tearing at it roughly, while on the radio a talk show discusses the suffering of women and children under capitalism.

In *Laberinto de lobos*, Terry attempts to reconcile the hardships of the Special Period on Cuba's younger generation. All three of his characters are "around thirty years old"[5] and were therefore born into the Revolution. They live within what Román De la Campa calls *transmodernity*, "an uncertain in-between modern and postmodern that also carries colonial traces—a non-synchronicity."[6] Life in Cuba, especially in the early 1990s, existed somewhere between the obsolete and the postmodern. Terry's characters live in Havana, the most modern city in Cuba, although several of them speak in a dialect that reveals they are not originally from the city.[7] The play occurs in a tiny, simple, two-room apartment satirically decorated with tourist propaganda posters, "encouraging the purchase of perfumes, drinks, and

Cuban cigars or forecasting a happy stay on the island."[8] The characters interact in this surreal, interstitial space.

In the first scene, Beatriz, clearly hung over from the party that disordered this room the night before, emerges from her bed and turns on the radio. Almost immediately, a radio announcer mentions the "grave economic and social crisis that affects the countries of Eastern Europe. . . . the abandonment of the principles of socialism . . . and the bitter consequences for the inhabitants"[9] of those countries. These contagious crises from the world outside immediately seep into the Cuban reality.

In their seminal work *Empire*, Michael Hardt and Antonio Negri argue that the world outside is part of our experience. They write, "Along with the global market and new global circuits of production has emerged a global order, a new logic and structure of rule—in short, a new form of sovereignty."[10] The authors contend that overall political autonomy has declined since the globalization of capitalist production and that a "series of national and supranational organisms united under a single logic of rule," known as capitalism, has engendered a "new transnational democracy."[11] Particularly since the break up of the Soviet Union, globalization—defined as the materialization of an interconnected global society inspired by world communications and accessibility—has provided direct challenges to what philosopher and novelist Kwame Appiah calls "an older political philosophy rooted in the nation-state."[12] New margins have been created through varying levels of participation in free markets and in democracy. Yet the interconnected nature of globalization means fissures elsewhere directly affect Cubans.

In Terry's play, Beatriz clicks off the radio just as an esteemed guest begins to discuss the "pessimism" pervading the people of the former Soviet Union and possibly Cubans, too. These first few moments decisively set the play in the Special Period in Cuba and situate its relationship within a global economic crisis. The audience now knows, if it did not already know, that Cubans hear about the outside world and have access to information that is not government propaganda. The events in Cuba and the Soviet Union were not unique or isolated but entirely intertwined. The political upheaval in the Soviet Union meant that the safeguards and assistance the Eastern bloc had provided to Cuba disappeared almost overnight. As Pérez explains,

> The collapse of the Soviet Union led immediately to retrenchment of existing international commitments and a moratorium on new agreements. Moscow found itself in a very much reduced capacity to fulfill previous military arrangements and meet existing commercial obligations. Even if the will had been present—and there is no evidence

> to suggest that it was—the wherewithal was not. The Russians turned inward, wholly absorbed with severe economic dislocation and deepening political instability.[13]

This "inward" turn left Cuba out. For the first time in nearly half a century, Cuba became entirely vulnerable to the variability of market forces. The Soviets no longer guaranteed credit for imports or markets for Cuban exports, as they had throughout the Cold War.

During the Special Period in Cuba, "a series of contingency plans conceived originally for use during a time of war"[14] ensued. At first, "Even the market seemed to conspire against Cuba," Pérez expounds, "as the price of oil increased and the price of sugar decreased, making a difficult situation worse."[15] Although an isolated island, Cuba now had to contend with global economics. Desperate plans to buttress the country against this enormous recession included national austerity measures, the decentralization of foreign trade, and an onerous rationing program. A series of measures was also enacted to manage the financial repercussions of the crisis and repair the economy. These incorporated difficult ideological shifts from collective to individual income sources. The measures included partially legalizing the dollar (later the euro and "peso convertible" tourist currency that can also be used as a Cuban peso), developing tourism, promoting foreign investments in Cuban projects, and allowing various types of self-employment. Terry establishes this complicated economic situation as the milieu for his play. For instance, his characters live in minimal space juxtaposed with lavish tourist accommodations. The prevailing cynicism of the era frames all of the interactions in the play.

Despite Cuban leader Fidel Castro's concession that globalization is an objective reality, the Cuban government has not fully incorporated the intervention by consensus that Hardt and Negri continually describe in their work. Cuba's ardent insistence on its self-rule and sovereignty have been critical to its national history since the nation gained its independence in 1898 and throughout its revolutionary society since 1959. The extended economic embargo by the United States, Cuba's decades of integrating its economy with the Soviet Union's, and its previous lack of global trading partners have definitely distorted the island's ability to navigate within a global economy. Hence, the country's attempts to modernize have often been derailed, disrupted, or fragmented, mostly due to economic and ideological factors. As García Canclini put it, Cuba is a place where "modernity has not completely arrived."[16] Modernizing projects in various stages that were tied to Soviet financing, methods, and equipment were deserted in the early 1990s. Cuba's fervent disassociation from capitalism has affixed it to the margins, leaving it noticeably sheltered from unbridled consumerism, but partially immobilized economically and politically. The burden of constructing a viable alternative to neoliberal globalization fell to the Cuban Revolution. *Laberinto de lobos* considers the fact that, "The watchword [after the Soviet collapse] was now '*Cuba contra todos*' [Cuba against everyone]," as Pérez notes.[17] Terry stages the effects this separation had on the everyday experiences of Cubans.

While playing a cassette by musician Charlie Parker in act 1, Terry's character Beatriz distastefully derides the guests of the previous evening, proclaiming that a friend sleeping with a French tourist will "rot in this country in the middle of nowhere"[18] if she is not careful. The music and her comments set the contradictions of partial globalization in relief: On this isolated island, there is still music by Charlie Parker, but it is only on cassette, an outdated technology by the 1990s; Beatriz's friend is dating a Frenchman rather than a Cuban; and Cubans seem immobile, left without options for earning a living. If her friend *is* "careful," she may be able to leave the island, affording her financial opportunities unavailable in Havana. The outside world, whether the former Soviet Union (via the radio), France, or the United States, is ever-present and imposes a continual renegotiation of the local.

In order to revive the Cuban economy in the 1990s, the nation entered into extensive joint ventures with foreign investors, mostly in its tourist sectors. Hotels, as Terry's characters point out, were renovated and beautified while other buildings declined into disrepair. Odd comparisons and contradictions abound. State-run restaurants, often impossible for Cubans to afford, sprung up all over major cities and beaches to attract tourists. Travel services were improved, tours created, and faster tourist intake systems developed because the country now relied on tourism as its greatest source of revenue. Average Cubans vied for tourism-related jobs rather than other positions because access to tourists meant access to greater income (tips), especially in convertible, rather than Cuban, pesos. Prostitution also increased tremendously. Cuban men and women sold what they had (their bodies) to make significant income quickly. Moreover, Cubans were often banned from hotspots in their own country, like the beaches at Varadero, so that the mostly European tourists would feel safe and relaxed there. The outside took precedence because it sustained the inside. This tourism surge also reawakened distasteful memories of outside influences during prerevolutionary Cuba (of casinos, the mob, etc.) and "set in relief the sharp contrast between deteriorating national living standards and affluent tourists," argues Pérez.[19]

In *Laberinto de lobos*, Beatriz embodies dichotomies like these. She is a prostitute who readily seeks out foreign clients; she is not from Havana but is living there; and her face, "even if a bit disfigured in an accident, conserves a good amount of her noticeable beauty."[20] Her language is often severe and foul. These contradictions only grow sharper when Felipe arrives with Sebastián. Both men are good-looking, but Sebastián, a lawyer, appears modest and stern. Felipe comments that Sebastián's bag makes him look like "a leader" and jokingly asks if Sebastian will dress like a revolutionary and give "an optimistic speech that's 150 pages long."[21] Here, Terry makes a bold, almost direct reference to Fidel Castro and his habit of wearing army fatigues and of addressing the Cuban people for hours on end. If "repetition leads to perpetual concealment"[22] as De la Campa claims, then Terry's reference is particularly accusatory.

When it is later revealed that Sebastián is exceedingly conservative, both politically and socially, the irony of his developing friendship with Beatriz mounts, reflecting what De la Campa might call "the social deficits created by globalization and neoliberalism."[23] Sebastián, who works for the state, represents the *experiential* encounter with revolution (as opposed to the ideological encounter that Marxist academics often promote) that must be reconciled with the postmodern economic reality on the island. Postmodernism, according to De la Campa, "is polysemic in the most equivocal sense: it absorbs a capricious array of methods and theories that can simultaneously signify difference and sameness, the old and the new, the self and the other, the radical and the conservative."[24] These binaries and any concept of the postmodern are exceedingly muddled in a country like Cuba. The island not only defies homogenous modernity but also lacks its own utopian vision. Globalized modernity exaggerates capitalism, as García Canclini asserts,[25] and these characters, on a socialist island, must struggle to participate.

Felipe explains that the party the night before was to celebrate their friend's marrying a Frenchman. He remarks, "Everything is almost ready: they only lack the completed paperwork. And to fly! Good-bye, underdevelopment! Cubana Airlines assures one's escape to the future."[26] Terry's commentary is notably polyvalent. For Felipe and Beatriz, leaving has become a unique privilege, and any engagement between a Cuban and a foreigner is viewed extremely positively—it signifies increased access to goods and possibly a ticket off the island. Furthermore, the idea that the future is elsewhere is key to the play in several respects. In the local sense, during the Special Period, Cubans came to feel as if they might not have a future on the island because earning a livable wage had become exceedingly difficult. This may have been due to what Renato Rosaldo calls "the various, unequal, and contradictory forms of modernity"[27] in Latin America. While García Canclini sees modernity as a "polemic or suspect project—with this mixture of heterogeneous memory and truncated innovations,"[28] the play's Felipe only wants to know if the "corpse of imperialism has passed or not"[29] so that there can be a future in Cuba. He is not particularly concerned with the "truncated innovations" cut off by absurd deindustrialization, simplifications, and other alterations brought on by the Special Period that emphasized Cuba's ongoing attempts at modernization. The bizarre modernity after postmodernity of the 1990s, part of what García Canclini refers to as, "an exuberant modernism with a deficient modernization,"[30] does not faze Felipe. He longs for what is next, for what might be, and does not attempt to reconcile present predicaments.

The varying levels of access and modernity in Cuba have made its predicaments all the more incongruous. For instance, although a lawyer, Sebastián lives with his mother-in-law, a common practice because Cubans faced (and still face) a severe housing shortage in Havana. In contrast, Felipe is extremely proud that he lives alone and, in particular, not with Beatriz, in the apartment he condemns as her "monument to promiscuity."[31] Felipe's rampant cynicism is undeniable, buoyed by his lucid comprehension that others are highly privileged in Havana. He drunkenly enacts a scenario in which a local, pretending to be a wealthy foreign tourist, offers him a bribe to open a certain mausoleum that is supposedly closed. Acting the part of a state guard, Felipe responds mockingly, "Dollars! Why didn't you tell me before? Do you want to go in or do you prefer that we bring the old guy to you?" (11). Unsurprisingly, the reticent and loyal Sebastián does not laugh. Felipe claims, "You already knew it. That's why you didn't laugh. But it is the truth" (11). Terry uses nothing but a pregnant pause to underscore Sebastián's and Felipe's evidently contrary views of their country's situation.

By the end of the act, it is clear that relationships with tourists could significantly improve the opportunities for average Cubans. Severe shortages of goods and services meant that earnings from the state were no longer sufficient to provide for daily expenditures after 1991. Many Cubans went hungry. Food lines were often hours long in oppressive heat, and many Cubans grew thin because they could not procure enough to eat. Massive cuts in electricity, transportation, and employment left Cubans in a state of shock. Just when local manufacturing became essential, technological shortfalls and difficulties obtaining spare parts impeded production. The new dual currency economy kept Cuban money from a sharp devaluation, but it also had critical social repercussions. There is still a palatable binary dividing Cubans *with* access to foreign currency and Cubans *without* this access. The consumer capacity of the convertible peso has grown substantially greater than that of the Cuban peso, both on the black market and in private business relationships. New patterns and social stratifications have been created; Cubans with friends and family members abroad who can secure remittances and encourage lucrative visits have a distinct financial advantage.

This phenomenon, of Cubans forging significant relationships with foreigners, is not new. The modern history of Cuba continually includes people leaving the island or solving problems with assistance from outside the country. Even independence leader José Martí was educated and wrote his greatest works from the United States, Fidel Castro met Che Guevara in Mexico. Beatriz explains that the party the night before was for Dorys, but she notes that Felipe is also engaged, to an Argentine millionairess. Without growing defensive, Felipe insists that his fiancée Cecilia is special because she is from Rosario, Argentina, as was Ernesto "Che" Guevara, a fact that Sebastián patriotically notes. When Beatriz disparages Cecilia for being "overly intellectual" and "conceited," Felipe defends his fiancée's position and inheritance. Yet in doing so, he also exposes the stark differences in economic prospects between foreigners and Cubans. He sarcastically inquires, "Do you believe that she became a millionairess selling caramels and hamburgers on the black market like Cubans do?" (13).

Cecilia's wealth far exceeds any that could be had by a typical Cuban. Beatriz only compounds the disparity, criticizing Cecilia for wearing "thousand dollar dresses" in Havana, "where people come in contact with two meters of fabric every two years" (13). For Cubans earning only pesos from the state, whose services and supplies rapidly deteriorated, life became exceedingly difficult at the end of the twentieth century. Reliable transportation disappeared, and fuel shortages resulted in extensive unemployment when factories closed. Because Cuba could not buy petroleum, the country ground to a halt; deindustrialization became necessary, with oxen and bicycles reintroduced for work and transportation. The postmodern gave way to the primitive. Cuba's youth were faced with increasing idleness, hopelessness, and despair; and while their longing for western goods had grown, their ability to procure them was rapidly dwindling. Pérez astutely describes the overall milieu of that decade this way:

> Cubans found themselves increasingly isolated and beleaguered. . . . Most of all it became increasingly difficult to go about normally in one's daily life, where so much of one's time and energy were expended in what otherwise and elsewhere were routine household errands and ordinary family chores, where days were frequently filed with unrelieved hardship and adversity in pursuit of even the most minimum needs of everyday life, day after day: hours on line at the local grocery store, hours waiting for public transportation, hours without electrical power. Vast amounts of ingenuity were applied simply to meet ordinary and commonplace needs—to *resolver* and *inventar* became the operative verbs of a people seeking ways to make do and get by.[32]

What happens to a people who constantly must resolve and invent just to meet their basic daily needs? How do they engage with people who do not have to do this? In Terry's play, foreigners and external access to money drive a noticeable wedge between these lifelong Cuban friends.

Felipe and Beatriz continue to argue about access to privileges as the play continues. Many goods and services made available to tourists for convertible pesos were simply unattainable for most Cubans during this period. Where they were once considered traitors, Cubans who left the island (especially those with money) were now encouraged to return to their homeland as consumers/tourists. In the early 1990s, for example, the Cuban government made over five times as many visas available for Cuban Americans as it had in previous years. These visits compounded the disparity—it was absurd to encounter tourists, Cuban American or otherwise, when one's own travel was highly restricted. Defining oneself as Cuban denotes a deficiency, or shortcoming, in Terry's play.

In order to relieve Sebastián of the position of "boxing moderator,"[33] Beatriz and Felipe decide to discuss the Spanish wine that Beatriz tasted on a trip with her Italian boyfriend Luciano. Sebastián observes, "I continue understanding. Dorys marries a Frenchman and leaves the country, Felipe marries a millionairess, and you marry . . ." but Beatriz interrupts him: "Cross me off the list of passengers. Luciano left me . . . I'm screwed."[34] This pattern of relations with foreigners and the profitable results are unambiguous. Beatriz's exclusion from this matrix elucidates why she has become a prostitute. Beatriz laments, "If we had gone to Italy, now I'd have my fashion magazine, I'd get up at ten in the morning, the servant would bring me breakfast in bed. . . . 'Wake up, woman, wake up.' The party doesn't last in a poor house" (15). Life outside the island is imagined as a leisurely utopia, while daily challenges continue within it.

Sebastián sarcastically encourages Beatriz, "Don't lose hope," and tells her exactly where to go to find a "tourist with an imbecile's face" to take her "a thousand kilometers from Cuba" because that is "in fashion" (16). Hurt but defiant, Beatriz insists she is nobody's whore and is in love with Luciano, who is not like men from Cuba, "not an angel or a shit, but distinctive" (16). It is also made clear that Beatriz holds foreigners in much higher esteem than she does Cubans. This offends Felipe, and, by extension, Sebastián and all Cuban men; Beatriz scoffs, "You're a rat if you tell yourself it's the same to be Cuban as it is to be Argentine or an Eskimo" (16). Finally, they toast, with Spanish wine, as Beatriz comments, "When one samples Pedro Domecq she knows that life is good" (17), reiterating that foreign goods, rather than Cuban products, signify the good life.

Terry also presents another point of view, creating a dialectic. Sebastián artfully defends life on the island. Despite enormous challenges, basic education and health care continue to be provided by the Cuban government to all citizens. Although sometimes mediocre, housing is available to all Cubans, and food rations assure at least the most basic sustenance. Because these social achievements have survived even the most arduous years of a market transition, they are hailed as permanent revolutionary successes. Cuban historian Julio García Luis insists, "It is admirable that, in this adverse situation, the nation didn't fall apart, didn't let itself be plunged into chaos, but protected all its citizens, preserved the strategic programs of the revolution and not only stood firm but also gradually, in a relatively short period of time, restored the growth capacity of its economy."[35] In addition, the Cuban people have avoided chaos and extensive violence even within this difficult period. The nonnegotiable nature of the Revolution has been reinforced by its survival, yet the long-term ideological cost of nonsocialist economic reforms and hard times remains to be seen. "Subsidized bread lines are not everything," Beatriz remarks,[36] directly criticizing arduous Cuban socialism.

Before Sebastián can respond to her criticisms, Beatriz asks Felipe if he has "found" Sebastián something to eat. Here, her choice of words is crucial, as procuring food became a daily challenge during the Special Period. Pérez duly notes that scarce fuel supplies after 1990 meant "blackouts were imposed daily, often lasting as long as eight and ten hours a day. . . . Electric water pumps, ovens, refrigerators, and freezers were rendered inoperative for hours at a time. Not only was it difficult to secure food, but it was becoming increasingly difficult to cook and preserve it."[37] As many Cubans did in the Special Period, Beatriz and Felipe hustle, barter, haggle, scheme, contrive, negotiate, and wait to get what they need and want. Bitterly reemphasizing the vast economic distance between wealthy foreigners and Cubans, Beatriz remarks that, while Cubans have only "hot nails" to eat, "in Cecilia's house the refrigerators are always full."[38]

As he drinks and grows more audacious, Sebastián finally criticizes Beatriz for not completing law school and for selling herself. She explains to him,

> You also want to live better, even if you don't say it. . . . I can't live this way. I don't want to. For you, who has seen nothing, all of this seems grand, but not for me. Zanja Street, or Campanario, or Egido, they seem like an inferno: an unbearable plague, the houses full of dirt, the trash strewn in the middle of the street, poor black people in flip-flops, with dreadlocks . . . they wear me out, Sebastián, they wear me out. [*Pause*] I like to buy perfume, to go out to a restaurant, to sleep in a hotel that's worth it. . . . And if I can't have it now, when am I going to have it? When I am fifty years old and they are rebuilding my face? When all of my skin is leathery?[39]

Beatriz sees her profession, and the access it provides, as her reaction against the scarcity and poverty around her. She does not believe in the promise of the future, and she fears the consequences of her own aging because her body is her greatest resource; she worries about what her options will be once she is older and less attractive. Sebastián's response illustrates his entirely contrasting views of Cuban society: he ruthlessly comments, "Beatriz is a whore who doesn't want to look at the face of underdevelopment, which is three times uglier than hers."[40]

Sebastián is empathetic with Cuba's poor, and he sees lessening their plight as an important socialist project. Economic flux and ongoing hardships made it clear that principles alone would not sustain the Cuban population after 1991. Cuba's "idealism" was tempered by fiscal pragmatism. "Survival . . . seemed to preoccupy the government," writes Pérez, "and indeed much in the Cuban response . . . was framed in a context of siege. This was the larger meaning of the *período especiál*, a condition that had originally been conceived as a response to war."[41] Terry's characters act as if they are besieged. Basic survival has changed their outlooks as well as their engagement with their country.

Within the first five years of the Special Period alone, the state made crucial concessions to capitalist formulas it had rejected for nearly five decades. These included alterations such as transforming large state agricultural enterprises into cooperative projects, the effects of which might not be understood for many generations to come. In a country firmly entrenched in its socialist ideals and its centralized government, these ongoing reforms are threatening even when necessary. Because foreign capital and tourism continue to provide for the island's financial survival, the ideological consequences of this industry have been veiled or ignored. The future is indeterminate, not mapped out. Adrián Lopez-Denis, a Cuban historian who recently immigrated to the United States, told me that the Revolution since the Special Period is a "week-by-week process," one that assumes an ever-changing logic of its own.[42]

Terry attempts to capture this moment of uncertainty—this strange, unsettling impasse—on stage. Beatriz reiterates the toll that the economic situation took on average people when she tells Sebastián, "Look at the women around here: they are young today, and tomorrow they seem like old ladies. All these problems, calamities, headaches, things that there aren't any of, things that are lacking . . . Surely I'll seem like an old woman at forty!"[43]

Beatriz is entirely consumed with the individual, personal damage of the Special Period. She never acknowledges Cuba as a communist or socialist collective, as a unified country. She attacks Sebastián for believing that his intelligence and refinement can help better his life on the island. She agonizingly declares, "You can repeat verses by Neruda from memory; but a janitor in a hotel earns more than you do, even if he has less brain than a mosquito. And what does Sebastián have . . . ? Your intelligence does not give you the power to buy a shirt that is worth it."[44]

Social and material matrices characterize domination for Beatriz. She has begun to define people and their success in terms of objects, possessions, and means. Sebastián reacts with disgust, disparaging "aristocratic whores" while viciously yet idealistically attacking hypocrisy in diplomacy, business, and love. Beatriz disagrees, expressing the highly capitalist notion that money is "the law of life in any system: what you have is what you're worth."[45] Their conversation dissolves into a series of brutal insults, leveled at Sebastián for being a socialist dreamer, and at Beatriz for succumbing to anti-Marxist materialism. Beatriz condemns Sebastián for "liking old things,"[46] framing Marxism as outdated, but she then plays a cassette of the Beatles' classic "Come Together." The song is a strange but vivid reminder that, no matter Cuba's level of modernization, the island is not in a time warp but experiences its own particular version of the present; although the Beatles are from another era, they are still widely played across the globe. "Global contemporaries all equally inhabit a late twentieth-century world," reminds Renato Rosaldo, a world that intelligently cites many periods and aesthetics. Fittingly, he observes that "to speak of certain groups as if they inhabited another century or millennium smacks more of metropolitan prejudice than considered judgment."[47]

Despite this contention, the irony remains that, as Beatriz notes in the play, "the whore has a telephone and the lawyer does not."[48] Still, the heat of attraction between Beatriz and Sebastián grows, and the two flirt and kiss. They clearly long for one another, in spite of their differing ideologies. Sebastián poignantly asks Beatriz the whore, "And how do I pay you: in dollars or in Cuban pesos?" (27). Beatriz maintains her agency and dignity, as she insists that theirs is a debt he will never pay and she will never collect.

The opening image of act 2 of *Laberinto de lobos* makes it clear that Sebastián has slept with Beatriz: even the loyalist has fallen for a whore. The once rigid Sebastián is clearly hung over, another blatant contradiction. Nothing has remained the way it seemed—Sebastián has let loose and Beatriz has sought an emotional connection rather than a financial arrangement. While arguing about Dorys, Sebastián reveals more paradoxes, when he remarks, "Contempt and envy . . . the people feel both things at the same time" (30). He bitingly remarks that when one leaves the island, "You go as a *gusano* [literally, "worm" but understood to mean a "traitor"] and you return as a butterfly, with your ass in a tourist taxi" (33), conceding to the absurdity of life for modern Cubans.

Sebastián's own desire to grow, his desire for a richer life, slowly surfaces as he chats with Beatriz:

> SEBASTIÁN: Every day I think that time passes. Second by second, but it passes. What are ten years? Twenty? A breath. Life goes by in a blink. In very little time I'm going to have to

ask myself: what did you see, what did you do, what did you enjoy?

BEATRIZ: And how are you going to respond?

SEBASTIÁN: That I was twenty, and then thirty, and then forty, and then old . . . and I only saw Paris in photographs!

BEATRIZ: Ah, so you also have these questions!

SEBASTIÁN: . . . I'm not like you. I never will leave this country . . . but I prefer not to tell anyone. Those who are always squawking that they aren't going, they are the first to shove off.

BEATRIZ: . . . Sebastián, you don't want to see.

SEBASTIÁN: To see what?

BEATRIZ: To see what's in the street, what is happening.

SEBASTIÁN: I see and I hate it all . . . and what? If the Revolution falls, you'll have to be a wolf, this country is going to change into a forest. Those that fall down are going to stay down. (36)

Sebastián seems to have accepted his country's condition, even if he is somewhat defeated by it. Although he will not consider leaving the island, he does not propose any way to fix its problems. Instead, he fully acknowledges Cuba's shortcomings but also that he is inextricably tied to them, a vital part of them, all the while lamenting the future. As a staunch supporter of the state, he represents the new Cuban conundrum without suggesting solutions. Rather, he points out the illogicality of the current situation, noting, "It seems like there are only two opinions: either you are corrupt, or you are an imbecile" (44). This character, who started with a clear investment in the state, appears more and more dichotomous as the play continues: when Beatriz dresses him up in clothes left by Luciano, Sebastián remarks, "Yes, I'm only missing a mansion in Beverly Hills" (42). At every turn, he is at once sarcastic, incisive, and straightforward, finally embodying the paradoxes in his experience.

Highly critical, cynical, and jaded, Felipe also recognizes the dystopian reality of the Special Period and does not imagine that he can remedy it. He explains his interstitial position this way:

> Socialism is the system of inefficiency; but capitalism is also not smooth. In this country, if a waiter serves you poorly, nothing happens. If a taxi doesn't want to pick you up, nothing happens. If a factory doesn't make its annual goals, nothing happens. If the stores are empty, nothing happens. But with [the capitalists] it's also not as easy as cake: in many streets of Europe you can find an old whore, dying from hunger, that at best seems like your mother or mine, and then you don't know whether to lie down and laugh or to lie down and cry.

> In which system do I stay? In neither and in both . . . What I can't do is try to straighten out the mess of others. (49)

He does not attempt to solve any social ills, and he is more concerned with surviving in spite of them by finding clever ways to conquer obstacles. He is not concerned with any greater good or national mission, but he works to better only his own experience.

As the possibility for local economic improvement wanes, any hope Terry expresses in the play seems to exist in the possibility of love as a refuge, specifically between Sebastián and Beatriz. Therefore, when it is revealed that Luciano is back in town and wants to see Beatriz the next afternoon, Sebastián desperately tries to convince Beatriz to stay with him. Sebastián grows so distressed by Beatriz's repeated refusals to stay with him that he brutally shakes her. With this physical act, the hopelessness pervading the piece devolves into violence. Felipe insists that Luciano's return was inevitable, as if there were no way out of this cycle. He tells Sebastián, "If this didn't happen today, it would've happened tomorrow, or the next week. I already know this story by heart."[49] Sebastián is forced to bitterly concede that Beatriz will belong to whoever can "buy her ass" (52). The outlook for Cuban relationships is grim and dispiriting.

The final stage moments do not relieve this discouraging sentiment. Alone, Sebastián turns on the radio, where an announcer discusses "an interesting interview with Silvie Vasallo, leader of the Movement of Young Communists of France," who then remarks, "Drugs, delinquency, inequities forcefully occupy their place inside the celebrated European nation" (54). Parallel to the opening moments of the play, this broadcast concerns the troubles facing the communists of Europe, many of which reiterate those of post-Soviet Cuba. Out of sheer frustration while hearing this, Sebastián angrily damages the beautiful Italian clothes Beatriz has given him. He outwardly rejects the suit as a metaphor for the foreign wealth that has destroyed the principles of his former classmates. To Sebastián, the suit represents the influence of materialism that has corrupted Beatriz's commitment to Cuba's socialist ideals and way of life. He indignantly refuses to play the part Beatriz wishes him to play, refuses to pretend that all is well by wearing this costume of affluence. Contrasting his humble clothing (or fatigues or a state uniform) the suit represents capitalism and its perversions, especially toward Cubans who have gone to extreme measures such as prostitution to attain goods. Despite valid frustrations with the system, Sebastián adamantly refuses to give up on the values of the Revolution. Hence, Terry's play indicates how pervasive systemic, economic, and ideological fractures have irreparably damaged personal relationships between Cubans.

Ignacio y Maria

Nara Mansur's play *Ignacio y Maria* depicts Cuba and an elsewhere as a means for comparison. The play centers on a pair of lovers who have been separated by economic circumstances: Maria remains in Cuba while Ignacio goes to Chile to make money. Although separated, both characters' identities are firmly located within the historical imaginary of the island and its specific geography. While Mansur's play is in no way realistic, its vivid poetry depicts modern Cuba as a place with determined cultural values strengthened by notions of what is within its borders and what is beyond them. The stage directions of *Ignacio y Maria* note that "Two geographic places are referred to: Havana and Santiago de Chile."[50] Neither location is physically represented, but the cultural and emotional terrain of Cuba in the new millennium quickly emerges as the foundation of the play. The work often reads like dual character stream of consciousness, with intertwined ideas and interjections of partial narratives. Key events include the characters' musings and malaise, Ignacio struggling to work, strange songs, Maria contemplating her value, a fight, nostalgia while looking at photos, dreams for the future, Maria aborting their son, complaints and recommendations, and an epilogue in which Maria metaphorically commits suicide by jumping to her death. The changing cultural constructs of socialist Cuba underscore all interactions between these lovers, as Chile becomes an exterior, "other" space used for distance and comparison.

Mansur chose to locate one Cuban character in *Ignacio y Maria* in Chile because of that country's historical interaction with socialism. The triumph of the Cuban Revolution undoubtedly paved the way for Marxist leader Salvador Allende's election as president of Chile in 1970. Like Castro, Allende was a leftist who sought the nationalization of Chilean industry and promoted collectivism and egalitarianism. He often took positions held by the Communist Party in Chile, a likely cause for the 1973 military coup that led to his death and the dictatorship of General Augusto Pinochet, which ended in 1990. While the first years of Pinochet's rule were marked by vicious human rights violations and repression, his government made market-oriented reforms that led to increased private investment and reduced the soaring inflation and economic decline that marred Allende's rule. Pinochet is credited with restoring the Chilean economy and initiating the profound capitalist, free-market successes the country has enjoyed throughout the last three decades. Cuba's most difficult years, especially the 1990s, were Chile's most prosperous.

Ignacio y Maria takes place during the harshest part of the Special Period in Cuba (between 1991 and 1997), years of great growth and optimism in Chile. The conditions facing these countries in this period could not have been more contrary: Chileans were reaping the benefits of their postsocialist era, while Cubans were struggling to craft a space to keep socialism afloat. Pérez insists that space is crucial within the Special Period: "space to adjust, space to adapt—space, in short, for Cuba to accommodate itself to the logic of changing international realities, and to which almost everyone on the island acknowledged Cuba had to acquiesce."[51] Was it really a necessity, as Pérez implies, that Cubans "acquiesce"—compromise, concede, comply? Pérez makes it sound as if Cubans resigned their agency in the process. The necessities created by the economic downturn in Cuba certainly fostered new social spaces, as intimate interdependency among individuals sharply differentiated the island from other cultures. People in Cuba still rely heavily on one another (more so than on the state) for help, food, or other needs, making the barter system a vital part of Cuban culture and the contact and trust that comes with it indispensable. These one-on-one relationships, these personal spaces, seem wholly incompatible with commercial neoliberal globalization and/or a long-distance romantic relationship like the one in *Ignacio y Maria*, but there is great personal agency within them. These are the conditions under which Ignacio and Maria interact.

The opening stage directions for *Ignacio y Maria* capture the nonrealistic essence of the play and frame the strange fractures that occurred during the Special Period. Though the characters' lives were closely intertwined while Ignacio was in Cuba, the breach between them seems enormous when he moves to Chile. These characters are miles from each other, yet Mansur writes, "Sometimes the characters get close. Sometimes they dance. Sometimes they talk to each other. Sometimes they deliberately talk to the audience."[52] In a polished staged reading of the piece at the International Latino Theatre Festival of Los Angeles (FITLA) I saw in 2003, director Paul Verdier guided two actors to do all of the above, including dancing together while talking to the audience directly. This style was wholly appropriate because the play deals with major rifts in a contemporary relationship between Cubans. The staging reinforced the surreal theatricality of this couple's separation, obscuring any spatial sense of distance, and complicating contact.

Director Julio César Ramirez and Teatro D'Dos (Theatre of/for Two) produced *Ignacio y Maria* in Havana in late November 2009. It was performed in the Sala Estudio (Studio Theatre) of the Centro Cultural Bertolt Brecht in Vedado, a tiny space suited to the company's minimalist aesthetic. The production launched an event that lasted until summer 2010, in which Teatro D'Dos celebrated two decades of their work in nominal spaces. In an interview with him I conducted in December 2011, Ramirez described the play as one that "comments on the Cuban reality, but with the poetry necessary to permit the re-creation of its themes through metaphor, through signs. For us it is essential to have a stage full of meaning, not a stage focused on a natural representation of a phenomenon."[53]

The Sala Estudio allowed Teatro D'Dos to effectively *share* the play with fewer than fifty audience members at a time, most within reach of the actors, as the typical spatial boundaries between stage and spectator dissolved. Ramirez claims that, "In the Sala Estudio, [Teatro D'Dos] became a dual axis, of proximity and complicity between public and spectators." He described the set for this "text full of poetry but with a submerged reality that overwhelms it" as having two defined spaces, one room and one rectangle, defined by two white pieces of carpet akin to "two pieces of canvas where a painter can fill in the colors of the space."[54] In the Teatro D'Dos production, the space defining Maria featured an ironing board and a radio, from which she and the audience members received up-to-date news. Ignacio's area comprised a rectangle, "where there [was] a chair for work, an electric stove, books and a coffee urn where Ignacio, while remembering, [made] coffee."[55] Ramirez adds:

> There are two islands in which the characters live solitarily. The confines of an island remain very clear visually. [Ignacio and Maria] dialogue from these islands and, clearly, this produces a different dialogue, a dialogue that refers to the total absence of communication as they mediate two geographies. . . . the characters experience the island of their own bodies, but it's important that those same bodies express a new circle of isolation, a barrier, an obstacle.[56]

Although Spanish is spoken in Santiago as well as in Havana, Maria tells Ignacio, "I want to become your interpreter,"[57] implying that their interactions now require mediation or translation, beyond the barriers Ramirez mentions. Though they are living under entirely different systems, the problems of place, of a hardly globalized Cuba, still define their relationship. Maria mournfully comments, "Nothing takes me near you, not even the bus."[58] This remark is layered in meaning: Ignacio is not only too far to reach physically, but now not even the notoriously unreliable Cuban bus system could possibly unite him with Maria. (Coupled with fuel shortages, a dearth of replacement parts for increasingly old, mostly Soviet vehicles often made public transportation on the island exceedingly unpredictable.) There is no way for Maria to get closer to Ignacio, physically and/or emotionally, given the spatial, economic, ideological, and social gulfs between them.

Ignacio and Maria's tight-knit Havana community is fractured once Ignacio leaves the island, yet its underdevelopment and poor infrastructure still haunt the lovers' exchanges. When Ignacio leaves for Chile, Maria is left with only his "new address: ignacio@hotmail.com."[59] Mansur's irony stings because personal computers are often illegal, scarce, and expensive in Cuba, where Internet access is highly restricted. However, Chile does not operate as Cuba does. This fracture is due to the fact that, as García Canclini explains, Latin America "did not arrive at *one* modernity but rather at various unequal and combined processes of modernization."[60] But it also elicits a deeper isolation, like the one Ramirez insisted on in his production. Any physical imagination of a concrete place, when so many have been crucial to this love affair, has been removed from Ignacio and Maria's relationship, lost somewhere in a one-sided entry into cyber space and the global market. Maria cannot join Ignacio there; she cannot fully participate in the modern space he inhabits.

Place also collides with history to mold the personal lives of Ignacio and Maria. When Maria asks Ignacio where he is, he replies,

> I want you to know that I am here. A bit more South than where I was before. . . . A bit more south of your throat. I am a reading instrument. A number in the statistics, during the strike where your father falls assassinated, the traitor who makes the mutiny dissolve in order to see you.[61]

With its physical position and its troubled history, Cuba constructs Ignacio's identity, yet he locates "place" and defines his space on Maria's body rather than on his own or in any country so that he can control it. Ignacio has become part of Cuba's emigration history. Because those who left the island were often regarded as traitors by those who remained there, Ignacio begins to view himself this way. However, he still questions whether anything will improve after he is gone. He complicates this position even further when he remarks, "I am a man of the Third World at an airport. An airport always resembles a place in the First World."[62] He expresses the fact that underdevelopment and economic disadvantage have made him an outsider, internally exiled by his Cubanness.

Cuba's economic, political, and social histories have designed Ignacio and Maria. While looking at photographs "either real or imagined," the couple has the following exchange:

> IGNACIO: This is Monte Barreto. It used to belong to my grandfather. Now there is a big development being built there.
>
> MARIA: This is the Arellano y Luz Park, "sombras nada mas," shadows only shadows, as the song says.
>
> IGNACIO: This is Che Guevara dead, in the small school of Higueras.
>
> MARIA: This is my father with his lantern in his hand during the literacy campaign.
>
> IGNACIO: These are Fidel and Camilo entering Havana on January 8, 1959. My mother is the one with the scarf.

MARIA: This is my grandfather handing over all the silver coins and the jewels of the family for the revolution.
IGNACIO: This is my cousin who drowned in the Almendares River.
MARIA: This is José Martí talking to the tobacco workers of Tampa.
IGNACIO: That's me in front of the Duchamps urinary. . . .
MARIA: A wounded dog. A genetic feeling. A hateful rain.
IGNACIO: Two adulterers getting into a taxi.[63]

Mansur blends family photos with political events, historical moments with private ones, and the national with the individual. These depictions shape Ignacio's and Maria's views of themselves. Their families have been part of the production of Cuban history and they are directly tied to it. Hence, Maria is incensed when Ignacio does not acknowledge the brutal history of Chile, but only its current attractions. She interjects, "And Allende? And the stadium where Victor Jara was? And the disappeared?"[64] It is clear that places and their histories bear enormous weight on this couple, as even Che Guevara and Ignacio's cousin are given equal, familiar consideration.

Ignacio and Maria refer to these photos because "To preserve a historic site, or certain furniture and customs," as García Canclini contends, "is a task with no other end than that of guarding aesthetic and symbolic models. . . . Their unaltered conservation would attest to the fact that the essence of that glorious past survives the processes of change."[65] As change is rampant, historical authenticity is privileged, intentionally marginalizing any spatialized view on this *island*, from which the outside world is always separated. Each character has a personal identity that is subsumed in a nationalist character constructed by time. The spatial imagination has been denied, leaving the impression of painful emotional distance in addition to the enormous physical distance between Ignacio and Maria. Director Ramirez asserts that the play is centered on "absence and the necessity of the man and the woman to fill the vacant spaces."[66]

Ignacio y Maria investigates, as Hardt and Negri have, how cultures "establish local identities that are in some sense *outside* and protected against the global flows of capital and Empire."[67] Yet Maria's first line in *Ignacio y Maria* is about "the humidity, the euro, and the war."[68] The play quickly establishes that Cubans, the vast majority of whom are literate, are well aware of Empire, aware that there is a prosperous world beyond their borders, a world they have been partially excluded from. Films and television programs from foreign countries are shown all over the island. Mansur's play even specifically refers to Jonathan Demme's thriller *The Silence of the Lambs*. While freedoms of speech and of the press are limited on the island, thousands of external images and objects still reach Cuba.

Because, by the 1990s, "directly or indirectly, tourism supported 300,000 Cuban jobs,"[69] vast external globalization has always permeated the nation's boundaries. Often from Europe or Latin America, items and their symbolic meanings have become mingled with Cuban culture. For example, in the play, while looking at slogans on the city walls, Maria reads:

> Socialism or death.
> Light beer keeps friendships.
> Pepsodent.
> Here, nobody surrenders.
> (*Very serious, with despair*) Give us back our son.[70]

Here, socialist dictums are seamlessly interspersed with product advertising and politics. The system, beer, toothpaste, and historical mantras revived for Elián González[71] are all given equal footing. The parallelism of these signifiers asserts that their signs are linked, that there is a reciprocal interplay between these slogans. Many advertising catchphrases are merely slogans for Cubans because recognizable ad campaigns and the objects they promote are rarely available on the island. The mention of Elián along with a list of products connects the boy with American-style consumerism. Yet, all of these items also become illusory signifiers entirely severed from the signs they indicate; their meanings become unstable, unpredictable, and unreliable when the products themselves are unattainable in Havana.

What happens to *people* in a society that sees advertising for products but cannot acquire these commodities? Some Cubans can afford simple items (e.g., toothpaste) that are manufactured outside the country, so it is not always poverty that limits their contact with the world market. Many obstacles to attaining consumer products are political, often directly tied to the reach of the U.S. economic embargo of Cuba. Store shelves are often empty; even for Cubans with money, necessary products are often unavailable. When significations, but not the items signified, reach the island, personal relationships and ideas are transformed. The access, jobs, prosperity, and transformations represented by these commodities separate those on the island from those abroad.

In *Ignacio y Maria*, Maria speaks of "new taxi drivers who once were pilots who flew to Moscow week after week."[72] Employment stratifications, which are crucial components of self and societal definitions, have been eroded by the economic isolation Cuba endures. Doctors lead vacation tours, teachers repair watches, and lawyers drive taxis because these positions pay more than state-funded jobs, and they pay in convertible pesos. Cubans are altered by what is outside of their reach, often assuming roles as human commodities. Dressed as a salsa cabaret singer, Maria expounds,

> Where does it say how much I cost?
> Here! In my belly button.
> And the discount . . . on my little bottom.
> Don't look at my cellulite
> For sale.
> I am the first one to be auctioned.
> The last one to be discounted.[73]

Because there is little else to sell, Cubans often sell themselves in their tourist economy—as performers, taxi drivers, guides, chefs, escorts, or prostitutes, often regardless of their educational backgrounds or other professional skills.[74] The outside alters the inside.

As poverty grew considerably throughout the 1990s, Cuba's underclass soon became its majority. Poor Cubans became an empowered collective, with access to social mobility because they were better equipped than wealthier Cubans to survive the stringent conditions of the Special Period. Many lower-income Cubans already knew the black markets and had valuable experience with street negotiations. Wherever the state fails to deliver goods and services, innovative Cubans fill these needs for those who can afford them. Private free enterprise reigns. However, the new convertible peso economy has brought noticeable benefits to those with the most solid revolutionary credentials. Those who work within the highest ranks of government often prosper; they have access to superior goods in a timely manner and are often given warning of circumstances such as impending shortages.

Although noticeably better than it was ten years ago, the considerable time and energy required for the average Cuban to procure daily necessities still makes life on the island exceedingly precarious and difficult. In general, Cubans rely much more heavily on each other than on their government, or as Rosendahl says, reciprocity:

> The scarcity and disorganization of the planned system created . . . reciprocity, patron-client relationships, and illegal and semi-illegal transactions. . . . The extended family, relatives, and close friends became an important means of survival. . . . Everyone . . . used his or her networks to enter into reciprocal relationships.[75]

Cubans turn to cultural values like sharing, trust, and communal ownership in order to endure the fluctuations of the market. The interconnected nature of activities such as bartering for goods and pooling funds continues to strengthen existing social relationships and to build new ones across the island. Although these communal efforts may seem appealingly socialist, private business relationships are generally prohibited or highly regulated (by exorbitant taxes) in order to preserve the dominance of the state. These seemingly opposing forces shape personal relationships in Cuba.

Cuba has also become a hub of international sex tourism in recent years. Cuban men and women prostitute themselves in exchange for lavish meals, unattainable foreign products, and the highest foreign currency wages in the country. The desire and need for limited or unavailable items compels Maria to see herself as a cheap commodity, defined by what another might pay for her. The play expresses how little she values herself and how a consumerist mentality insidiously causes disidentifications. Throughout *Ignacio y Maria*, commodity fetishism creates unbearable tension for Maria. She explains to the audience,

> Each time I look at a woman, that I talk to her, I look at her accessories, her tight blouses, her broaches, her earrings. . . . I want her accessories to be mine. I'd like to take them away from her. Or better yet, to have them come by themselves to the drawers of my bedroom chest. To my ears, [*with a scream*] to the interior of my being!!![76]

Maria is plagued by the schism created by these unattainable objects that identify a woman. Objects, and how to obtain them, have come to define her. Unlike in other cultures, this direct relationship with accumulation is relatively new to Cubans. Living within the Revolution and its economic reforms, Maria has only recently been exposed to market forces, to a consumer culture and its limits under the Special Period. Still, she feels distraught that she does not know whether Ignacio "has shampoo and what brand."[77] Her nonparticipation in the global marketplace divides her from Ignacio, from herself, and from much of the world. Images of things she cannot obtain, things outside of Cuba, become torturous reminders of her limitations and of her confinement.

The paradox in the overwhelming oppression that comes from underdevelopment and seclusion, coupled with the education to understand these obstacles, acts as Maria's tormentor. For example, Maria knows the Paris neighborhood she would most like to live in, but admits "a square meter costs approximately all the salaries I'll never make in my life."[78] For an educated Cuban like Maria, knowledge is not necessarily power—rather, it can poignantly expose deficiencies and impossibilities. Ignacio's final advice to Maria only compounds these paradoxes: "I have one last thing left to tell you: don't forget to buy oil. And remember to put oil in your food, Maria. Think how important oil is for the brain, for motors. No plane can fly without oil, Maria, so go and buy oil. A big kiss" (34). Ignacio's suggestion immediately invokes politics and the global economy; fuel and cooking oil are often scarce or incredibly expensive in Cuba, and therefore unobtainable for Maria. Like many Cubans, Maria does not own a car. The brains and motors in Cuba do not have much access to oil but may not function without it; hence, Ignacio's ironic counsel cuts to the core of the country's plight. Ignacio mentions a plane, although it is unlikely that Maria will ever fly off the island. As he is clearly part of another system, Ignacio's "kiss" has no means of reaching Maria.

Maria and Ignacio struggle as they recognize what is exceptional about and what is missing from their center, Cuba. While still a place where relationships are key, Cuba's economic crisis has drastically altered the country over the last twenty years. The markers that made Cuba specific and recognizable have shifted. Foreign items have acquired greater value and more prestige than Cuban ones. Traveling within the country is nowhere near as enviable as traveling outside it. For many, leaving has become more desirable than staying. Ramirez notes that Cubans "live a life full of absences" due to modernity and what he calls "the extravagant individuality and its affliction of the modern world."[79] In her revealing book *Real Life in Castro's Cuba*, the former U.S. ambassador to Cuba, Catherine Moses, writes, "Cubans have been seeking refuge [off the island] . . . for generations. The young have been driven to it by their lack of hope for the future, and others have seen it as the only way to escape the political and economic difficulties that make life nearly impossible. . . . People who have no means of leaving fantasize about ways out."[80] Moses also points out that extensive migration and exile have been integral parts of Cuba's historical landscape and social reality since the 1930s—the phenomenon is not new. Yet there are Cubans who remain on the island *willingly*, patriots who believe in a better Cuba, who foster their defiant hope with their personal sense of nationalism. For example, Moses writes of a man who made a conscious decision to stay—he tells her, "Someone has to change this place."[81] In Mansur's play, Maria admits that "affection" for Havana "attracts her like a magnet," leaving her without "the time, nor the feeling, nor the education to pack [her] bags and leave."[82] Yet fragmentation and attachment permeate Maria and create feelings of internal exile on the island. She realizes, "I could drown, flee, escape toward another exile, to another climate drier, less gray. And far away. Who will be there? And you? And you?" (6). Combined with their estranged circumstances, her separation from Ignacio has already fractured her sense of self and exiled her internally, conditions she acknowledges she would carry with her to any country.

These conditions render it difficult to locate what is real in Cuba; the bizarre, the surreal, and the illogical frequently converge to frame reality. Rapid changes and nonlinear development have caused fissures in coherent thought. The pastiche and bricolage of disconnected modernizations within postmodernity have been astounding. Mansur expresses this in her play, as Ignacio is forced to question, "What am I to her? Am I real or the fiction she has available to make everything more credible?" (5). As in many countries, perspectives in Cuba are skewed by misinformation, hunger, worry, and insecurity. Maria laments that she does not "know how to live in [her] body" (20). She is bound by her homeland, her exclusion, and her love for Ignacio, and these layers trouble her identity: "I am not a mother, not an exile aristocrat, not an aborigine with magical powers, not a virgin, I'm not a laborer, I'm not a peasant, I'm not an intellectual. 'I am only a fly locked in the cupboard'" (18). Maria struggles because she fits none of these archetypes. Instead, she defines herself by her feelings of inferiority and her confinement. Her intellect and experiences are ultimately and irrevocably transformed by existing on the margins of the global market and on the fringes of economic integration. The dichotomies in Cuba leave Maria in strange suspension—her moments of hope are tempered by despair, her ambitions by fear, her imagination by stagnation.

These and other questions emerge from the collision of the psychological and material realities of life in Cuba that are expressly depicted in this piece. The play reaffirms theorist Karen Shimakawa's claims that extensive globalization determines shifts in temporal-spatial relations,[83] profoundly altering the structures of identification. Mansur's characters describe the experience this way:

> IGNACIO: I want to forget the present. What is the past? What is the future? It doesn't make any sense. This can't be fixed.
>
> MARIA: This silence and this trip, without a return, was assigned to me. . . . But a little bird tells me that everything will change. . . . but I only know how to look at the past.[84]

Both Ignacio and Maria express that permanence is impossible and that slippages are all around them. They wrestle with their interpretations of time but cannot actively define their relationships in space. Maria feels incapable of being part of recent changes and therefore feels threatened by them, while Ignacio lives only for change but cannot control it. He cannot fully engage in the present moment, while she can only connect with the past.

In a section entitled "Maria's First Monologue: The Abortion," Maria explains that "In the same hospital that they took blood from my finger as a child, they now take the son of Ignacio. The son that I won't have."[85] She does not directly voice why she has made the decision to abort their baby, but it clearly emerges from her increasing isolation and despair. She performs the monologue "on a platform with stereotyped gestures," speaking directly to her "comrades."[86] This construction reveals how deeply the state, with its political and economic realities, is subsumed in her identity and in her decision to have an abortion. Her choice is not unique—Pérez explains that in this difficult period in Cuba, "fertility rates had declined to what perhaps may have been the lowest levels in the twentieth century. The number of abortions increased. Between 1988 and 1990, there were nine abortions for every ten births."[87]

Neither Ignacio nor Maria can escape the paralyzing interval that Cuba is encountering. Maria cannot progress in Cuba, and Ignacio cannot progress without it. Its stagnant condition defines them both, as Maria reveals the depth of the frustration and confusion within her muddled identification. In the "Second Monologue: Words from a Generation," Maria explains:

> I feel lethargic, I never have extreme moods nor extreme feelings. Nothing ever happens to me and I never happen to anybody or anything. . . . I am motionless. Immobilized, stopped, frustrated, incapable, asleep, drowsy, yawning, eating, copulating, tired, aggressive, tolerant, sad, longing, deluded, satisfied, dissatisfied . . . they succeeded!! But not that much. . . . I'm perfectly prepared to do nothing, to draw, to photograph, to write the project of illusion, of the future which I'm not capable of giving myself in this life or in the one beyond. But even then I always find the possibility of turning defeat into victory. Am I a revolutionary? Am I sick or am I healthy?[88]

Maria does not know what the standard is—she can no longer answer basic questions about her own identity. All levels of recognizable representation break down, creating Maria's intense paralysis and dissatisfaction.

The progress and abuses that currently lead to a global space of "flows" rather than of "places" leave a profound mark on those for whom the flow is disrupted, fractured, or complicated. Cubans wait to be a part of a future they cannot predict, some hopeful and others defeated. Cubans in their twenties, thirties, and forties have experienced nothing but the Revolution. As they age, their dreams fade, along with the hopes of pursuing them. Maria cannot envision the future of Cuba and/or how she might fit into it. Although Ignacio claims "Depression goes with the territory, pure topography" (33), Maria's struggle for optimism endures. Yet, ultimately, she is unable to imagine her future positively.

At the end of the play, Maria commits suicide. In the epilogue, she states:

> I jump from the tall wall because he's down below and he is . . . So beautiful!!!! I can't bear his absence and the distance any longer. I fall from the wall. . . . [From Death] Fallen down here, I resemble a mixture, like a soft egg omelet on the concrete floor, spread out like a stain, an error, a horror between the force of gravity and love. Farewell to all. (35)

Her falling action implies that gravity (as a motion force and also "of the grave") controls her, that she is somehow involuntarily, uncontrollably meeting her death. She claims she does so because Ignacio is "down below," using a spatial construct (south?) to express her fervent desire to find any way, even death, to reach him. Because of the daily conditions she faces and the identity fracture these engender within her, Maria hopelessly takes her own life.

Ignacio does not necessarily fare any better than Maria does. She leaves him entirely depleted and isolated: he remarks, "I had already given her all my tears, some other day. I didn't have any left. I have nothing left. And now I am all alone" (35). The text ends with an inscription on the seawall in Havana, with an impassioned wish for basic control of one's identity and destiny. It reads, "I am not asking God to change the events, but instead to change me concerning all things. So I'll be able to guide my eternal sleep instead of enduring it" (35). Mansur does not outwardly critique the system or its challenges, but one's responses to it. This plea for greater agency, for the genuine ability to alter one's own experience, is the crux of the play.

Nara Mansur's work astutely reflects the paradoxical, often absurd conditions Cubans have endured and the staggering toll these conditions have on their personal lives. The disillusionment and isolation engendered by the political and economic situation on the island pervades the personal. In *Ignacio y Maria*, Mansur adamantly reinserts *lives* into the discussion as the only lucid indicator of global progress or struggle. Her characters are alienated, damaged, and displaced by adjustments to their positionality. The very nature of their Cuban identities has been problematized. Mansur questions what remains for Cubans, products of nationalism, in a globalized world where sovereignty has been weakened. She investigates how even educated people so restricted from the rest of the world for nearly half a century could possibly interact in a global society. Ramirez explains that Cuban audiences for the Teatro D'Dos production were "emotional" and "very close to Ignacio and to Maria. Many *were* Ignacio and Maria. . . . All of us are a little like them and that's why people could relate to their passions, their absences, and their disagreements."[89] These viewers understood the eventual self-destruction of two people. As the conditions of the Special Period slowly erode both Ignacio's and Maria's spirits in the play, Maria poignantly notes: "We begin to eat the sad dinner/we begin to eat our naked bodies."[90]

Transformed Identifications

Fidel Castro once commented that he feared globalization would bring about the "depersonalization and dispiritedness of individuals."[91] Both *Laberinto de lobos* and *Ignacio y Maria* probe the cost of preserving the Revolution against the unsentimental forces of globalization and its inherent economic pressures. Because globalization challenges territorial characteristics, it also presently endangers personal identities connected with national constructs. The reassignment of the power of the nation-state within a globalized economy has caused colossal, disconcerting ruptures in a tightly controlled society such as Cuba. Cubans are at once cut off from, but inevitably part of, an interconnected geoeconomic (and geopolitical) world. Miguel Terry and Nara Mansur investigate how recent generations of Cubans, those raised within the Revolution and of working age during the Special Period, have been affected by the economic conditions they endure and how these conditions circumscribe their personal relationships. While Felipe and Beatriz constantly reinvent themselves and renegotiate their identities in order to survive, Maria aborts a child and commits suicide because she can no longer reconcile her "self." Written about what could arguably be viewed as the harshest ten years of the Special Period, these pieces present bleak examples of the toll the circumstances took on identifications. Together, they contribute to the history of life in Cuba in the 1990s and they complicate how those who identify with a socialist revolution might integrate globalization into their views of themselves.

Unmarked storefront advertising "*hoy hay kerosen*" (today there's kerosene), Santiago de Cuba. The availability of state-subsidized goods varies daily in Cuba, making long-term planning difficult. Sellers often list their offerings to alert locals when crucial items are in stock. Unmarked storefronts like this one are common. **(All photographs in this gallery were taken by Christopher Stackowicz.)**

Sign at the entrance to La Cobija (The Refuge), a state-funded center for artists, Havana. This "sociocultural project," housed in a crumbling multistory former courthouse, offers painting, martial arts, music and dance classes, a children's theatre group, art studios, and ample rehearsal spaces. The sign reads, "Without culture, freedom is not possible."

El Teatro Mella (Mella Theatre) from the street, Havana. The Teatro Mella, founded in 1961, holds up to fifteen hundred patrons and is used for theatrical events, dance and music concerts, children's shows, and other presentations. Once a cinema, it was rededicated in honor of Julio Antonio Mella, a Cuban Communist Party founder who struggled against President Gerardo Machado. Assassinated in Mexico in 1929, Mella is considered a revolutionary hero and a key historical figure.

Interior, El Teatro Mella, Havana.

Workers taking a break, Santiago de Cuba. Under a crude painting of revolutionary leader Che Guevara, these men relax and jest as they take a break from their work at a warehouse. Note the game of dominoes under way at the folding table on the right.

Dancers rehearsing at La Cobija, Havana. These boys are a testament to Cuba's dedication to the arts. This photograph was taken on a sweltering afternoon, as they rehearsed in this dilapidated room with an uneven floor, no air conditioning, and no available drinking water. Yet, in an area where the housing shortage has made space scarce, La Cobija is indispensable.

Teatro El Sótano (Basement Theatre) from the street, Havana. The Teatro El Sótano could be a modern example of a Cuban "*salita*," or pocket theatre. It is a small, hard-to-find, unassuming venue in the residential neighborhood of Vedado. It is also the permanent home to the acclaimed theatre company founded by Afro-Cuban singer and actress Rita Montaner. Often used for Havana's biennial international theatre festivals, it is known for presenting cutting-edge, contemporary Cuban plays.

Interior of the Basement Theatre, Havana.

Bicycle taxi on Obra Pía Street, Havana. Bicycle taxis like this one serve both tourists and Cubans, but often at different prices; Cubans pay much less than foreigners. The proprietors find creative ways to attract attention. Some use horns or musical instruments, others sing or chant about their maneuvering skills. Some use broken English or German to comment to passersby, hoping to lure customers.

(Left) Afro-Cuban rumba, Callejon Hamel, Havana. Callejon Hamel is a pedestrian alley in the Cayo Hueso neighborhood. The corridor serves as the seat of Afro-Cuban rumba in Havana and is covered with imaginative, poetic, and often provocative statues and murals. Because tourists have discovered its hypnotic, open-air rumba performances, hustlers and prostitutes have followed.

Graffiti near the Capitol Building, Havana. “Give me cable,” beckons this plea for Internet connectivity. The Internet, if available to Cubans, is highly controlled and often erratic or sluggish due to limited bandwidth. There are absurdly long lines and frequent outages at scarce and expensive public terminals, despite repeated calls for greater access.

Interior of El Teatro Trianon, Havana. Often used as a cinema on weekdays, the eleven-hundred-seat Trianon Theatre in Vedado is also home to Teatro El Público, a theatre company known for its brash and unconventional productions. The stage version of *Fresa y Chocolate* (from the story by Senal Paz and later made into the famed 1993 film *Strawberry and Chocolate*) premiered here.

Cuban slogan featuring the likeness of José Martí, Santiago de Cuba. Depictions of Cuban poet and independence leader José Martí (1853–95) are emblematic on the island and in Miami. The Cuban Revolution consistently incorporates Martí's philosophies, writings, and achievements into its rhetoric. The lyrics of the patriotic Cuban song "Guantanamera" come from a poem in Martí's book *Versos Sencillos* (Simple Verses), and his far-reaching influence can be seen throughout Latin America.

Classroom, Cayo Granma, Santiago de Cuba. This one-room, rudimentary schoolhouse provided the students pictured with one lead teacher and two assistants. The literacy rate in Cuba is more than 20 percent higher now than before the Revolution and one of the highest in the world.

The former El Cine Megano, Havana. On the corner of San Martín in Centro Habana, only five hundred yards from the Capitol building, stands the rundown Cine Megano. Until it was closed in 2011, its darkness typically sheltered the destitute, transvestites, illegal immigrants, and addicts. Cuban playwright Abel González Melo writes about the misery that inhabited this space in his play *Talco*.

Tourist rumba, Callejon Hamel, Havana. Another view of the popular spot where Cubans and tourists mingle.

Window display at the Peerless department store, Havana. The items displayed in the window of this former American-style department store illustrate the peculiar mixture of products for sale in Havana.

Balcony above the Prado, Havana. There is both an institutionalized and a popular culture of watching others in Cuba. *Vigilancia*, vigilance or watchfulness, is expected and rewarded. Communities count on people paying attention to their surroundings in order to expose crime and report problems, but the practice is often viewed as intrusive snooping for the sake of gossip.

Mural linking the Castro brothers, Havana. This mural, which reads "Together with Fidel and Raúl, Revolution," was one of the few instances of the direct mention of Raúl's rule or his relationship with Fidel. Most slogans and graffiti refer to Fidel, the Revolution itself, or deceased leaders such as Che Guevara, Camilo Cienfuegos, Julio Antonio Mella, or José Martí.

Fruit seller's cart passes by the scaffolding on a building, Santiago de Cuba.

The Centro Cultural Bertolt Brecht, a cultural center named for the great German playwright, Havana. In the midst of the residential neighborhood Vedado, this busy location features a café, two main theatres, and one tiny experimental studio. The venue houses plays, musical performances, comedies, and shows for children, among other events. It is a principal location for events during the international theatre festivals and is often sold out.

Decaying wall, Santiago de Cuba. What remains on this disintegrating plaster is the unfinished dictum "Fatherland is . . ."

4

Revolution from Afar

Cuban American Perspectives

> [Relational space] . . . is another space . . . actually lived and socially created spatiality, concrete and abstract at the same time, the habitus of social practices. It is a space rarely seen for it has been obscured by bifocal vision that traditionally views space as either a mental construct or a physical form.
>
> —Edward Soja, *Postmodern Geographies: The Reassertion of Space in Critical Social Theory*

On 13 August 2006, Cuban president Fidel Castro celebrated his eightieth birthday, although recovering from major surgery and ominously absent from view. Miami Cubans who identify as political refugees danced in the streets at the news of Fidel's failing health but were also forced, yet again, to acknowledge his spectacular longevity as Cuba's charismatic leader. Their reaction added another episode to the problematic relationship between Cuba and the United States that deeply informs the entire Cuban diaspora. Cuba's reach extends far beyond the Miami-Havana nexus that Juan Flores insists is "incomplete without Washington, and New York, and by extension San Juan, Los Angeles, Mexico City, Madrid, Tokyo"[1] and, recently, Caracas or Beijing. Yet it is also clear that Cuba's "borders have proliferated, all the while showing their limited ability to contain, arrest, or limit the historic and present exchanges that continue to sneak through its cracks."[2]

Years of exchange and influence have permanently linked the island to its northern neighbor. However, since the Cuban Revolution of 1959, decades of unresolved political clashes, ideological disagreements, economic sanctions, and immigration crises have marred the two countries' once affable political, financial, and social affiliations. According to scholar Román De la Campa, the Cuban Revolution has certainly, "found its primary source of inspiration in confronting American brawn"[3] and to date, nearly a dozen American presidents have encountered a resolute, fiercely independent Fidel Castro. Political differences have had a profound effect on Cubans at home and in the diaspora. While more than one million former Cuban citizens live in exile *in* the United States, I contend that other Cubans have been undeniably exiled *by* the United States. This chapter investigates how the experience of this postmodern dislocation is making itself heard in the theatrical language of two contemporary Cuban American playwrights, Rogelio Martinez and Nilo Cruz, both of whom concentrate on the interstitial space of the blended subject. They are a part of an ongoing conversation by a prominent group of Cuban American playwrights (including María Irene Fornés, Eduardo Machado, Carmelita Tropicana, Caridad Svich, Dolores Prida, and Jorge Cortiñas) writing about identifications, exile, and the island.

While exile can serve as a space of potentiality or a ground of possibility, it can also engender wrenching estrangement—its participants are not fully at ease in any country. Since the Cuban Missile Crisis, Cuba has been notably positioned as peripheral to the United States. The individual, personal consequences of Cuba's position are manifest in many Cuban American plays, including *Illuminating Veronica* by Rogelio Martinez (2000) and *Hortensia and the Museum of Dreams* by Nilo Cruz (2004). Both plays engage the ways in which various views of the United States as a "home" to the exiled are translated, transferred, and transformed by Cubans in the United States and in Cuba. Martinez and Cruz vividly express the tension of living at a murky, hyphenated crossroads.

Both Martinez and Cruz come from families that were ruptured by moves from Cuba to the United States. Rogelio Martinez came to the country with his mother when he was nine years old, during the Mariel boatlift of 1980, but his father was unable to join them until ten years later. Nilo Cruz left Cuba before his tenth birthday; he emigrated from Matanzas to Miami with his parents, leaving two older sisters behind on the island. Clearly, these two playwrights were children when they emigrated and did not make personal or political decisions to leave Cuba. *Illuminating Veronica* and *Hortensia and the Museum of Dreams* are included here because they take place in Cuba, but at the time they were written (in the early 2000s), neither Martinez nor Cruz had ever returned to the island. Unlike many other Cuban American writers, both Martinez and Cruz must fictionalize Cuba entirely or rely on their memories and research about their native country. Both authors rely on their intimate and immediate knowledge of life as Cuban Americans in the United States, allowing them to complicate the experience of exiles from the other side—looking inward at Cuba rather than outward from Cuba.

Martinez and Cruz reaffirm what Edward Soja contends, that "'life-stories' have a geography too; they have milieux, immediate locales, provocative emplacements which affect thought and action."[4] Both playwrights contend with lives left elsewhere and lives rebuilt in new surroundings. Their plays accentuate the hope for reconstitution of the self and of the homeland within multiple competing exile conditions (internal, external, by a country, and within a country). Both artists write about modes of self-imposed exile and exile *by* the United States, for those inside Cuba and outside it. Their works continually complicate notions of repatriation and assimilation, as they incorporate a keen personal awareness that these challenges exist both inside Cuba and in exile. Cubans on the island have had to reexamine and transform their identities, as have those Cubans who left the country.

In his play *Illuminating Veronica* (2000), Rogelio Martinez explores Cuba just after the Revolution, when the title character remains on the island although her family has relocated to Miami. Martinez portrays Veronica's exile within Cuba, her efforts to embrace the revolutionary socialist system, to reenvision her home and family, and to reconcile the personal sacrifices she will have to make to participate in Cuba's newly constructed society. He positions Veronica's cultural and personal memories as a dialectic between her view of the United States, of the world, and of herself. The play emphasizes the interplay of history (both personal and political) and geography. In *Hortensia and the Museum of Dreams* (2004), playwright Nilo Cruz depicts a pair of siblings as they return to Cuba seeking recollection, recuperation, closure, and conservation. Sent together to the United States as children without their parents, their separate homecomings are observably burdened by questions of identification and belonging.

Both plays engage complicated questions about the connections between place and personhood; they examine how Cubans in the United States view themselves and how they view Cuba (in memory and in actuality) and their relationships to it. The characters search for ways to traverse the deep ideological divides between homeland and exile. Wrestling with what theatre scholar Una Chaudhuri calls "the unsentimental recognition of home *as* a discourse, replete with ideological antecedents and consequences,"[5] *Illuminating Veronica* and *Hortensia and the Museum of Dreams* illustrate how the enduring, intricate relationship between the United States and Cuba has irrevocably shaped identities in both countries. Martinez and Cruz use the stage to boldly articulate experiences of hybridity and of transculturation (mutual borrowing and lending between cultures) that circumscribe their characters.

Illuminating Veronica

Cuban American playwright Rogelio Martinez was born in Sancti Spiritus, Cuba, in 1971 and left the island by boat, via the port of Mariel, nearly a decade later. He and his mother relocated to Union City, New Jersey, an area known for its significant concentration of Cuban immigrants, second only to Miami. Martinez completed his undergraduate studies at Syracuse University and he later earned his MFA in playwriting from Columbia University. An alumnus of New Dramatists, his works have been developed and presented across the United States, by theatre organizations such as the Public Theater, the Oregon Shakespeare Festival, the Mark Taper Forum, the

South Coast Repertory, Primary Stages, and the Atlantic Theater Company. Martinez's plays include *All Eyes and Ears*, *Fizz*, *Learning Curve*, *I Regret She's Made of Sugar*, *Arrivals and Departures*, and *Union City*. He received the Princess Grace Award in 2001 and has earned NEA/TCG and Sloan Foundation grants, as well as several prominent theatrical commissions. The Denver Center Theatre Company premiered his play *When Tang Met Laika* in early 2010, and he wrote a new play, *Wanamaker's Pursuit*, for the Arden Theatre Company in Philadelphia's 2011 season. Martinez also teaches playwriting at Montclair University, Goddard College, and Primary Stages, where he is a member of the Strelsin Writer's Group. He currently runs the Hispanic Playwrights in Residence Lab at INTAR (International Arts Relations, Inc.) in New York City.

Martinez's play *Illuminating Veronica* begins in Havana in December 1960. It is an unsentimental, complicated (rather than nostalgic) view of Cuba's past. An educated but very sheltered woman in her early thirties, Veronica has chosen to remain in Havana after the Revolution although her birth family emigrates to Miami. She, her husband Manuel, and their former maid, Rosario, stay and support the Revolution. Manuel works for the Ministry of Culture and is promised a promotion from his job as a censor to a position editing books to "put them in a socialist context." Veronica, who is pregnant, learns that proving her allegiance to the Revolution will require putting her bourgeois past behind her, even if that includes betraying her marriage—Manuel's boss, Pepin, insists that Veronica sleep with him to prove her dedication to the Revolution, and to garner favor for Manuel. She reluctantly agrees to the affair and to relinquishing her ties to Havana's old society. Yet Veronica also demands that Pepin hire her, making her case by explaining that she already does half of Manuel's work. Instead Pepin uses Veronica's now counterrevolutionary collection of books (such as Proust's *Remembrance of Things Past*) as justification to question Manuel's loyalty and to fire him. When the government begins moving rural Cubans into large homes in Havana, an old man named Ernesto and his twenty-something granddaughter Sofia are assigned to half of Veronica's house. Once they move in, Manuel, who blames Rosario (now their neighbor) for spying on him, is disillusioned and disgusted. He admits to Veronica that he never wanted her to work, and that he has arranged for them to be smuggled out of Cuba. In the next scene, two men take Manuel away, making it clear that Veronica has exposed his plan to leave the country. She chooses the egalitarian ideals of the Revolution over her marriage, suffering great personal losses in order to participate in the new collective. Five months later, Pepin visits Veronica (now the mother of triplets) and explains that he was fired for supporting her application to work for the Ministry of Culture. This reality tests Veronica's belief in the growing egalitarianism promised by the Revolution. Yet soon after he leaves, Veronica embraces Sofia and Ernesto as her new family and, along with her three sons, celebrates her commitment to the Revolution and its future.

Although the story is geographically contained in Havana, powerful links between Miami and Havana anchor this play. Miami was undoubtedly the most prominent destination among Cuban émigrés of the era. According to Cuba historian Louis Pérez, "Miami began as an imitation of Havana in the 1920s and 1930s, then was imitated by Havana during the 1940s and 1950s; in the 1960s it was a copy of a copy that was copied."[6] Cuban culture dictated much of Florida's imaginary, just as American culture shaped a great deal of Cuba's aesthetic. A simple, visual example is that much of Key West reflects early-twentieth-century Cuban architecture, while much of the architecture in Havana imitates the American Art Deco style of the 1920s.

De la Campa, however, questions the particular choice of Miami as a popular exile destination to begin with. He writes, "I am not sure why Cubans went there instead of New York, Europe, or Latin America. . . . Perhaps it was the unconscious return of the possessive gaze: Cubans looking to Miami as the United States historically looked at Cuba."[7] *Illuminating Veronica* investigates precisely how the Cuban characters who remain in Cuba respond to this gaze. Educated and pregnant, Veronica remains on the island because she defines revolution as Chaudhuri does, as "a painful turn in a long, ongoing narrative that has a logic of its own."[8] For Veronica, the "turn" Chaudhuri mentions can only develop meaning within a particular cultural narrative—in Martinez's play, that narrative includes the unambiguous division between Cuba and the United States after the Revolution. Theorist Edward Soja best explains the schism of the revolutionary narrative, in terms of space:

> Those seeking the demise of capitalism . . . tended to see in spatial consciousness and identity—in localisms and regionalisms or nationalisms—a dangerous fetter on the rise of a united world proletariat, a false consciousness inherently antagonistic to the revolutionary subjectivity and objective historical project of the working class. Only one form of territorial consciousness was acceptable—loyalty to the socialist state. [9]

Martinez's work traces the processes of re-identification, of forming the new loyalties the Revolution demands of Veronica, of her marriage, of her home. The first stage picture is that of Rosario, ex-housekeeper of Veronica's now departed family, standing on a chair attempting to dust an heirloom chandelier. The bourgeois past immediately collides with the revolutionary present. Veronica compares Russian revolutionary Vladimir Lenin's portrait on the back of the book she is reading with that of American movie star Yul Brynner, even though the familiarity that had formerly allowed the United

States and Cuba to influence each other, "to imitate each other, to borrow from each other, to become somewhat like each other"[10] had already been irrevocably altered. In these brief moments, a theatrical framework is created; both the past and the present, as well as the Soviet Union and United States, are ever-present in this Cuban world, despite their obvious antagonisms.

Cubans on the island live with what May Joseph asserts is the "impossibility of full citizenship by constituting its absences, its longings, its elsewheres."[11] Their citizenship originates from a cultural rather than a geographical identity, as Soja suggests. The book Veronica has chosen to read comprises translated letters between Lenin and Soviet writer and activist Maxim Gorky at a time when reading Russian authors was highly recommended in Cuba. The book being a long-distance correspondence between two people in separate physical locations adds another important theme to the play, while keeping Russia foregrounded. The book insists that distance does not extinguish conversation. Veronica's comparison of Lenin to Brynner signals that American culture remains ubiquitous as well. She soon reveals that she and her husband are the only members of her immediate family and friends who did not leave Cuba for Miami. An ideological rift, followed by physical separation, has fractured her former family and exiled her from them. Her local, territorial consciousness and its cultural influences have prevailed over her familial relationships.

The vestiges of a different life, of a prerevolutionary (and capitalist) society are still visible in Veronica's home, despite the vast political changes around her. Several paintings, a lavish chandelier, and many European books adorn the stage—abandoned objects that once belonged to Veronica's family. Although they readily acknowledge that it is a symbol of their previously bourgeois existence, Veronica and Rosario admit their sentimental attachment to the chandelier. Veronica remarks, "It's part of my family now" and insists, "If my father could have stuffed it in his suitcase he would have taken it with him."[12] Veronica insinuates that she will create a new family. Household objects and correspondences by mail with her departed family are her only links to a former life, a former self.

This is a major shift for Veronica, who has never been an independent woman. Although highly educated, Veronica concedes that she led an incredibly sheltered life before the Revolution; she divulges that she never ventured out alone because she could not have found her way back home. This metaphor is the foundation of Veronica's experience in the play. Her view of herself has changed. Her refusal to go to Miami was a profound, initially solo venture and, because of it, Veronica is entirely unable to return to or to recuperate the home life she once knew. The very definition of *home* becomes incredibly malleable throughout the play. Despite her revolutionary resolve, Veronica grows pensive while poring over her father's copy of Proust, confessing, "All of a sudden I miss home."[13] When her husband Manuel reminds her that she is "home," she gently concedes, "Yes. I know. Isn't that silly."[14] Veronica suffers from what Chaudhuri calls "*static* exilic consciousness," the condition of being homesick while at home. Chaudhuri notes, "Here the sentimental image of home—as an actual place correlated with a strong and desirable emotional experience (the sense of 'belonging')—unravels."[15] As it unravels, the play raises important questions about the nature of home, about what a home entails, and whether or not it can be (re)constructed (physically and emotionally) in exile.

Although Soja suggests that in the recent past, "national patriotism and citizenship were usually couched more in a cultural than a geographical identity and ideology,"[16] Martinez's Veronica views Miami as a physical space, complete with unfamiliar objects, that is distinctly disconnected from Havana. Manuel hands an already open letter to Veronica and tells her, "It's a letter from your father in Miami. Telling you how life there is—he has a new Cadillac." Manuel seems impressed by this information, but Veronica's contempt for the American lifestyle is immediately clear, as she flatly responds, "As if that's what life is."[17] The United States is only a consumerist text to Veronica, a fractured dystopia that has been determined, corrupted, and transformed by commodity capitalism and personal hubris. She disagrees with Manuel, firmly asserting her opinion in a way she has not previously. However, the play suggests what Jimmy Porter noted in John Osbourne's *Look Back in Anger*—that there is inherent difficulty in not being American while living in an American age.

No matter how many Cubans create enclaves in the United States, Veronica realizes that Florida can never replicate Cuba. Because all her friends and family have left, Manuel contends that Veronica does not "belong" in Cuba, but belongs "with [her] father" (i.e., in Miami).[18] The United States is never far from their consciousness. Yet Veronica deems it impossible to cultivate what De la Campa calls "an alternative Cuba through Miami."[19] Her view corresponds with Foucault's insistence that, "we live inside a set of relations that delineates sites which are irreducible to one another and absolutely not superimposable on one another."[20] A rift between the couple emerges as Manuel embraces the connections between the countries, the transculturations, openly discussing with his boss, Pepin, "how the Yankees just lost the World Series to the Pirates."[21]

The fissure between Manuel and Veronica deepens when other cultural markers are considered, such as the books Manuel has been charged to rewrite. His list includes *Remembrance of Things Past*, whose "title alone is counterrevolutionary" because, according to officials, "the past is not worth remembering."[22] Memory has become suspect. This sentiment not only applies to the Cuban Revolution, which often focuses on the future of Cuba rather than its past, but also refers to personal memories of those who left the island. Manuel declares, "We can't stop to think about [the past] when we're making our own way in the world."[23] The emphasis on Manuel and Veronica's "*own* way in the world," as unique and separate from their heritage, is key because their friends and families are now palpably absent. While Manuel struggles, Veronica has been exiled *to* where she belongs, not *from* it.[24] She discredits the past, moving away from her dependent, unassertive self. The egalitarian ideals of the new Cuban Revolutionary society shift her view of marriage and her capabilities.

Manuel does not express the same sense of belonging Veronica does. Rather, he is highly critical of Cuba and notes the manufactured fear in the country when he comments that the recurring air raid sirens are "a false alarm every day."[25] Manuel's skepticism about any threat the United States poses to Cuba creates a nuanced incongruity. The connections and the antagonism between Cuba and the United States are conveyed simultaneously, as Veronica demands, "I want color television, Manuel. . . . My father has one in Miami." No matter her ideology, Veronica's desires are still fueled by American-style consumerism.[26] These kinds of contradictions trouble her identifications. Manuel's immediate response reiterates his earlier opinion—"Then maybe that's where you belong."[27] Manuel's comment could be staged as sarcastic or hopeful. He ignores the fact that "the immediate purpose [of departing for Miami] was to get away from an uncertain—and in some cases threatening—future, but it was also a way to communicate opposition to Castro's regime," what De la Campa calls "a way of voting with one's feet."[28]

The United States remains in the conversation, as a palpable adversary, when Veronica meets Pepin, the Minister of Culture and Manuel's boss. Pepin reminds Veronica to keep her eyes open for Yankee imperialism and blames Cubans' lack of "taste" on "what's left of Yankee influence,"[29] highlighting the once closely intertwined relationship between Cuba and the United States. Pepin accuses Veronica of clinging to her privileged past because she has not destroyed a painting that her aunt left behind. He claims Veronica believes, and maybe hopes, that those who left are "going to march back in." He firmly warns her, "You can't live in two worlds,"[30] flatly rejecting Chaudhuri's notion of "inhabiting two or more homes simultaneously."[31] Veronica's memories torment her and she implores Pepin,

> Do you ever get—do you ever remember things from your past. Things you had forgotten. Like a painting has the—to remember what you were like. It happens sometimes when I'm alone. I go into my older sister's room—she has this little music box that I open and Schumann plays. And just as it gets—I think she's going to walk through the door. I wait and wait, but she never comes back.[32]

Veronica's memories forge a critical link to her identity and to her relationships with her family. She directly relates certain items to her former self. Yet she also acknowledges that she is in a holding pattern, waiting for something to change. She still calls a space in her house her "older sister's room" although that sister is no longer present. If, according to Chaudhuri, Veronica's home exists in relation to a familiar group of people, what becomes of it without those people? She is uncertain about the *stability* of home; or to put it another way, she has a deepening *suspicion* that home is an unstable container, depleted without one's memories.

This exile from her family and her former self grows deeper, as Pepin insists Veronica "can't have revolution under the values taught to [her] by [her] father."[33] He goes on to demand that Veronica "prove" to him that she can "let go of everything" in her past in order to secure a promotion for her husband. This rejection of her previous bourgeois values includes sleeping with Pepin so that he will promote Manuel. Veronica negotiates her own new identity, proving she can overcome her bourgeois past, as well as what Chaudhuri calls "the power of place."[34] As her formidable response, Veronica violently slashes her aunt's painting with a knife, signifying her willingness to brutally relinquish the past while recognizing her personal power to choose to do so.

Despite this strong display of her will to transform and to join this new society, Veronica's self-definition remains geographically centered, tethered to her home and her desire to reterritorialize it. Her adamant sense of place reemerges as she insists, "I was born in this house"[35] when Rosario explains that there is ample room for the government to house other families there. Rosario, like others, gruffly points out that Veronica is "too sentimentally attached . . . to the way things used to be,"[36] as the audience witnesses her fervent effort to transform her thinking, to reimagine herself.

Within a month, Veronica significantly modifies her view of her home. She brazenly informs Pepin,

> This isn't even my house. Everything in it belongs to my father. Is it too much to ask to be taken seriously? Papi thought it was. Then I read Marx and quickly learned everything Papi had taught me was wrong. Submission. Grace. Weakness. They were nothing but antiquated beliefs. Now there are new ideas. Fulfillment. Equality. Strength. Ideas that have taken hold of me. That have filled me. And I don't ever see me letting them go.[37]

Revolutionary knowledge has altered Veronica's perspective. She now demands personal respect and recognition, ideals that were never important to her before. She has enacted a "transformation of the family," according to Chaudhuri, "from a living receptacle of the individual's memory to the site of its being forgotten."[38] Yet rather than simply forgetting the beliefs instilled in her by her family, she vehemently and actively rails against them. Veronica views herself as having been enlightened, having been schooled anew about agency and female participation. However, the price of her ideological reeducation and her new national identity is her familial one. Veronica understands this as a binary relationship—she decides she must shed one identity in order to incorporate the other. While exiling her family, she exiles herself from her past.

The play moves forward in time and Veronica, now seven months pregnant, expresses her disgust that Manuel has still not provided the color television he promised her. She feels utterly betrayed, misled by "another broken promise."[39] Manuel, on the other hand, has begun to appreciate the markers of the past. He realizes, "There is an inherent value to things old. They contain within them years and years of survival" (137). Where he once criticized Veronica for her sentimentality, he begins to cling to what came before. He seems desperate to recover another time, to return to the relationship they once had. Veronica bitingly implies that Manuel only values his individual survival rather than having any sense of a collective and that he has not appreciated the Revolution. Their differences in perspective are immense; Manuel finally asserts, "I can't live here—I want to go" and explains that pouring cement for seventy hours a week since losing his government job was not "what he bought into" (138). Veronica insists that Manuel does not understand the immense sacrifices that are called for, and she reminds him that she "gave up her family" (138) to further this revolutionary project. Manuel then informs his wife that he has arranged for their clandestine departure to Miami. During an impassioned exchange about his plan, Veronica painfully admits that she thought her husband was "another man" (139). The contrast of staying on the island as opposed to leaving for Florida has fractured their relationship, leaving no room for complicated or gendered nuances. Veronica and Manuel take sides against one another.

Veronica's reaction to sudden explosions is also particularly revealing. Remnants of her hope resurface, as she exclaims, "My father. . . . He's come back" (141), assuming that Cubans in the United States have decided to attack the island. She excitedly believes that her father has not abandoned her and will reclaim his homeland. She believes he could reinstate the "dynamic adaptation and accommodation" that Pérez notes existed between the United States and Cuba for centuries before the Revolution.[40] The explosions are not an attack after all, but are the celebratory fireworks of Cuban carnival. Yet the scene exposes Veronica's innermost feelings; the audience glimpses the naïve hope she has preserved underneath her burgeoning feminist, revolutionary exterior. It signals that her past has not been entirely eradicated from her personality and may never be.

The deliberate conflation of celebration (carnival) with destruction or aggression (a military attack) exposes a major paradox of the Cuban Revolution and of exile: does the past have to be obliterated for a reenvisioning of the future? Veronica further illustrates this contradiction as she tells Manuel,

> I always thought that all those books would change the way people think. That people would look at me not as a woman with a wealthy family but as one with no past. That you would look at me not as your wife but as your equal. That all of you would trust I'd find my way home—it might take me hours but I would eventually come home.[41]

Veronica's questions about how to create equality, belonging, and kinship are essential to her redefinition of herself and her definition of revolution. She slowly becomes aware that her past gender dynamic with Manuel could indelibly mark her future despite great changes, and she struggles to accept this paradox.

Manuel also discloses contradictory ideas, as he tries to accept that the past has become irrelevant. While talking with Sofia, a girl from the countryside who moves into Veronica's home with her grandfather, Manuel remarks, "History begins with Fidel." Sofia cleverly responds, "I suppose it will end with him as well" (143), emphasizing her understanding of just how little control rural Cubans in particular had over their situation in the early 1960s. As the only character who seems to calmly accept and comprehend the complicated nuances of the Revolution, Sofia informs Manuel, "Everything is up for grabs now. It's not the same. It's not what you're used to" (144).

Shortly after this exchange, the ideological differences between characters in the play become especially tumultuous. Veronica notifies government authorities of her husband's plan to leave the country, resulting in his arrest and imprisonment for five years. It is unclear whether she does this out of spite, out of fear of his departure, out of fear for her own safety if the government views her as his accomplice, or due to her fervent belief in the egalitarianism of the burgeoning new society. (A complex blend of these motivations seems most probable.) Although not without turmoil, Veronica's actions privilege her new liberated identity over her dependent old one.

Rosario makes it clear that Veronica can never return to the past. She lucidly reminds Veronica, "Your father will never accept you as you are" (147). Rosario also rationalizes the losses required for Veronica to move forward, as they share the following conversation:

> ROSARIO: Veronica. Do you remember when your father left? At the airport. All of us were there.

VERONICA: Yes. Why?
ROSARIO: You didn't want to kiss him good bye but I gently pushed you forward until you had to.
VERONICA: That kiss is all I have left.
ROSARIO: I want you to kiss your husband good bye so you can get on with your life. (147)

In this context, letting go of personal relationships—particularly those with her father and her husband, the males who have led her—becomes required for Veronica's life to progress. De la Campa asserts that "nationalism begets a sense of isolation, if not arrogance, that may well keep all Cubans from any sense of belonging."[42] This is the crux of Veronica's exilic experience. Her internal exile, complete with emotional isolation, seems required for change. Her perplexed state of continual development reflects Pérez's notion of national identity, "not as a fixed and immutable construct but as cultural artifact, as contested."[43]

What implications do these kinds of identifications have? What, if anything, remains? Memories comfort, inform, torture, revive, and destroy Veronica and others. Sofia's grandfather Ernesto has also been deeply affected by the ideological changes in Cuba. Displaced from the countryside to the city, he comments that the plans for the revolutionary government's continuation translate into a long stay in Havana, "away from the country. Away from where I belong."[44] Sofia quickly advises him, "The old belong where there are people willing to take care of them" (149). Ernesto is perceived as intertwined with others, a context from which Veronica has labored to remove herself. The fracture of the self that accompanies the new politic in Cuba is undoubtedly widespread and touches all classes. Veronica poignantly invokes her own eager transformation and its ongoing, accompanying loss, as she tells Sofia, "Isn't it funny how you can forget something that meant so much to you growing up. . . . Waking Papi up every morning. Duty. The duty towards my family. I haven't felt that way in a long time" (149).

By the end of act 2, it is especially evident that every character's previous perceptions of America have been considerably altered by the Revolution. Veronica explains how her father reacted when, as a five-year-old child, she told him she "belonged" where there was snow:

> I told him I wanted to go to a place where everyone walked on clouds. He said it wasn't a cloud they were walking on but water. And I said, even better. He smiled and took me to a lake, threw me into the water and yelled for me to walk. And as much as I tried I couldn't. At that time my father was incredibly nationalistic. Nothing was better than Cuba and he was going to prove it to me.

She continues, "My father must be senile. He now believes in things he once told me were false" (150). Opinions have been turned upside down. The supposedly safe haven of exile also creates a torturous longing for the homeland, while those who have remained "at home" must reimagine it, and themselves within it. Veronica criticizes the changes in her father's beliefs without acknowledging the vast changes in her own.

A similar yearning for connections and belonging drives Sofia to offer to become Veronica's family. She tells Veronica, "I don't want to give up the chance to have something genuine" (151). She implies that because they have not had sincere relationships with their actual relatives, family must be chosen or fabricated. An earlier reference to Goldilocks reemerges here, as the characters admit that no one knows how the independent, lost girl's search for identity and belonging was actually resolved. This metaphor bolsters the provisional, unfixed nature of the postmodern exile identity. Goldilocks tries out the trappings of different identities to find one that is just right. Her story implies that there is an uncertain exploration and an unknown future subsumed in the search for identifications.

In the final scene of the play, Veronica divulges her pointed understanding of precisely how any ideology enacts change. Speaking about Pepin and power, she remarks, "That's what this whole thing is. Taking an idea that is pure and corrupting it until it gets you what you want" (152). Veronica's naiveté now eradicated, Pepin tells her, "Part of a Revolution is learning—growing." Skillful adaptation has become a most necessary tool. Pepin continues, "We haven't yet learned what to do with those of us who are genuine. It's a lesson we'll have to learn if this is going to work" (152). He does not explain what *genuine* means in this context or how one might recognize it in a world with relationships turned upside down.

The fracture of Veronica's home is completed by the last letter she receives from her father. He writes that "memory either narrows a place to the point of disappearing or causes it to grow in your imagination" (157), yet he does not reveal which has happened for him. He admits that he can find no way to retain actual experiences. Although he remarks that his friends in Miami "want" Havana, he reveals, "I've decided to let go because for me Havana is a house on a quiet street—a house that no longer belongs fully to me. Street by street or room by room they've taken Havana from me" (157). His most chilling admission is that his own daughter grows faint in his memory—part of the "narrowing" he mentioned. He feels he must relinquish Veronica, along with Cuba itself, to live fully in the present. Veronica reads his explanation in a letter:

> Last night I forgot what you look like and though the thought of forgetting you rattled me a little I soon decided that you were like the house that no longer belonged to me. With love, your father. PS. This is my

last letter to you. I have grown sentimental and I am embarrassed by everything I do or say in respect to Cuba. (157)

Veronica's father has incorporated the "combination of nostalgia and refusal" that De la Campa argues defines the Cuban community in Miami.[45] He has chosen to become a part of "a project that quickly went beyond the rejection of the old," according to De la Campa, "toward the creation of an alternative community, another homeland, perhaps a Cuba we never had or could have, in the United States."[46]

The letter makes Veronica aware of her father's decision to embrace another community and eradicate his past. Hence, in a brief exchange between Veronica and Ernesto, Veronica adopts a new family, a new father, a new identity. "The possibility of being exposed," writes theorist Zdravko Mlinar, "to the near infinity of places, persons, things, ideas, make it all the more necessary to have a center in which to cultivate one's self."[47] This impetus drives Veronica to replace her lost relatives with those who already share her house and accept her choices. Families become interchangeable. Veronica resituates her home life in order to reterritorialize what is local, the world inside her home, so that it incorporates her newly embraced agency.

The scene appropriately ends with the sound of Veronica's triplets crying, of the family that will surround her in the future. The end of the play reveals Veronica's attempt to firmly reinvent herself and her home, no matter what her father and the others who left decide to do. She remarks,

> The man who wrote that letter and his friends. When they come back we will turn off all the lights and close all our doors and then we will hope they don't recognize their old homes. That they have forgotten them. We will hope they go away.[48]

Although Veronica's hope for their return remains, her point of view has changed. The alteration of her identity and belonging have come full circle. She no longer seeks a reunion and a return to past relationships but instead favors those she has recently established. Veronica's home has become "a place of discovery, a place to be discovered"[49] rather than the site of her physical and metaphoric exile from her family and her self. Both Veronica and her father forge new alliances that disregard the old and reject those who were once so vital—acknowledging that it is impossible to belong in both worlds. The rupture is severe enough that it has destroyed Veronica's ties and made them impossible to restore, yet it has also created significant new bonds to replace them.

The play does not assert whether or not this level of severity is necessary to form new political and gender identifications, to belong when exiled. Veronica's future will reflect Chaudhuri's inquiry about whether revolution is "an exercise in futility, a charade, an eyewash . . . or a radical change, altering the basic conditions of living."[50] Martinez's work demonstrates that these tensions remain unresolved because, as Ann Pelligrini contends, "Processes of identification are the subject's constitutive condition. Through identification, individuals effectively solder their egos to others, both real and imagined."[51] *Illuminating Veronica* depicts the problematical journey toward a somewhere or someone else, rather than an arrival at any fixed identity.

Hortensia and the Museum of Dreams

Nilo Cruz was born in Matanzas, Cuba, in 1960. His parents had initially supported the Revolution, but they grew concerned as it became more Marxist. Cruz's father was imprisoned for attempting to leave the island when Cruz was two years old; upon his release, the family fled to Miami. Cruz wrote poetry in his teens and attended community college in downtown Miami in the early 1980s, where he met a theatre professor who inspired him to write plays. He later met Cuban-born playwright María Irene Fornés, who invited him to join her playwriting workshop at INTAR in New York and introduced him to the faculty at Brown University. Cruz eventually studied at Brown, earning his MFA. in playwriting in 1994. In 2001, Cruz returned to Florida as the playwright-in-residence at the New Theatre in Coral Gables. There, he wrote his Pulitzer Prize–winning play, *Anna in the Tropics* (2002), which moved to Broadway and was nominated for a Tony Award in 2004. Cruz was the first Latino playwright so honored. His other works include *Night Train to Bolina* (1995), *Two Sisters and a Piano* (1998), *A Bicycle Country* (1999), and *Lorca in a Green Dress* (2003). His plays have been produced by New York's Public Theatre, Pasadena Playhouse, McCarter Theatre, and South Coast Repertory Theatre, among others. Cruz has won numerous prestigious awards, including a Kennedy Center honor for New American Plays and a Rockefeller Foundation grant. Like Martinez, Cruz lives in New York City and is an alumnus of New Dramatists. He has taught playwriting at Brown University, Yale University, and the University of Iowa.

Nilo Cruz's play *Hortensia and the Museum of Dreams* (2004) takes place in Havana in 1998. Estranged twins Luca and Luciana, who have a physical condition that slows their aging processes, return to Cuba after more than thirty-five years in the United States The twins were on the Pedro Pan flights (Operation Peter Pan), the clandestine exodus of roughly fourteen thousand children from Cuba in the early 1960s. The Catholic Church organized these departures of children, without their parents, when it was rumored that children would be sent to Soviet-style work camps to support the Revolution. The children were placed in Catholic homes or orphanages in the United States until relatives or their parents could reclaim them.[52] In 1998, a rare papal visit affords Luca and Luciana the right to travel for eighteen days to the island, where they have separate but intertwined experiences as they seek to deal with troubling childhood memories and to find closure. Luca stays with his *tio* (uncle) Lalo and experiences the difficulties of daily life in Havana during the Special Period. He finds a Cuban lover (probably a prostitute) named Delita, who helps him understand the conditions in modern-day Cuba. Luciana encounters Havana as a tourist, escorted around the city by a Cuban guide while staying in a hotel. Luca's and Luciana's adventures expressionistically overlap and coincide onstage, although they are detached. When Luca attempts to meet with Luciana, she flees Havana to the town of Santiago de las Vegas, where she meets Hortensia and her twenty-something sons, Basilio and Samuel. Hortensia has lovingly created a Museum of Dreams, filled with letters describing the miracles and wishes of everyday Cubans. She and her sons assume Luciana is there to write about the museum and to gain the church's support because Cuban authorities, especially one General Viamonte, view the museum's spiritual overtones as suspect. Viamonte interrogates Hortensia and Luciana, insisting that the state will allow no such public (state-supported) museum. Hortensia continues to collect stories of miracles and encourages Luciana to seek her own miracle—reconciliation with her brother, Luca. As both Luca and Luciana confront the incestuous relationship they had in the past, miracles from the museum mirror their journey. When Luca and Luciana are finally reunited in the last few minutes of the play, they reconcile and are ready to learn how to be normal siblings. Safely back in the United States, Luciana and Luca send Hortensia a letter about their own "miracle," their reconciliation, to add to her museum.

Hortensia and the Museum of Dreams takes place during Pope John Paul's historic first visit to Cuba. The papal visit serves as an important backdrop by which two Cuban American exiles visit their homeland. The papal gesture indicates Cuba's growing openness and its increasing desire to participate in the outside world. Modern Cuba—constituted by its fervent determination of sovereignty, its isolation and its shortages, its cultural exports, and its diasporic community—drew international focus in 1998 when it acknowledged all religions on the island and permitted their practice. Because absences make what *is* in Cuba as relevant as what is *not*, this historic moment of candor and tolerance signaled the willingness of Cubans on the island (and outside it) to imagine the country differently and to accept change.

Hortensia and the Museum of Dreams deals with the loss intrinsic in exile, and especially within the experience of children who, as part of Operación Pedro Pan, were brought to the United States from 1960 to 1962. Cruz explains that Luca and his estranged sister Luciana "should look younger than their actual age, as if their lost childhood has stopped them from aging."[53] Cruz physically presents their bodies, as Ann Pelligrini might describe them, "as contested discursive site[s] through which ideological concepts are naturalized as biology."[54] Although Cuba has changed a great deal in the thirty-five years since the siblings were on the island, they do not appear much older. This is incongruent with the Cuba they now encounter. It is no longer a place of revolutionary hope and excitement and instead has been forever marked by the Revolution's successes and failures. The economic hardships of the Special Period are evident in its long food lines, intermittent blackouts, and crumbling architecture, yet Cubans soldier on. They suffer and struggle to survive, forced to weigh their commitment to revolutionary ideals with their practical concerns about everyday needs such as food and housing.

The Cuban American siblings in the play embark on separate, very personal journeys, as they seek to make sense of their abstracted childhood, one shadowed by duality and partial identifications. Where the United States was once the utopia they dreamed about, they now imagine Cuba as their utopia. As Chaudhuri astutely articulates, their Cuban "identities have to be negotiated out of a welter of myths and stereotypes and desires and dreams and daydreams."[55] The Cubans these siblings meet face a similar challenge. After nearly forty years of revolution, many are torn about the capacity for the socialist country to thrive on its own. The stresses of the Special Period have made them question Cuba's fervent anticapitalist, isolationist positions. Cubans love their country but long to modernize, to integrate with the rest of the world, and to benefit from its goods and services.

Cruz specifies that the performance space for his play should have "a feeling of openness" and that a Tibetan bell should be used "as a way of suspending reality."[56] While there are brief moments of theatrical realism throughout the piece, ambient sounds and commingled spaces often create an impressionistic, dreamlike stage environment. For instance, the piece begins with Luca and Luciana both on stage, but completely unaware of each other. They share the space but are clearly in separate environments while having simultaneous, parallel travel experiences. They go from the United States to Cuba, but their physical environment on stage does not change. Hence, the mental and emotional landscapes make up the foreground, rather than any specific place. Luca and Luciana also write in travel journals and impart these thoughts directly to the audience. Cruz uses theatrical elements like these to express the paradoxes and complexities of exile and reterritorialization, amid a loss of immediate geography. Questions about the crucial relationship between place and personhood emerge immediately, making it clear that exile has hybridity at its core.

Luca and Luciana come to the island with different purposes and distinct visions of their *cubanidad*, or Cubanness, a cultural identity that emphasizes diversity within the contexts of strong nationalism and anti-imperialism. (Because they left the island involuntarily as children, their departure is not viewed as political but circumstantial.) Luca explains to Cuban airport agents that he has come to the island to visit relatives, with whom he will stay. Luciana discloses that she is a journalist and will stay at the Hotel Capri. One sibling has come home as a Cuban returning from the United States, the other has come to Cuba as an American tourist. Their varied perspectives are instantly evident: the Hotel Capri, once run by Miami mobsters, was open only to non-Cubans at the time. Locals were not permitted to stay there and were usually not permitted on hotel grounds.

Luciana's choice signifies that, as Chaudhuri contends, "tourism is a method of experiencing other places in terms one already understands, a method of canceling out unfamiliarity."[57] Does an exile inherently approach with a remembered, or possibly imagined, familiarity with his or her country? Both Luca and Luciana note the "same old" things in Havana, recognizing the city's streets and seawall. However, Luciana insists, "I didn't come here to retrace the past, I came to see the new generation . . . The new island."[58] Her statement raises questions about what is "new" in contemporary Cuba for her to see (despite its newness to her) and how her past may be reflected or obscured there. Along with changes since the Revolution began, Luciana's remoteness is used to reiterate Chaudhuri's view that the meaning of exile is usefully ambivalent, that "exile is branded by the negatives of loss and separation; on the other [hand] it is distinguished by distance, detachment, perspective."[59] Considering the contentious relationship between the United States and Cuba, the twins struggle with an amalgam of their memories and of their perceptions of the island. This is not the Cuba they left behind in 1961. Instead, it is a country that has been through many phases of influences, triumphs, and repression. The Special Period tempered Cubans' hopes to shape their futures by significantly diminishing their power to do so. Rather than looking forward, they had to concentrate on meeting immediate needs. Luca and Luciana have changed, too, yet they are partially stuck in a time gone by. Like Cuba, they want to move forward but cannot do so without reconciling the past.

Basic privileges afforded to him in the United States alter Luca's view of Cuba. In a section entitled "A Place Called Home," Tio Lalo explains to Luca that, "It's better to bathe in the morning because the electricity is cut off after six."[60] Although he was aware of difficulties in Cuba since the end of Soviet subsidies, Luca is startled. The reality of daily life in Cuba in the 1990s is conveyed, as basic services were unreliable. This reality is directly contrasted with Luciana's posh experience of the island—the hotel receptionist informs Luciana that her "tour guide" will be Ramón. (Because Luciana is American and, thus, suspicious, she is required to have an escort.) Here, Luciana represents part of the "sociocultural world of the audience watching"[61] in the United States, with controlled tourist-only access to the island (if permitted access at all).

Since departing Cuba in the 1960s, these Americans have had little contact with the island. In the following scene, entitled "Maps and the City," the siblings grapple with memory:

LUCA: I'm remembering the streets . . .
LUCIANA: The streets are remembering me . . .
LUCA: Blue skies, faded awnings, orange tiles . . .
LUCIANA: The world is not forgetful . . . A sidewalk never forgets to be a sidewalk . . . A tree never forgets to be a tree.[62]

Luca and Luciana question whether their memories are affected by whether or not one is remembered. They desire an exchange, or conversation, of memory. Chaudhuri observes, "Although the act of returning home is an archetypally regressive act—'going home is always going *back* home,.' . . . it is used . . . not to recuperate identity but rather to stage the difficulties, even impossibility, of such a recuperation."[63] Cuba's isolation since the Revolution means much of the terrain has remained as the twins remember it, but they are surprised by its severe decay, especially because their bodies have not deteriorated with age. Nevertheless, they encounter a less dogmatic, much more nuanced Cuba than the one they left in 1961. Although Luca reveals that he and Luciana should "settle the past,"[64] Luciana seems more concerned with the memories and impressions she can presently cull from the island. Luciana remarks, "In a secret way I'm collecting faces, streets, and romantic corners."[65] Like many tourists, she is far more interested in what she can take from Cuba than what she can offer it. She does not see her role as a contributor but as a recipient.

Cruz's metaphor of Havana as "a sleeping madam who lost her pearl necklace"[66] exposes the loss that pervades Luciana's experience. Her exile is complete in her definition of herself, when she tells Samuel, "I'm not from here. I'm from the United States" and insists she is on the island "for the Pope's visit."[67] She does not admit that her trip has any personal significance, nor does she divulge that she was born in Cuba. When Samuel's brother, Basilio, insists that Luciana's birthplace, "makes [her] one of [them]," she tellingly does not respond. She resists the "new hybrid identity" that May Joseph suggests may "continuously produce discursive critiques of the state, of patriarchy, and of capitalism."[68] She clings to her American experience and will not identify with the material and ideological struggles, decay, and confusion she witnesses around her, as she is still unable to accept these traits in herself.

Basilio and Samuel, both in their twenties, explain to Luciana that their family has been treated with suspicion "because of all the letters [they] sent abroad."[69] These letters reveal that, even before Luciana's arrival, the world abroad was always present and viewed with anticipation by these brothers. The young men were seeking support for the museum from beyond Cuba's borders, a comment about the outside world bolstering even Cuba's most intimate projects. Basilio welcomes Luciana to his mother Hortensia's house and to the Museum of Dreams in the same breath, conflating the two. The "museum" of "dreams" sounds like a place where unrealized dreams come to permanently reside and where realized dreams linger in limbo. It is a metaphor for the paralysis of Cuba itself at the end of the twentieth century.

As Néstor García Cancilini asserts, "It is not the same thing, of course, to preserve the memory in individual form or to pose the problem of assuming a collective representation of the past."[70] Museums aim to represent collectives. Yet, as Chaudhuri contends, "Only those things are put in a museum that have no 'organic' place within a society, because they either belong to a different time or a different place."[71] If dreams belong in a "different time and place" than present-day Cuba, the picture is bleak. Basilio's welcoming of Luciana is completed by the "sound of a large wave,"[72] a persistent reminder that Cuba is, psychically and metaphorically, an island and, quite possibly, an unaltered museum of another era. As Patricia Ybarra asserts, "Within Cuban American drama of the 1990s, the rendering of the sea as a liminal borderland . . . ingests and reimagines travel and the travelogue as chronicles of immobility and stalled motion."[73] The sea as a boundary insists that even though Luciana has come, Basilio is not going anywhere. During the Special Period, the outside world cannot fully penetrate this environment and remains distant.

Meanwhile, Luca tells his Cuban lover Delita why he does not really know how old he is—he explains that he and his sister suffer from an aging disorder. He explains that his "body has stopped recognizing"[74] his age. He implies that he has been physically unable to grow because of severed identifications. When Delita asks Luca why he is so "gloomy," he asserts that he is "just trying to adjust." He continues: "Everybody tried to prepare me for this trip. They told me about the power being cut off, the shortage of food. How buildings are falling apart. How people live double lives. . . . Well, nobody ever can tell you how it affects you inside."[75]

Luca's remark highlights the privilege he has known in the United States and echoes his past, during which he was forced to "adjust" to a life outside Cuba. He is dejected because he is confronted with what Soja identifies as "urgent awareness of geographically uneven development and the revived sense of [his] personal political responsibility for it."[76] Luca's intense memories of the island as it was thirty years before must be painfully reconsidered. Because Luca appears much younger than his age, the audience is confronted with the physical paradox within Luca's observation: although Luca still appears youthful, the years have drastically altered the world around him and his perception of it. The ethereal nature of these conversations materializes again, as the end of this scene is punctuated by the border—the sound of a large wave that "takes Luca and Delita away."[77]

Like her brother, Luciana is unable to "return completely" to her homeland, as Guillermo Gomez-Peña put it.[78] In a journal entry she shares with the audience, Luciana is exploring Cuba as a tourist and adventurer rather than as a native. She is utterly lost while at "home" in Cuba and describes how "the thrill and the fear of the unknown take over."[79] Here, the play explores what it means to be lost in one's native country. The specific language Luciana uses—that her homeland is "unknown" to her—pointedly reflects her bewildering experiences on the island. When Luciana meets Hortensia, Hortensia calls her "a woman from a foreign country."[80] Only Luca consistently positions Luciana as a native of Cuba. He tells an absent Luciana, "I went back to our old house. I found you in every room. Even if you have chosen to remove yourself, you were there in the patio, in the living room, standing by the window."[81] The place is marked for Luca and, in his estimation, his sister still belongs in it. Luca's memories are crafted around Luciana's presence, in sharp contrast with her choice to distance herself from Cuba and to see herself as an American outsider.

Basilio quickly reminds Luciana that, for his generation, the United States is always present in the Cuban psyche. He flippantly remarks, "I told [Samuel] he doesn't want a wife, he wants a Girl Scout" (21), revealing his specific cultural knowledge of American scouting. Even Basilio and Samuel, born within the Revolution and therefore too young to remember any other system, understand and use American references. If they do so only for Luciana's sake, it becomes evident that her American background changes the conversation between them. This highlights how the close proximity and historical relationship between the United States and Cuba mark both Cubans and Cuban Americans. Basilio, Samuel, Luciana, and Luca are all constantly aware of two countries, influenced by two sets of ideas and values—exile is not necessary for this duality to emerge.

This moment is juxtaposed with Tio Lalo explaining to Luca why he and his sister were sent to the United States. Lalo describes the perception on the island: "Everybody thought there was going to be a war, you see. And there were rumors that the government planned to send children to work on Soviet farms, so [your mother] wanted to protect you" (24). The binary between the United States and the Soviet Union emerges here—the United States was perceived as a safe haven for the children while the Soviet Union was feared. Yet the attempt at finding a safe haven in the United States caused the twins' greatest calamity: their incestuous relationship. It looms much larger than the threat any Soviet work farm may have been. This passage also notes Cuba's position between the super powers and anchors Cuba's difficulties within the Cold War framework. Cuba is isolated. Because they leave the island, Luciana and Luca suffer a parallel isolation in exile. Being Cuban isolates them once they are in Ohio, and living in the United States isolates them anew once they are in Cuba. Like Cuba, they are trapped in between, existing in an undefined, interstitial space where they cling to each other.

Despite Luciana's fractured childhood, Hortensia insists, "Oh, the body never forgets love, Luciana. It has its own time and memories." She goes on to say, "And the old days come back, like a forgotten season and restore all of what I was and am" (26). Hortensia's descriptions reflect Luciana's journey as much as they do her own. These memories on and in the body seem particularly poignant because Luciana's body has not aged normally. Time has not passed as usual. Basilio soon shares a memory with Luciana, a file of "a few of the miracles that came last month." One memory in particular is staged. A man named Faustino appears as the lights change and the Tibetan bell chimes. Wearing an old straw hat, he begins, "On the ninth of September my father left the country and told me to take his little statue of the virgin to the wilderness and place it in the river" (27). Departure to a foreign land is central yet again, clearly part of the entire Cuban experience. As if transported elsewhere, Luciana walks to center stage and recites poetic dialogue about journeying and feeling lost. She admits, "No, I can't go on pretending" (28). It becomes obvious that a particular memory plagues her. Then Luca and Delita appear. Luca carries a suitcase and opens it as he asks Delita, "Tell me what do you want to eat?" (29). This suitcase is completely stuffed with American food and toiletries. Luca ironically adds, "I told you I came prepared" (29), and he did, by consumerist standards. Delita eats a biscuit and quizzically comments, "They taste like paradise" (29). Cuba was often envisioned as a paradise, with its warm tropical weather and sandy beaches. Ironically, Delita's perception of the United States, with its abundance of goods, has now become the ideal.

To soothe Delita's extremely emotional reaction to the abundance before her, Luca gently says, "We have everything we need, and what we don't have we'll do without" (29). Here, this comment is framed as a decidedly Cuban mentality rather than an American entrepreneurial spirit. Cubans, as represented by Delita and Hortensia, are more concerned with what Jon Erickson notes as "a relationship to *being* rather than with *having*" (31). Although Luca has a suitcase full of products and Luciana has the freedom to travel, the access and excess of American capitalism has not soothed the emotional ruptures of their exile and isolation. They do not have a relationship with each other. To an island that has few material goods, they come seeking recuperation, a reconciliation that could never happen in the United States, despite their wealth of possessions.

The angst that the trip to Cuba has created for Luciana is evident when Samuel and Basilio share parts of her travel diary aloud. They note that she "just want[s] the trip to end," that she is "in a quandary" that causes her to wander through the streets (30). The psychic toll of rediscovery, of attempting to reconcile the past, has disoriented her. Yet she also writes, "Here, I can only anticipate the gifts that come with each day, whether it's a walk to the square with Basilio or a smile from Samuel" (31). She acknowledges that Cuba offers time, that the pace on the island is much slower than in the United States, and that human connections are therefore paramount.

Yet it is Luca's intense longing that seems to beckon to his sister. She faces the pinnacle of her identity crisis, just as Luca enters the stage and remarks,

> I went to the house we used to visit every summer. . . . The place looked withered and old, as if the sea had entered the house. . . . The old swing was still there swaying in the breeze . . . And the hum of mother's song in the air, telling you to come back. (32)

Because of his estrangement from Luciana, Luca chooses to imagine his sister through his early childhood memories from Cuba rather than in the present, clearly equating her with Cuba's locations and climate. Luciana tells her far-off brother, "Because I can only love you best when you're far away, I've chosen to love you in the distance" (33). This is also true of Cuba, of her experience of exile from her homeland. The rupture caused by involuntary relocation, combined with the ominous secret of the incest in their childhood, creates an internal exile in Luciana that mirrors her physical stagnation. Her identity is in turmoil, as she begins to understand her condition. She tells Hortensia, "Little by little I realize why I am playing this role, why I can't face myself. . . . Why I am living a lie" (35). She slowly discovers that she has been exiled from her own feelings as well as from her country.

Luciana's quest for self-discovery and recovery is complicated by General Viamonte, who ruthlessly interrogates her and Hortensia. Although Hortensia insists that Luciana is "not a foreigner" because she was born in Cuba, the general replies, "She's a foreigner to me!" (37), marking Luciana's distinct difference from those who stayed on the island. Viamonte also points out that the process of childhood exile manufactured identifications: "the Pedro Pan project, they called it, like the children's book about the boy who runs away to never-never land and never grows up" (38). Because their childhoods were irrevocably altered, many Peter Pan survivors who were separated from their families and raised by strangers abroad feel as if they never fully experienced childhood.[82] Even if sarcastically, Viamonte positions the United States as a faraway land where all is supposedly well, a utopian "Never-Never Land" where no one ages and new, joyous identifications can be created. Yet the story of Peter Pan does not end well. The others around him, whom he loves dearly, do grow up—they become adults and leave him behind, stifled by his immaturity.

The general later refers to Luciana as a "tourist" and asserts,

> We live in an age of reason, of natural science. We take pride in the real. Our system gave me a pair of shoes, a home, a refrigerator. If compañera Hortensia wants to call our accomplishments miracles, then these are the miracles that need to be exhibited in her museum. (39)

Viamonte firmly situates practical, material accomplishments of the Revolution in opposition to hopes and dreams. His edifying and unsentimental assessment of modern Cuba troubles Luciana's utopian vision of her homeland. Viamonte also points out that Luciana's visa is for journalistic purposes, yet she is not in Havana following the pope. When Luciana insists she came to see Hortensia because Hortensia wrote to her in the United States, the general explains that the letters were intercepted and never left Cuba. He attacks Hortensia, saying, "You live in a world of fantasy, with angels and spirits, and you don't want to face reality" (39). He claims that, because "nobody wants tourists" in this small town in the eastern part of the island, the museum was voted down. Its purpose and merits were not discussed. As a government figure, Viamonte's blatant rejection of dreams, of faith and hope at a time of opening in Cuba, is an especially revealing comment on state bureaucracy, one that directly contrasts with Hortensia's (i.e., the people's) idealistic project.

Upon their return to the museum, Luciana criticizes Hortensia's passivity in the face of the general:

> LUCIANA: (*With contained anger*) It seems like this whole island is always waiting! Waiting! Waiting for something to happen. And nothing ever happens. Who's going to be the first one to stop waiting! Who's going to be the first!
>
> HORTENSIA: You have your ways . . . You come from a different world.
>
> LUCIANA: No, I come from the same world.[83]

The women's disagreement over the form of resistance, of action, reflects their unique perspectives. The play insists that Cubans have a different worldview than Americans. It raises the pointed question May Joseph asks—"How are hybrid identities shaped in excess of, and in relation to, the boundaries of nation?"[84] It is indicative that in this exchange, Luciana reveals her understanding that her two experiences, as a Cuban exile and as a hyphenated American, are not separate. She acknowledges her connection with a Cuban world just as Hortensia denies it. While Hortensia now views Luciana as different, Luciana has begun to see herself as a part of Cuba, as within its revolutionary purview. She finally considers both her American experience and her Cuban experience as parts of the same whole.

This characterization affirms Homi Bhabha's observation that identification is "always the production of an image of identity and the transformation of the subject in assuming that image."[85] Luciana gradually accepts her Cuban identity. Yet the complexity within this identification emerges soon after their discussion, when Hortensia tells Luciana about a Cuban mantra, "You must learn to endure what you can't change."[86] This type of resignation does not sit well with the typically innovative, entrepreneurial American ideal. When Hortensia gently asks Luciana why she chose to stay with them in Oriente (rather than remain safely in Havana), Luciana replies, "Because for a moment I needed a sense of place, to belong."[87] Hortensia wisely informs Luciana that, "everything in life is trying to find its place but also its absence. And already from the beginning the absence had begun."[88] What *is not* is as significant as *what is*. Then, without any prior knowledge or discussion of Luca, Hortensia suddenly encourages Luciana to go find her brother. This surreal moment, filled with Hortensia's premonition, intuition, and compassion, concludes their intense exchange.

The most impressionistic scene in the play, entitled "Entering the Night without Electricity," takes place in near darkness. Cruz creates two conversations that overlap considerably, often making it unclear exactly who is being spoken to, or being spoken of:

> Delita: You must not remember much about this place.
> Basilio: You're almost American . . .
> Luca: Are you saying that I'm American?
> Basilio: You were so young when you left.
> Luciana: But I don't feel American.[89]

What does it mean to "feel" Cuban or American? These cultures coexist in the characters' bodies, perspectives, and memories. Their self-definitions are both chosen and circumstantial.

Both Luca and Luciana experience what Mae G. Henderson calls "the outsidedness of insidedness."[90] The siblings are trapped between rootedness and estrangement, in their homeland, in their adopted nation, and within themselves. Their dichotomy of consciousness is due to, as Chaudhuri argues, "the most fundamental rift between the figure of America and the old discourse of exile . . . from the grim reality of home—and homelessness—that greets the already unhomed immigrant."[91] Delita exposes a crucial nuance of exile when she admits, "I never thought that life would be difficult up there" (in the United States). Luca replies, "It was. I remember it as if it was yesterday. A cold town in Ohio. An old building falling apart . . . Children and more children. The stench of urine."[92] Luca incisively dismantles the fantasy that America is a paradise. Luciana poignantly adds, "In Ohio my heart was circumcised."[93] Clearly, the sense of trauma that De la Campa considers has molded these exiled adults. Cruz decisively echoes De la Campa by dismantling the notion that only positive traits and experiences are obtained abroad.

Luciana and Luca's young-looking bodies act as the sites of inscription of their exilic experiences. When Basilio asks Luciana if she loves Luca, she replies, "He was my mother, my father, my brother, my sister, and also nothing. Nothing. So he could be everything. Everything. On his mouth the seaside. On his eyebrows my old school."[94] She explains that in exile in Ohio, her brother became all she had and wanted. He became the vessel for her memories, physically as well as emotionally, crucially and continually reconfirming her identity. The incest that caused their estrangement from each other is gently revealed, as evidence that their reconciliation could only occur on Cuban soil, where they were still innocent. Reconciliatory action is only possible, as De la Campa explains, because "behind their anxieties lies a need to come to grips with a complicated national history that affected them so deeply at an age at which they could not act for themselves."[95]

In an ethereal scene called "Mercedita's Miracle," a woman relays that, after her husband was shot by rebels, she sent her children abroad because she "wanted them to be safe." She explains that San Cristobal came to tell her that her children were, in fact, "safe in a small town up North."[96] The United States is viewed as a useful point of intervention, a safe haven from rebels and strife. It is faith (in the north and in San Cristobal) that reassures this lonely mother in Cuba. However, it is in the United States that Luca and Luciana unknowingly transgress, allowing their attachment to one another to grow incestuous. This contradiction plagues them. In addition, the timeline is unclear for Mercedita, Luca, and Luciana—it is unclear how long the children must stay away to remain safe and whether staying away too long can render them unsafe. Moreover, there has been no path for safe return established.

As music plays and Luciana says farewell to the museum, she reads, "I write this as though I am claiming and taking back with me a box of embraces . . . A box of dreams . . . A jar of memories."[97] The notion of claiming, or reclaiming, one's heritage is crucial in various theoretical frameworks. Yet taking something back infers it was once lost, once separate from the individual. Cruz's play seems to suggest that it was never disconnected, never missing entirely. In fact, during a reprise of brief moments from Luciana's experience in Cuba, Hortensia remarks, "They come with invisible suitcases full of maps,"[98] clearly acknowledging that those returning know something is there and only seek the direction to reclaim it. Cuba has been "mapped," charted in some way, and therefore seems recoverable. As she leaves to find Luca, Luciana declares, "Now it was time to find my way back to what I had left behind,"[99] keenly aware of the journey of repossession, the journey to recover something absent.

When the siblings finally meet again face to face, they share the following exchange:

> LUCA: Do you regret our past?
> LUCIANA: I regret nothing. But you and I . . . We have to find a way.
> LUCA: I'm learning how to be your brother again.
> LUCIANA: You never stopped being that.
> LUCA: For a long time I had thought about this moment, when we would finally talk.
> LUCIANA: Me, too. I thought I had to find a way to tell it to myself, like a children's story that explains the world.
> LUCA: And how would the story go?
> LUCIANA: Two children dressed up in airport dreams. Two children who thought the world was going to end. Two children who only had each other.[100]

For Luca and Luciana, the airport was thrilling, filled with anticipation, but it was also the beginning of a violent rupture from their homeland. It marked a continually shifting border that these siblings spent their lives negotiating. For them, this border signified a constant state of transition, an interstitial space in which they still reside. Their exile shielded them from the changes in Cuba but also engendered the incest that eventually led to the considerable separation between them. Within the play, this fracture also creates their vivid fantasies about a distant, special reunion.

Despite fear, loss, displacement, and disjuncture, Luca and Luciana remain imaginative and hopeful, optimistically childlike. They embrace what Chaudhuri describes as the "possibility of entertaining two or more cultural contexts simultaneously"[101] and find comfort in it. The play ends with the miracle they send to Hortensia. In it, Luca and Luciana describe themselves by their professions (salesman and journalist, respectively) and by their present addresses (one in New York, the other in Rhode Island) rather than by their nationalities or by their past affiliations. They finally create self-definitions that do not include the rigid spatial binary (United States vs. Cuba) that caused them such turmoil. Instead, as a borderland entirely constituted by boundaries and its own daily transformations, Cuba becomes the ideal physical location for their personal reconciliation and renewal. Cruz uses the intersection of space and time as a border where subjects with ties to two identifications constitute crucial acts of self-representation.

Staged Pluralities

If, as De la Campa suggests, "the most realistic way to inhabit one's nation . . . is to recognize the conflictive pluralities it contains,"[102] then the characters in these plays prosper. Their geographical and emotional displacements are eventually subsumed into their daily realities. De la Campa's most difficult question is eloquently posed by these dramas: "Can exiles ever recapture a lost past, or register suspicions about historical events that engulfed everyone, most of all themselves?"[103] *Illuminating Veronica* and *Hortensia and the Museum of Dreams* defy closure by refusing to resolve key paradoxes like these. The binaries become untenable as identities are not clarified, but further complicated. Constant loss and expectation frame multiple and incomplete identities, creating intricate levels of hybridity within these subjects.

The result of the theatrical layering of discreet spatial and temporal domains in these plays is the exposure of the enigmatic qualities within all recognizable relationships. Going back to Cuba, or remaining there amid profound changes, helps these characters deconstruct their experiences in order to reveal and celebrate new possible paths of identification. Ultimately, Martinez and Cruz use unfixed, yet confined stage spaces to challenge, incorporate, and overcome the radical insecurities of displacement. Their works position the theatrical voice of the hybrid immigrant as intact in its own right while also characterized by what has been left behind. *Illuminating Veronica* and *Hortensia and the Museum of Dreams* are significant for various audiences because they focus on the simultaneities that, as Soja suggests, "intervene, extending our point of view outward in an infinite number of lines connecting the subject to a whole world of comparable instances."[104]

Although only ninety miles separate Cuba from Florida, the extreme division of the two countries over five decades has created acute dislocations for Cubans, both on the island and living in the United States. Merely being in the United States isolates Cubans—the embargo separates them from their families, their culture, and their heritage, while complete assimilation to American standards is expected, encouraged, and rewarded. However, remaining in Cuba isolates Cubans as well, due to their limited access to the outside, especially to the United States. Exiles constantly float in between, fervently trying to incorporate pieces of two disparate cultures into individual, reconstituted hybrid identities shaped by profound emotional ruptures and losses. Many people experience a dichotomy of consciousness, brought on by the residue of previous associations mingling with the present and the future. These plays posit how and why exiles manufacture new identities and spaces, actively fusing together the past and the present in the hopes of creating viable futures.

5

Para Siempre

Staging the Future

> The Cuban model doesn't even work for us anymore.
> —Fidel Castro, interviewed in *Atlantic Monthly*, 18 Sept. 2010

Fidel Castro's perplexing remarks in recent interviews have raised vital questions about Cuba's direction. Despite claims that his remarks were misinterpreted, a frail but alert Fidel acknowledged to the Associated Press that Jeffrey Goldberg had in fact accurately quoted him in the *Atlantic Monthly* conceding the failure of the "Cuban model" he had invented and perpetuated. Indeed, Fidel seemed to be reversing course, disparaging the very system he embedded in Cuba's life. However, Julia Sweig, a member of the Council on Foreign Relations who accompanied Goldberg for the Havana interview, clarified that Fidel "wasn't rejecting the ideas of the Revolution [so much as acknowledging] that under 'the Cuban model' the state has much too big a role in the economic life of the country."[1] It is possible that Fidel was creating space for his brother's recent reforms (self-employment, alterations to travel restrictions, etc.) and signaling his support for modifications to the country's economic model. While Fidel's strategy still derives from ideology, his tactics and those of Raúl, have become increasingly pragmatic.

Over a decade ago, in his speech saying good-bye to Pope John Paul II after the pope's historic visit to Cuba, Fidel acknowledged that Cuba had to avoid seclusion at all costs. He expressed that the future of the island nation, bound by geographic and material limitations, would be shaped by its relationships with other countries; the outside would affect the inside. Yet he has never suggested *what* that future, following decades of revolution, could look like. Likewise, the artists included in this book do not view the destiny of Cuba as fixed or inevitable; although unsure of what is to come, they do not posit a way out of the island's daily conundrums nor admit any kind of defeat. Cuba's revolutionary society has persisted for so long that it has predictably undergone great transformations and taken on fresh nuances. One of the society's most profound accomplishments is that it appears constant. The ideals of the Revolution have often been reconfigured and reconstructed to suit the current moment—they revolve and evolve, unhinging concrete definitions and ensuring their own continuity.

On Transition

Cuba is currently governed by a bureau of soldiers. As longtime commander of the armed forces, Raúl Castro enabled a smooth transition when Fidel stepped aside. That is Raúl's legacy. Six years after Raúl's rise to power, questions about whether or not he has the charisma and the admiration of the people necessary to run Cuba have subsided. Although some insist that Fidel still rules from behind the scenes, others maintain that he has entirely yielded power to a new group of leaders. Upon visiting Fidel in 2010, Sweig noted, "Fidel is at an early stage of reinventing himself . . . primarily on the international stage. . . . He has time on his hands now that he didn't expect to have. And he's revisiting history, and revisiting his own history."[2] Fidel has slowly assumed the role of elder statesman, making space for revisions to some of the rigid stances associated with him. While most agree that Raúl may modify the economic models created by Fidel, there may be little room for major political or social adjustments while Fidel is still alive. Moreover, serious doubts remain about how long Raúl's new collective can sustain power over the meager Cuban economy after Fidel dies.

The phrase *Cuando Castro desaparezca*—literally, "when Castro disappears," expressing possibility—is often used when discussing the future of Cuba. A subtle yet theatrical exit, possibly a "fade out," and the ongoing nature of Castro's influence are implied. The effects of more than five decades of Castroism (possibly more if the present group continues to lead) will undoubtedly be felt in Cuba and throughout Latin America for many generations beyond the lifespan of *El líder máximo* (The Great Leader). It is wholly apparent that Fidel has irrevocably shaped Cuba's identity in all global forums, especially within the Caribbean and Latin America and in opposition to capitalism and to the United States.

It is my contention that the term *post-Castro* has needed to be redefined since 2006. Where it once essentially meant "after Fidel," it should now include Raúl Castro and other revolutionary figures as well, otherwise the post-Castro future would simply mean more Castroism. Fidel's *gradually* failing health, which signaled the inevitable acceptance of his mortality, may have foreshadowed his country's peaceful future. When Fidel became too ill to rule Cuba in the summer of 2006, the fierce figure modestly relinquished "provisional" power of Cuba's one-party communist system to his brother, Raúl (then defense minister). Without obvious fanfare or sway, the island quietly experienced an organized governmental succession, with Fidel allowing his then seventy-five-year-old brother to take the helm and preserve the legacy of their revolution. Planned since the early 1990s, this much-anticipated redesignation of power came surprisingly gently, due to Fidel's intestinal surgery rather than any political upheaval. Little changed immediately on or off the island, but Fidel effectively stepped down—a yielding that many (Cuban playwright and author Reinaldo Arenas among them) had been anticipating for half a century but thought would only come with the octogenarian's death.

Within months, dozens of predictions of massive change were squelched. Leaders throughout Latin America expressed their concern for Fidel's health and sent messages of solidarity to Raúl and his ministers. Critics such as former U.S. Assistant Secretary of State Thomas Shannon and Bush administration State Department Cuba Transition Coordinator Caleb McCarry made statements to news outlets insisting that the transfer would not work.[3] On the island and in Miami, speculation was (and continues to be) rampant among Cubans about whether Fidel is on his deathbed or already in his grave, as few specific details about his medical condition are ever revealed. Yet each day, Cubans still focus on their *own* survival much more so than on Fidel's. Their transition has not yet fully transpired, and their relationship to the state has not yet been effectively changed.

Will the island's defiant reputation as a mouse that roared remain intact without Fidel's indignant leadership and the U.S. blockade? When Fidel is deceased, the Cuban nation (at home and in the diaspora) will unquestionably find itself at a major crossroads, where legacies, opportunities, problems, and fears abound as well as collide. The revolutionary chapter of Cuban history will continue with alterations after Fidel, like a scientific innovation that incorporates previous achievements and builds on them. But a new, postrevolutionary phase of Cuba's history could also begin. This phase might entail a degeneration, a chaotic improvement on the previous fifty years, a repetition of its efforts, or most likely a combination of these responses.

Staging the Future

Writer Reinaldo Arenas (1943–90) vividly explores questions about Cuba's future and what a transition might mean to Cubans on the island in his short play *Traidor* (Traitor, 1986). Although older than the rest of the works in this study, the play is highly significant because it is set in the future rather than the past or the present, depicting the moment "after" the regime has ended. Arenas is the only Cuban playwright I have encountered who looks this far forward. His courageous work instantly provokes a discussion about Cuba's present conditions and its future because it takes place just after "the dictator's" death, opening up every possibility for political change on the island. However, Arenas's piece is not joyful or celebratory. Instead, it cynically views participation and nonparticipation, as well as revolution, in retrospect, while straightforwardly indicting of all forms of absolute authority. Despite the fact that it was written over twenty-five years ago, *Traidor* remains exceptionally relevant because it unabashedly considers a highly problematic transition, a reality even more likely today than it was when it was first produced.

Like his famous stories and essays, *Traidor* bears the imprint of the discrimination Arenas endured as an openly gay intellectual in Cuba, which led to his imprisonment for nearly three years (1973–76) and, later, to his emigration to the United States during the Mariel boatlift of 1980. (Notably, in August 2010, Fidel Castro admitted in the Mexican daily *La Jornada* that the persecution of gays in Cuba was a "great injustice."[4]) Arenas's major works include critical essays, poems, short stories, and *Pentagonia*, a five-book series depicting postrevolutionary Cuba. Once exiled, Arenas became an outspoken advocate of artistic and intellectual freedom for all Cubans. After several years of living with AIDS, Arenas committed suicide in the United States in 1990. His autobiography, *Antes que anochezca* (*Before Night Falls*), was highly lauded when published in English in 1993. A film version of the book was released in 2000 to critical acclaim; directed by artist Julian Schnabel, the film starred Academy Award winner Javier Bardem as Arenas.

Arenas's play *Traidor*, written in Miami in 1986 and published in English, is set in Havana during the interval when a "new" system is initially endorsed in Cuba. Another revolution has occurred, and Arenas does not specify exactly what has happened, but the overwhelming power of the island's government remains. It is initially unclear if *Traidor* is actually about the transition into the Cuban Revolutionary government (in 1959) or out of it sometime in the future. The main character in the piece is a nameless "Old Woman" of seventy being interviewed by a journalist. It is "recommended" that the Old Woman be played by a man *dressed* as a woman who is not "grotesque" in any way.[5] This choice compounds the fracture of identity that the Old Woman will bring to light throughout the piece—as is often the case in Cuba, nothing is quite as it seems. Both a man and a woman are strangely present at once, resulting in a subject experience that is dominated by contradictions and duality. The Old Woman's references to a man could signify her representing both characters simultaneously, or possibly expressing her own masculine ideas in the guise of a female persona. The choice and this character are both transgressive. *Traidor* depicts the nonstable, non-unified self; in this case, the self that is created under repetitive totalitarianism.

On a screen behind the Old Woman, Fidel Castro is shown giving a speech while a crowd responds with a rousing ovation. The Old Woman explains, "Now that the dictator has fallen, was overthrown, or got tired, everyone talks, everyone can talk. The system has changed. . . . Now it turns out that everyone was against him" (114). The right to speak, to directly voice one's thoughts and opinions, is of immediate concern. Arenas makes it deliberately unclear whether the Old Woman is speaking of the transition from the Batista to the Castro era or from the Castro era to some other when she comments that the "system has changed." It is only evident later that she is speaking from a post-Fidel perspective, but the obscurity has already given the audience a brief chance to understand key parallels between these two transitions as well as Arenas's critique of power in general. This ambiguity prophetically serves the piece, when we realize that, despite its new leaders, the "new" government being described closely resembles the previous one. Arenas implies that Fidel's government has become similar to that of Batista. The Old Woman's intense skepticism about any new regime, coupled with the continuing pervasiveness of the old one, emerges in her remarks: "If you're allowed to speak your mind today, it's because there's nothing to criticize, nothing to say. Otherwise they . . . (*She instinctively points to the screen*) they'd stop you. *They* have poisoned everything, they're everywhere . . . Now, whatever will be done will be because of *them*. For them or against them, but always because of them" (114). The play ponders just how long the residue of any political era may remain, whether acknowledged or not. This is the incredible double bind of the play: the hold of one government on the next, and the fact that reactions and rectifications often circumscribe the future.

The Old Woman then adds, "Once again I hear people talk of liberty. They even shout it. That's bad. When one shouts 'liberty' that way, generally the opposite's desired. I know. I saw" (114). The "I" she speaks of is already complicated by her dual-gendered appearance and then further obscured by her removed role as witness. Her lucid and resolute refusal to participate in the current fervor is based on her personal, firsthand knowledge of how unlimited power operates. It also serves as her prediction about power to come.

Traidor and its author's personal history serve as constant reminders that there are, and always have been, intense consequences for disloyalty to the state in Cuba. Within the play, a handcuffed man appears on the screen, amid whistles and shouts of "*¡Paredón! ¡Paredón! ¡Paredón!*"— shorthand for "Put them against the wall (*paredón*) and shoot them" (115). The Old Woman acknowledges that it is assumed she will "cooperate by saying what [she knows] . . . about one of the victims" (115). Yet the definition of *cooperation* is not clarified. The Old Woman immediately rephrases this reference, calling this victim (it is still unclear who she is talking about) a "'double victim' . . . or 'triple' . . . or rather a 'victimized victim'" (115). She does not explain further. The fact that she is a man dressed as an Old Woman could mean that she is the "double victim" incarnate, not able to embrace either identity fully. She could be interpreted as the embodiment of Arenas's exile, a physical representation of the fracture of not belonging in either place or to either sex. Her camouflaged presence continually defies closure by acknowledging its own artifice and amalgamation, pointing out her own lack of stability and the theatricality of this transition. The "double" or "triple" victim might refer to the fact that several regimes may have already or will someday oppress this person. It is Arenas's insistence that this experience is likely repeatable, even under the next government.

The Old Woman returns to her description of the victim she had previously mentioned, admitting that "the more furiously he worked, the more he hated the system. He didn't do it out of devotion, but out of hate . . . He loathed all of it!" (116). This paradox forms the larger questions posed by the play, about exactly what constitutes a revolutionary or a traitor. Arenas questions who the traitors are and to what entities; he then complicates any understanding of loyalty and patriotism. In a time of political flux, loyalties are often obscured and patriotism misaligned. The French Revolution cemented this notion. Arenas's work asserts that revolutionaries are inherently transgressive traitors, who, like scientific innovators, advocate for new systems to replace older, established ones.

The Old Woman soon points out the political cul-de-sac the victim experienced: "In the military service, what could he refuse to do if everything was official, patriotic, revolutionary, that is, essential?" (117). She continues, "He was a man, and he had to live, that is, he needed a room, a pressure cooker, an extra pair of pants. You wouldn't believe me if I told you that the issuance of a coupon to buy a shirt involved a political privilege" (117). When everything—even access to something as simple as a shirt—is wrapped up in one's revolutionary stance, Arenas insists, there are no alternatives. Vacant obedience becomes a plausible and possibly transgressive way to fulfill one's role as a revolutionary citizen: I obey but do not comply. The play boldly considers where a revolutionary citizen/participant stands *after* the revolution, under its successors. The Old Woman poignantly describes one man's diplomatic tightrope walk. She explains that, "Since he didn't talk, he didn't contradict himself like the rest who had to correct or deny what they said today the next day . . . And since he didn't contradict himself, he became a man of trust, of respect" (117). Yet she does not reveal *who* trusts him and what actions they trust him to do, only that his obedience earns him respect.

The play makes it clear that this man's passive submission was extremely costly. Growing bitter, the Old Woman, with a man constantly visible underneath, laments the victim's (or any victims') brutally fractured personal identity when she confronts the young journalist who is interviewing her with this caution:

> Do you know what fear is? Do you know what hate is? Do you know what hope is? Do you know what impotence is? Take care of yourself. Don't trust; don't trust anyone. Not even now, even less now. Today when everything encourages confidence is the right time to distrust. Later it'll be too late. Afterward you'll have to obey. (118)

Although she has agreed to the interview, she warns the journalist about the current conditions. Her suspicious pessimism highlights her fear that all governments are the same, that the revolutionary process may in fact take on the cyclical meaning of the word "revolution," a revolving or return to an original point where it started. A man masked in woman's clothing, she attempts to caution others because of her own experience. She eerily divulges,

> Sometimes he himself had to take care of the [search] lights and the guns—clean them, polish them, check over the objects of his subjection. . . . And with how much discipline he did it! One'd say it was a matter of his real self not showing through these acts. (118)

Arenas then wrote, "*The character of the Old Woman appears [on the screen], but thirty years younger, saying,* 'Calm down. For God's sake, wait. Don't say any more. They can hear you. Don't ruin it all with your anger" (118). The tone is desperate and frightened, but the description of the image is unclear. Arenas does not specify whether this version of the Old Woman, thirty years earlier, is actually a young woman or possibly a young man dressed as a woman, with the man showing through as he does in the present version. The Old Woman on stage before the audience then repeats the dialogue verbatim, but much older than her filmic image. Her theatrical reiteration of the same advice thirty years later reinforces the persistent, insidious nature of both subjugations (the victim's and her own) and the repetitive tendency for power to be abused. The Old Woman also exposes the extraordinary depths of self-conflict this man faced, quoting him as saying, "Don't you realize that by betraying myself to this degree, I'm going to stop being me? Don't you see I'm a shadow, a puppet, an actor who never comes down off the stage where he plays a dirty role?" (121). The Old Woman is a symbol, the incarnation of what the victim has stopped being. Her "role" and the portrayal within/underneath her persona act as corporeal reminders of a self divided—by gender, exile, and political exigencies—for many years.

Her passion deepening, the Old Woman ultimately confesses:

> And I'd say, "Wait, wait. . . . And he knew how to wait. Until the moment came. (*Pause. Total illumination.*) The moment when the regime was overthrown, and he was accused and condemned as a direct agent of the tyranny. All the evidence was against him, and he was condemned to the maximum penalty, death by shooting. Then, standing before the firing squad . . . , he shouted, 'Down with Castro! Long live liberty! . . . Cries that the press and the world called *cowardly cynicism*, but that I . . . can assure you, were the only authentic thing he said aloud in his entire life. (121)

In a moment of ultimate illumination, this "man" whose life has been governed by submission and fear, is executed for the same vigilant obedience it tormented him to enact. It is unclear what the Old Woman was pleading with him to wait for, but evident that Arenas imagined an abrupt, definitive end to the Castro era in Cuba. It now appears that the regime's power may fade out over time, making it exceedingly difficult to predict who is a traitor, how one might be judged, and what might come after the regime.

The irony of this tortured man's deception is further multiplied by the final moment of the piece. In total darkness, the Old Woman's voice, which could be the voice of many Cubans, is heard remarking anew, "I know. I saw" (121). Whether an active participant or affected witness, the Old Woman is profoundly manipulated by the myths, assurances, and realities of Castroism. They are her lived experience. Historical and actual violence (metaphorical, physical, and emotional) permeates her memories, creating her staunch skepticism about the future.

Arenas's view was decidedly dark. His play reflects the modern contradictions of life in Cuba, where beautiful beaches are often restricted but education and health care are provided, where government permission is required to rent out rooms and drive taxis, but every Cuban has a roof over his/her head. Arenas wrote of a Cuba where dissent was often grounds for arrest or harsher punishment. Written after he safely left the island, *Traidor* confronted the system Arenas experienced before 1980, which he viewed as having created scarcities for purposes of political control. His work asserted that Cubans were obviously weary after years of calls for sacrifice, long lines for basic necessities, and promises of a better future.

Traidor insists that nothing short of Fidel's death would begin a transition on the island. It does not posit how the leader might die, but there is no indication in the piece that his death would be suspect. (For all intents and purposes, Arenas's work suggests that the transition is sparked when the leader dies in power, of natural causes.) Arenas reveals that there is no guarantee that any alternative system or leader would promise abundance or even significant change. The repetitive nature of the governments Arenas portrays implies that the Revolution itself has not served as a feasible substitute for the system it replaced (Batista's crony capitalism), nor will the system that replaces the Revolution be a sustainable alternative to over fifty years of Castroism. The playwright's view is pointed and boldly subversive, yet Raúl Castro's recent and uneventful ascension to power has partially undermined the scenario Arenas presented in 1986. It is not yet known whether Raúl is part of the next (and therefore, according to Arenas, equally suspect) government, or merely an extension of the existing one.

Reforms and Consequences

The transition of power to Raúl Castro and the army in 2006 did not radically alter everyday life on the island, despite ongoing reforms and revisions. The Revolution still floats, yet is fixed; it repeats, as Benitez-Rojo noted, but continually adjusts.[6] Those adjustments are imperative. The economic severity facing Cuba was amplified in 2009, when a decline in nickel prices combined with the global recession to significantly diminish tourism and reduce remittances. Due to a destructive hurricane season, Cuba also had its worst sugar harvest in nearly a century. There were palpable reactions. Public protests were escalating: Las damas de blanco (the Ladies in White), an opposition group of wives and female relatives of jailed dissidents, swelled their Sunday marches in Havana, and jailed Afro-Cuban mason Orlando Zapata Tamayo began a hunger strike (leading to his death in 2010), inspiring other prisoners to stop eating. Small but important reforms—such as increasing Internet access and visits from Cubans living abroad, as well as revoking the cell phone ban as of April 2008—helped to buffer what Archibald Ritter has called the "gerontocratic paralysis"[7] facing a country whose centralized economy had never been self-sustaining. Cuba had begun drifting away from discourses of survival (necessary as part of two decades of the Special Period) and toward discourses of change, requiring an uneasy evaluation of its fundamental properties.

Part of this assessment includes incorporating self-employment into the system in Cuba. The revival of a lapsed experiment that had begun in 1990, the government's recent plan to lay off 500,000 state workers and reorient them for jobs in the private sector was called a "breathtaking gamble"[8] by Edward Schumacher-Matos of the *Washington Post*. Yet the state insists it is not seeking to change the fundamental way Cuba operates nor to enter the free market. Economists agree that a shift of that kind would require a major adjustment in the way the private sector is viewed and treated in Cuba. Private businesses are not yet seen as a strategic part of the Cuban economy. The state strictly regulates small businesses, requiring licenses, imposing high taxes, and prohibiting advertising while ignoring obstacles like access to credit. Farmers are now allowed to lease land from the government, but most lack vital farm machinery, fertilizers, and herbicides. *Casas particulares* (houses that rent rooms to foreign visitors) can now be rented out in their entirety (previously, Cubans had to live there with their foreign guests). Although highly regulated, and often subject to intrusive inspections, *casas particulares* can now hire staff and eventually operate like upscale bed and breakfasts. Restaurants run in private homes, known as *paladares*, are now permitted to hire staff that are not family members, to serve up to twenty patrons at a time (up from twelve), to expand their menus to include restricted items like steak or lobster, and to set their own prices. However, taxes on revenues are roughly 15 percent, sales taxes are near 5 percent, and payroll taxes are 25 percent.[9] Many new business ventures on the island fail due to general inexperience and/or the absence of training. Cuba's severe economic circumstances have led to the government's attempt to formalize these potentially lucrative parts of the underground economy. The reforms reflect an effort to modernize without abandoning socialism, to collect revenues while maintaining the government's ideals.

But reforms and revisions also have profound social consequences. Material realities change relationships, trouble subjectivity, and disrupt fixed images of the future, often splintering personalities and wreaking havoc on identifications. Amelia Rosenberg Weinreb has written of how the two-currency system and its underground market engender secret identities and transform Cuban social behavior. Weinreb insists these dimensions of lived existence are usually ignored in foreign policy, resulting in "unsatisfied citizen consumers"[10] who resist state domination. The dual economy forces ethical Cubans to perform basic economic illegalities in order to improve their individual situations. These Cubans are politically invisible and powerless as a collective. Yet these same economic concessions have also ensured the system's survival, along with the day-to-day survival of many Cubans. In these and many other ways, the Cuban Revolution engages the world while retreating from it, participates while isolating itself, and continually engenders hope without proposing a defined course for the future. Its paradoxical, moment-by-moment adaptability is exactly what has made this unpredictable revolution durable. It is built on complicated contradictions.

External Entanglements

If "the Cuban nation must not be deprived of its links with other people," as Fidel Castro insisted in 1998, the United States and its Cuban diaspora must remain in the discussion. The triumph of the Revolution in 1959 broke the mold of how "small, relatively poor states are supposed to behave in world politics"[11] and the assumption that the United States will be able to control Cuba after Fidel Castro's death has been vanishing since 1989. As Cuba secures political and financial support from countries such as Venezuela and Brazil, while further developing strong economic ties with China, Spain, and the rest of Europe, the supposition that Cuba will be "more pliable after Fidel Castro passes away"[12] is certainly waning. Predictions of chaos made by opponents of the Castro regime simply have not materialized. Instead, Cuban exiles seeking personal reconciliations, as in the plays by Cruz and Martinez, are most common.

The United States' ongoing policy of blockading Cuba until Fidel's imminent demise has allowed eleven presidents to circumvent difficult questions about America's real interests in the island, while having little effect on Fidel's power there. Insisting that the Castros are completely removed from Cuban politics has prevented the United States from having a participatory influence in *crafting* any post-Castro scenario. All U.S. plans are based on responding to what happens *after* a transition, not how to be an integral part of the process. Due to their unwillingness to alter this policy, Americans in power do not have significant relationships or real influence with the key players who may decide Cuba's future. Case in point: in December 2009, American Alan Gross was arrested in Cuba for allegedly delivering unauthorized satellite Internet connections to Jewish groups on the island. Gross received financial support from programs linked with USAID, an organization known for the covert political nature of its foreign ventures. Collaboration with U.S. programs is a crime in Cuba; this is a fairly transparent reality many dissidents readily acknowledge. Despite diplomatic efforts, the United States has been unsuccessful in securing Gross's release. In this instance, Cuba seems particularly eager to demonstrate its refusal to take orders from the United States.

Raúl Castro's decision to release fifty-two political prisoners in July 2010 may appear like a missed opportunity for the United States to enter a dialogue about change. However, discounting Raúl's gesture highlights the fact that President Barack Obama does not want to spend political capital in Latin America; Cuba is not worth public debate because it is not a direct threat to the United States or any other country. Because Obama assumed he needed to win Florida to get reelected in 2012, domestic politics necessitated forgoing a chance to alter the dynamics between the United States and Cuba. However, during his second term in office, Obama could easily use executive prerogative to (a) lift various restrictions imposed by the embargo (on phone service and travel, for instance) and (b) remove Cuba from Bush's "Axis of Evil," a list of countries suspected of state-sponsored terrorism.

The growing xenophobia within the prevailing national discussion on immigration in the United States also weakens the country's ability to promote positive changes in Cuba. Cubans no longer feel particularly welcome in the United States, and many have instead emigrated to Spain, South America, and Caribbean countries. Many think that Washington is so overwhelmed by terrorism, war, and problems in the Middle East that it now only desires a stable transition in Cuba, rather than an ideologically compatible one. Recent efforts to lift the American travel ban by inserting it into a bill with food provisions got notable support from farm states eager to sell more food to Cuba (food was exempted from the embargo in 2000). Food provisions were included to deal with the specific reality of trading with Cuba, a nation greatly hindered because it does not have credit and must pay in cash. Pro-embargo Cubans with considerable power in Congress—such as Rep.

Ileana Ros-Lehtinen (R-Florida), Sen. Robert Menendez (D-New Jersey), Reps. Lincoln Diaz-Balart and Mario Diaz-Balart (R-Florida)—have held enough sway to prevent change, even though the majority of Cuban Americans now agree that the embargo has failed.

The U.S. travel ban is particularly significant because tourism has become central to all Caribbean economies. Cuba is no exception—the island welcomed millions of tourists in 2010, in addition to lucrative visits from Cubans living abroad. Globalization has guaranteed that capital flows where it can profit, so Cuba must prove that it can yield income for itself and others. Cuban officials have been encouraging foreign investments, partnerships, and exchanges wherever they can; for example, most major hotels on the island have already been sold to international corporations from countries such as Spain, Germany, and France. The Canadian tourist industry is planning to add resorts and time-shares to its offerings on the island and, once the embargo is lifted, cruise ships will surely restore Havana and Santiago de Cuba to the popular ports of call they once were. The island must convince investors that it is a safe, stable place for their money to grow, a difficult task when its political future after Raúl's tenure is entirely indeterminate. Tourism and retirement homes alone will not usher Cuba into the twenty-first century economically because of the country's significant debt. Many of these economic relationships recall the Batista era, when the majority of the island was owned by non-Cubans. The island's leaders do not have free market experience to compete with foreign entrepreneurs, a serious deficit that compels external consultation from a cross-section of fields and countries. Therefore, it is not yet understood exactly what these relationships could yield for contemporary Cubans.

Fidel's Legacy and What Comes Next

A 2004 Research Brief compiled by the Rand Corporation (an American think tank), entitled *A Legacy of Dysfunction: Cuba after Fidel*, suggested that Cuba will face, "an alienated younger generation, a growing racial divide, an aging population, and a deformed economy" when Fidel Castro "departs."[13] Ultimately, the study speculates that a new, post-Castro communist regime might falter, making way for the Cuban Armed Forces (FAR), "arguably Cuba's most important institution,"[14] to assume control due to a lack of laws restricting the power of the state. Because the military already operates the majority of Cuba's agricultural, tourist, construction, and telecommunications activities, the military's transition to power has not been transformative but simple. In the last five years, Raúl Castro's government has dismissed prominent revolutionary officials such as Air Transportation Minister Rogelio Acevedo, Foreign Minister Felipe Perez Roque, and Vice President Carlos Lage and replaced them with military brass. Undoubtedly, Cuba is already governed by its armed forces. However, the Rand Corporation concludes that the constructiveness of the military's role will "be contingent not only on post-Castro succession dynamics at play within Cuba but also on U.S. policy and the actions of the Cuban-American community."[15] Associated Press writer Anita Snow noted that "the island's socialist political and economic systems will endure long after [Castro] is gone."[16] This may be why, according to Tony Karon of *Time* magazine, "in the interests of stability and preventing bloodshed, the U.S. Coast Guard has reportedly made contingency plans to stop any flotilla of exiles trying to sail back to the island [from the United States] to reclaim property seized . . . decades ago."[17] Younger members of Cuba's exile community, however, have defied their parents and grandparents by seeking ways to promote modern reforms in Cuba rather than to rectify grievances from the nation's past. Unlike their elders, they travel to Cuba and have developed relationships with friends and family there. Their decision to look forward rather than backward may be the most noteworthy component of Cuba/U.S. relations as Fidel "disappears."

Another key question is whether or not a transition from an aged state-run system to some sort of fledgling, hybrid system that combines market reforms and liberalization with authoritarianism is possible without widespread bloodshed and corruption. Is the orderly evolution toward participatory democracy (promoted by Cuban youth) possible? French revolutionary history would insist it is not. Writer Oakland Ross of the *Toronto Star* comments, "The new face of the Cuban revolution wears scholarly eyeglasses, sports a trim moustache in place of a beard, speaks excellent English—and wasn't around on Jan. 1, 1959, when Fidel Castro seized power. . . . The island's revolutionary faithful now include a crop of younger men and women . . . who have no memories of life before Castro because they weren't born yet."[18] While Cubans between eighteen and thirty-five years old are educated and motivated, their leaders were brought up in a state without free markets or widespread access to information. This critical younger demographic, clearly concerned with the future (jobs, technology, opportunities for links beyond the island) must obtain the necessary experience to lead. Some have argued that they are the demographic most discontented with the current state of affairs in Cuba, the least loyal to the revolutionary government. However, the daily hardships they have faced may also make them the best-equipped, most self-reliant generation yet to advance the Revolution, from whom the dominant message is "nothing is about to change here."

Yet there has already been change; Fidel has been noticeably absent from national celebrations since 2007. There are no hours-long speeches at public rallies to mark workers' holidays, but Cuban soldiers are present en masse. It is highly implausible that any other candidate could rise to prominence under Raúl Castro's regime. However, Raul's role may simply be to bring the country through a peaceful transition, paving the way for either expressed military rule or elections after Fidel's death or his own.

Because Fidel Castro has proven to be one of the greatest political strategists of all time, another fundamental question persists: Is what is presented to the Cuban and foreign public what is really happening in the Cuban government? Because the Cuban Revolution claims that "the future needs to build upon the past," as José Quiroga notes,[19] the fact that the past includes constant adjustments and reconsiderations bodes well for the nation's future. By this standard, the future might be flexible, shaped by the revisions, negotiations, and transculturations that have been hallmarks since the Special Period in Cuba.

Most Cubans are focused on their daily lives at present, taking a "wait and see" approach rather than demanding immediate political change. Some revolutionaries view any transition after the Castro brothers as a chance for socialism to fully take hold of their nation, as an opportunity for a modern, global socialist system (possibly like Sweden's?) to realize its full potential once the U.S. embargo is lifted. Others view the regime's exit as a chance to either return to the island or to leave it. Enormous cultural and economic identifications threaten to make it impossible for Cubans in the diaspora to reunite with the island; therefore, interstitial subjects will be fundamental to Cuba's future. Constructing communities not based on nationhood (a notion skewed by Cuba's isolation and dual market) will be essential. Yet after nearly sixty years of ardent self-determination, it is exceedingly difficult to imagine that decisions about Cuba's future will come from outside the island. The crucial problem will be how the Revolution, from the inside, might integrate external ideologies, economic models, and social constructions to create hybrid or blended subjects who can better its future.

Revolving and Evolving

As evidenced, a wide range of voices is needed to best represent the effects of Cuba's ongoing revolutionary transformations in the present, the past, and any imaginable future. The playwrights included in this book move away from discourses of ideas within Cuba and focus on the everyday realities on the island, on the lived consequences of those discourses. They concentrate on the inside as it encounters the outside. They depict lived experiences in order to generate a new conversation, one about individual destinies, outcomes, and aspirations within Cuba's existing frameworks. These artists investigate personal ruptures and achievements, emphasizing the ongoing processes by which Cubans adapt and adopt. They view Cubans as much more than people caught in an experiment—these are an active and interested people, seeking to shape their own lives while boldly acknowledging the enormity of restructuring their well-rehearsed identities.

As Arenas explains in *Traidor*, people who left Cuba in the early years of the revolutionary project were considered deserters and often called *gusanos* (literally, "worms"). However, those who remained on the island and faithfully participated as the state grew more overbearing are viewed as traitors by Cubans in the diaspora. Both groups are implicated, irrevocably marked by the Revolution and its double binds, the inversions created by its confusing fluctuations and incongruities. The theatrical voices of the playwrights that have stayed on the island as well as those in exile have been fashioned by the residue of these areas of contestation and their "revolving" discursive loops. In their efforts to depict what's happening inside the country, these playwrights also complicate the world outside, documenting the intense effects of globalization within Cuba as well as beyond its borders. Hence, the stage provides a vital, adaptable space for these contemporary artists to negotiate shifting identities and the meanings of revolution, rather than making them concrete. The theatre does not bring these topics to a close, but instead positions identifiable precursors for future theatrical and political deliberations. These dynamic plays prove that theatre is a necessary, counter-hegemonic medium in which to upend, debate, complicate, and challenge ongoing considerations about Cuba and revolution, from inside and out.

Notes
Bibliography
Index

Notes

1. Overture: Cuba and the Evolution of Revolution

1. Dominguez, "*Cuba teatro*," 5.
2. Torrance, "Brothers at War," 292.
3. For a comprehensive study of Arrufat's textual choices and a comparison with the original Greek text, see Torrance, "Brothers at War."
4. Cano, "*El teatro cubano*."
5. Castro, "*Palabras a los intelectuales*."
6. García Luis, *Cuban Revolution Reader*, 271.
7. Lievesley, *Cuban Revolution*, 40.
8. Pérez, *On Becoming Cuban*, 130.
9. Trento, *Castro and Cuba*, 16.
10. Lievesley, *Cuban Revolution*, 74.
11. Trento, *Castro and Cuba*, 18.
12. Leal, *Breve historia*, 15.
13. Ibid., 30.
14. Ibid., 61.
15. For more information on Cuban stock characters, see Rine Leal's description of "Los 'diablitos' salen al escena" in *Breve historia;* and Lane, *Blackface Cuba*.
16. Leal, *Breve historia*, 121, 123–26.
17. Ibid., 126–28.
18. Trento, *Castro and Cuba*, 22.
19. García Luis, *Cuban Revolution Reader*, 1.
20. Lievesley, *Cuban Revolution*, 52.
21. Pérez, *On Becoming Cuban*, 197.
22. Fidel Castro quoted in García Luis, *Cuban Revolution Reader*, 60.
23. Trento, *Castro and Cuba*, 26.
24. Ibid., 29.
25. Lievesley, *Cuban Revolution*, 5.
26. García Luis, *Cuban Revolution Reader*, 25.
27. Lievesley, *Cuban Revolution*, 27.
28. Fidel Castro quoted in García Luis, *Cuban Revolution Reader*, 68.
29. Ibid.
30. Lievesley, *Cuban Revolution*, 11.
31. García Luis, *Cuban Revolution Reader*, 89.
32. For more information on Cuban theatre history in this period, see Freire, *Teatro cubano (1927–1961)*.
33. Castro, "*Palabras a los intelectuales*."
34. Paterson quoted in Lievesley, *Cuban Revolution*, 14.

35. Bonefeld and Tischler, *What Is to Be Done?*, 5.
36. García Luis, *Cuban Revolution Reader*, 122.
37. Lievesley, *Cuban Revolution*, 33.
38. García Luis, *Cuban Revolution Reader*, 126.
39. Bonefeld and Tischler, *What Is to Be Done?*, 131.
40. García Luis, *Cuban Revolution Reader*, 117.
41. Ibid., 169.
42. Bonefeld and Tischler, *What Is to Be Done?*, 6.
43. Lievesley, *Cuban Revolution*, 94.
44. Ibid., 84.
45. García Luis, *Cuban Revolution Reader*, 177.
46. Ibid., 4.
47. Dominguez, "*Cuba teatro*," 9.
48. García Luis, *Cuban Revolution Reader*, 209.
49. Ibid., 211.
50. For an in-depth discussion of Teatro Nuevo, see Boudet, *En tercera persona*, 79–100.
51. For in-depth information about productions by Teatro Escambray, see Leal, *Breve historia*, 153–62.
52. Lievesley, *Cuban Revolution*, 102.
53. García Luis, *Cuban Revolution Reader*, 219.
54. Lievesley, *Cuban Revolution*, 159.
55. García Luis, *Cuban Revolution Reader*, 224.
56. Lievesley, *Cuban Revolution*, 114.
57. García Luis, *Cuban Revolution Reader*, 231.
58. Ibid., 243.
59. Ibid., 270.
60. Ibid., 272.
61. Lievesley, *Cuban Revolution*, 125.
62. Bonefeld and Tischler, *What Is to Be Done?*, 171.
63. Ibid.
64. Carlos Lage quoted in García Luis, *Cuban Revolution Reader*, 276.
65. The peso convertible (CUC) is state issued currency (introduced in 2004) that serves two purposes—it can be used in the tourist economy, or in the local/peso one. It is worth significantly more than a Cuban peso (MN), so items cost much more if paid for using CUCs than MNs. As of 2011, the peso convertible was equal to the dollar, 1USD:1CUC. One U.S. dollar, however, was worth roughly 25 Cuban pesos, 1USD:25MN. So using CUCs to pay for items listed in MN means spending a great deal more than the average Cuban would. For example, the tickets to most plays in Vedado are either $5 CUC (for tourists) or $5 MN for locals; locals pay roughly 20 cents while tourists pay 25 times as much.
66. For further discussion of the social consequences of the dual currency economy, see Lievesley, *Cuban Revolution*, 125, and Ritter, "Shifting Realities."
67. Ibid., 162.
68. Ibid., 180.
69. Scott, *Domination and the Arts of Resistance*, 25.
70. Ibid., 17.
71. Ibid., 156.
72. Ibid., 157.

73. Here I refer to Bataille's and Foucault's notions of transgression as an intrinsic component of modern/postmodern life. It is Chris Jenks's definition of *transgression* as a "deeply reflexive act of denial and affirmation" of "the bounds or limits set by a commandment or law or convention" (2) that I invoke here. For further discussion of transgression, see Jenks, *Transgression*.
74. Scott, *Domination and the Arts of Resistance*, 139.

2. Staging Revolutions: Past and Present Conversations

1. *Webster's Encyclopedic Unabridged Dictionary of the English Language*, rev. ed., 1996.
2. LaRousse, *Diccionario de la lengua española esencial*, s.v., "revolución."
3. Weiner, *Dictionary of the History of Ideas*, 153.
4. Kuhn, *Structure of Scientific Revolutions*, 6. Subsequent page references are cited parenthetically in text.
5. Lievesley, *Cuban Revolution*, 9.
6. Ibid.
7. Kuhn, *Structure of Scientific Revolutions*, 17.
8. Weiner, *Dictionary of the History of Ideas*, 156.
9. See Lindner, "Hallucinatory Realism" for references to Weiss's notebooks.
10. Mansur, *Carlotta Corday*, 6.
11. Pelligrini, *Performance Anxieties*, 10.
12. Parham, "*Marat/Sade*," 236.
13. Mansur, *Carlotta Corday*, prologue.
14. Jenks, *Transgression*, 180.
15. Jenks, *Transgression*, 94.
16. Ibid., Mansur, *Carlotta Corday*, 3.
17. Corazzo and Montfort, "Charlotte Corday," 33.
18. Jenks, *Transgression*, 182.
19. Corazzo and Montfort, "Charlotte Corday," 35.
20. Chaudhuri, "*Marat/Sade*," 218.
21. Here Mansur refers to the Revolution's National Literary Campaign, in which teachers and students from Cuba's metropolitan areas were sent to the countryside to educate the population.
22. Mansur, *Carlotta Corday*, 5. Subsequent page references are cited parenthetically in text.
23. Chaudhuri, "*Marat/Sade*," 219.
24. Ibid., 222.
25. Mansur, *Carlotta Corday*, 2. Subsequent page references are cited parenthetically in text.
26. Chaudhuri, "*Marat/Sade*," 224.
27. Mansur, *Carlotta Corday*, 7.
28. Chaudhuri, "*Marat/Sade*," 217.
29. Weiss, *Persecution and Assassination*, 14.
30. Mansur, *Carlotta Corday*, 7.
31. Ibid.
32. Ibid., 11.
33. Parham, "*Marat/Sade*," 236.
34. Corazzo and Montfort, "Charlotte Corday," 47.
35. Mansur, *Carlotta Corday*, 7.

36. Parham, "*Marat/Sade*," 236.
37. Mansur, *Carlotta Corday*, 7. Subsequent page references are cited parenthetically in text.
38. Chaudhuri, "*Marat/Sade*," 224.
39. Parham, "*Marat/Sade*," 237.
40. Ibid., 238.
41. Mansur, *Carlotta Corday*, 13. Subsequent page references are cited parenthetically in text.
42. Jenks, *Transgression*, 92.
43. Godinez, "Toward a Revolution?"; Svich, "Flower in Havana."
44. Del Pino, "Buendía, virtuosismo a los veinte."
45. For an in-depth discussion of the Cuban *teatro bufo* style, see Leal, *Breve historia*; and Lane, *Blackface Cuba*.
46. Carrió and Lauten, *Charenton*, 4.
47. Ibid.
48. Quiroga, *Cuban Palimpsests*, 29.
49. Carrió and Lauten, *Charenton*, 5.
50. Ibid., 9.
51. Taylor, "Framing the Revolution," 82.
52. Carrió and Lauten, *Charenton*, 11.
53. Carrió and Lauten, *Charenton*, 15. Subsequent page references are cited parenthetically in text.
54. Taylor, "Framing the Revolution," 82.
55. Silverman, "Subject," 157.
56. Carrió and Lauten, *Charenton*, 22. Subsequent page references are cited parenthetically in text.
57. Dufrenne, "World of the Aesthetic Object," 135.
58. Carrió and Lauten, *Charenton*, 43. Subsequent page references are cited parenthetically in text.
59. Dirlik quoted in Taylor, "Framing the Revolution," 87.
60. Carrió and Lauten, *Charenton*, 55. Subsequent page references are cited parenthetically in text.
61. Dolan, "Gender Impersonation Onstage," 5.
62. Quiroga, *Cuban Palimpsests*, 26.

3. Revolution under Siege: Theatre, Globalization, and the Special Period

1. Pérez, *Cuba*, 385.
2. García Luis, *Cuban Revolution Reader*, 5.
3. García Canclini, *Hybrid Cultures*, 266.
4. For a more comprehensive discussion of the practice of *jineterismo*, see Kempadoo, *Sun, Sex, and Gold*.
5. Terry, *Laberinto de lobos*, 7.
6. De la Campa, *Latin Americanism*, 64.
7. Migrations to Cuba's major cities, especially the capital and Santiago de Cuba, have been commonplace since the Special Period began in the early 1990s, by those seeking higher paying jobs in the tourist sector. Habaneros (Cubans from Havana) typically look down on Cubans from the countryside.
8. Terry, *Laberinto de lobos*, 7.
9. Ibid., 8.

10. Hardt and Negri, *Empire*, xi.
11. Ibid., xii.
12. Appiah, quoted in Sassen, *Globalization and Its Discontents*, xv.
13. Pérez, *Cuba*, 382.
14. Ibid., 383.
15. Ibid., 384.
16. García Canclini, *Hybrid Cultures*, 1.
17. Pérez, *Cuba*, 387.
18. Terry, *Laberinto de lobos*, 8.
19. Pérez, *Cuba*, 390.
20. Terry, *Laberinto de lobos*, 8.
21. Ibid., 9.
22. De la Campa, *Latin Americanism*, 107.
23. Ibid., 82.
24. Ibid., 57.
25. García Canclini, *Hybrid Cultures*, 22.
26. Terry, *Laberinto de lobos*, 9.
27. Rosaldo, introduction, xvi.
28. García Canclini, *Hybrid Cultures*, 3.
29. Terry, *Laberinto de lobos*, 10.
30. García Canclini, *Hybrid Cultures*, 41.
31. Terry, *Laberinto de lobos*, 10. Subsequent page references are cited parenthetically in text.
32. Pérez, *Cuba*, 387.
33. Terry, *Laberinto de lobos*, 14. Subsequent page references are cited parenthetically in text.
34. Terry, *Laberinto de lobos*, 15.
35. García Luis, *Cuban Revolution Reader*, 271.
36. Terry, *Laberinto de lobos*, 17.
37. Pérez, *Cuba*, 386.
38. Terry, *Laberinto de lobos*, 17.
39. Ibid., 19.
40. Terry, *Laberinto de lobos*, 19.
41. Pérez, *Cuba*, 395.
42. Lopez-Denis. Personal conversation, 17 Oct. 2006.
43. Terry, *Laberinto de lobos*, 20.
44. Ibid., 21.
45. Ibid., 22.
46. Ibid., 25.
47. Rosaldo, introduction, xvi.
48. Terry, *Laberinto de lobos*, 27. Subsequent page references are cited parenthetically in text.
49. Terry, *Laberinto de lobos*, 52.
50. Mansur, *Ignacio y Maria*, 3.
51. Pérez, *Cuba*, 399.
52. Mansur, *Ignacio y Maria*, 3.
53. Ramirez, Email interview, 4 Jan 2012.
54. Ibid.
55. Ibid.

56. Ibid.
57. Mansur, *Ignacio y Maria*, 4.
58. Ibid.
59. Ibid., 33.
60. García Canclini, *Hybrid Cultures*, 103.
61. Mansur, *Ignacio y Maria*, 6.
62. Ibid., 20.
63. Ibid., 22.
64. Ibid., 33.
65. García Canclini, *Hybrid Cultures*, 109.
66. Ramirez, Email interview, 4 Jan 2012.
67. Hardt and Negri, *Empire*, 45.
68. Mansur, *Ignacio y Maria*, 4.
69. Stokes, "Cuba Samples Globalization," 4.
70. Mansur, *Ignacio y Maria*, 4.
71. Elián González was a six-year-old Cuban boy rescued at sea off the coast of Florida in 1999. His mother had drowned while trying to bring him to the United States. The boy, who was initially housed with relatives in Miami, became the center of a major immigration controversy when his father, Juan González, demanded Elián return to Cuba. A U.S. federal district court ruled that the boy's relatives could not petition for his asylum, yet they refused to release him. In June 2000, the boy was forcefully seized by federal agents and returned to Cuba. The diplomatic tempest, followed by all major media, exposed complex flaws in U.S. immigration policy and deep divisions among the Cuban American community. For further information, see the *Congressional Record* of the 106th U.S. Congress, volume 146, part 4.
72. Mansur, *Ignacio y Maria*, 7.
73. Ibid., 13.
74. See my discussion of *jineterismo* earlier in this chapter.
75. Rosendahl quoted in Brundenius and Weeks, *Globalization and Third World Socialism*, 99.
76. Mansur, *Ignacio y Maria*, 14.
77. Ibid., 20.
78. Ibid., 21.
79. Ramirez, Email interview, 4 Jan. 2012.
80. Moses, *Real Life in Castro's Cuba*, 104.
81. Ibid.
82. Mansur, *Ignacio y Maria*, 20. Subsequent page references are cited parenthetically in text.
83. Shimakawa, *National Abjection: Asian American Body Onstage*, 243.
84. Mansur, *Ignacio y Maria*, 11.
85. Ibid., 25.
86. Ibid.
87. Pérez, *Cuba*, 385.
88. Mansur, *Ignacio y Maria*, 27. Subsequent page references are cited parenthetically in text.
89. Ramirez, Email interview, 4 Jan. 2012.
90. Mansur, *Ignacio y Maria*, 31.
91. Fidel Castro, Speech of 25 Jan. 1998, in García Luis, *Cuban Revolution Reader*, 290.

4. Revolution from Afar: Cuban American Perspectives

1. De la Campa, *Cuba on My Mind*, vi.
2. Rivera-Servera and Young, Introduction, *Performance in the Borderlands*, 2.
3. De la Campa, *Cuba on My Mind*, 13.
4. Soja, *Postmodern Geographies*, 14.
5. Chaudhuri, *Staging Place*, xiii.
6. Pérez, *On Becoming Cuban*, 502.
7. De la Campa, *Cuba on My Mind*, 23.
8. Chaudhuri, *Staging Place*, 153.
9. Soja, *Postmodern Geographies*, 35.
10. Pérez, *On Becoming Cuban*, 6.
11. Joseph, "Diaspora," 7.
12. Martinez, *Illuminating Veronica*, 98.
13. Ibid., 103.
14. Ibid.
15. Chaudhuri, *Staging Place*, 11.
16. Soja, *Postmodern Geographies*, 35.
17. Martinez, *Illuminating Veronica*, 99.
18. Ibid., 100.
19. De la Campa, *Cuba on My Mind*, 9.
20. Michel Foucault, qtd. in Soja, *Postmodern Geographies*, 17.
21. Martinez, *Illuminating Veronica*, 101.
22. Ibid., 103.
23. Ibid.
24. Chaudhuri, *Staging Place*, 12.
25. Martinez, *Illuminating Veronica*, 106.
26. For more on the historic influence of the U.S. consumer on Cuba, see Pérez, *On Becoming Cuban*.
27. Martinez, *Illuminating Veronica*, 106.
28. De la Campa, *Cuba on My Mind*, 26.
29. Martinez, *Illuminating Veronica*, 111.
30. Ibid., 113.
31. Chaudhuri, *Staging Place*, 212.
32. Martinez, *Illuminating Veronica*, 113.
33. Ibid., 114.
34. Chaudhuri, *Staging Place*, 56.
35. Martinez, *Illuminating Veronica*, 116.
36. Ibid.
37. Martinez, *Illuminating Veronica*, 124.
38. Chaudhuri, *Staging Place*, 107.
39. Martinez, *Illuminating Veronica*, 132. Subsequent page references are cited parenthetically in text.
40. Pérez, *On Becoming Cuban*, 6.
41. Martinez, *Illuminating Veronica*, 142. Subsequent page references are cited parenthetically in text.
42. De la Campa, *Cuba on My Mind*, 14.
43. Pérez, *On Becoming Cuban*, 8.
44. Martinez, *Illuminating Veronica*, 148. Subsequent page references are cited parenthetically in text.

45. De la Campa, *Cuba on My Mind*, 9.
46. Ibid., 64.
47. Mlinar, *Globalization and Territorial Identities*, 4.
48. Martinez, *Illuminating Veronica*, 158.
49. Chaudhuri, *Staging Place*, 135.
50. Ibid., 163.
51. Pelligrini, *Performance Anxieties*, 10.
52. For more information on these departures, see Conde, *Operation Pedro Pan*.
53. Cruz, *Hortensia and the Museum of Dreams*, 4.
54. Pelligrini, *Performance Anxieties*, 6.
55. Chaudhuri, *Staging Place*, 147.
56. Cruz, *Hortensia and the Museum of Dreams*, 5.
57. Chaudhuri, *Staging Place*, 150.
58. Cruz, *Hortensia and the Museum of Dreams*, 9.
59. Chaudhuri, *Staging Place*, 12.
60. Cruz, *Hortensia and the Museum of Dreams*, 9.
61. Chaudhuri, *Staging Place*, 97.
62. Cruz, *Hortensia and the Museum of Dreams*, 10.
63. Chaudhuri, *Staging Place*, 92.
64. Cruz, *Hortensia and the Museum of Dreams*, 10.
65. Ibid., 11.
66. Ibid.
67. Ibid., 13.
68. Joseph, "Diaspora," 5.
69. Cruz, *Hortensia*, 14.
70. García Canclini, *Hybrid Cultures*, 140.
71. Chaudhuri, *Staging Place*, 120.
72. Cruz, *Hortensia*, 14.
73. Ybarra, "Havana Isn't Waiting: Staging Travel during Cuba's Special Period," 59.
74. Cruz, *Hortensia*, 15.
75. Ibid., 16.
76. Soja, *Postmodern Geographies*, 34.
77. Cruz, *Hortensia*, 16.
78. Gomez-Peña, *Warrior of Gringostroika*, 21.
79. Cruz, *Hortensia*, 16. Subsequent page references are cited parenthetically in text.
80. Ibid., 17.
81. Ibid., 20.
82. For more information about the children of Operation Pedro Pan, see Conde, Yvonne M. *Operation Pedro Pan: The Untold Exodus of 14,048 Cuban Children*. London and New York: Routledge, 1999.
83. Cruz, *Hortensia*, 41.
84. Joseph, "Diaspora," 4.
85. Bhabha, *Location of Culture*, 45.
86. Cruz, *Hortensia*, 42.
87. Ibid.
88. Ibid.
89. Ibid., 44.
90. Henderson, *Borders, Boundaries and Frames*, 17.
91. Chaudhuri, *Staging Place*, 200.

92. Cruz, *Hortensia*, 45.
93. Ibid.
94. Cruz, *Hortensia*, 46.
95. De la Campa, *Cuba on My Mind*, 55.
96. Cruz, *Hortensia*, 48.
97. Ibid.
98. Ibid., 49.
99. Ibid.
100. Cruz, *Hortensia*, 52.
101. Chaudhuri, *Staging Place*, 212.
102. De la Campa, *Cuba on My Mind*, 19.
103. Ibid., 55.
104. Soja, *Postmodern Geographies*, 23.

5. *Para Siempre*: Staging the Future

1. Julia Sweig quoted in Goldberg, "Fidel: 'Cuban Model,'" 2.
2. Ibid., 4.
3. Associated Press, "U.S. official: Castro has 'serious' health problems. "*CNN*, 11 Aug. 2006.
4. Saade, "Soy el responsible," 26.
5. Arenas, *Traidor*, 112. Subsequent page references are cited parenthetically in text.
6. Benitez Rojo, *Repeating Island*.
7. Ritter, "Shifting Realities in Special Period Cuba," 229.
8. Schumacher-Matos, "We Must Staunch Cuba's Coming Crisis."
9. "Capitalizing on Cuba" (editorial), LATimes.com, 15 Sept. 2010, accessed 4 Oct. 2010.
10. Weinreb, *Cuba in the Shadow of Change*, 168.
11. Fernandez, "Cuba: Talking Big, Acting Bigger," 84.
12. Brenner, "Cuba after Fidel," 6.
13. Gonzalez and McCarthy, "Legacy of Dysfunction," 1.
14. Ibid.
15. Ibid., 2.
16. Snow, "Cuba's Castro Dismisses Illness Reports."
17. Karon, "Cuba Comtemplates Life without Castro."
18. Ross, "Rallying Cuba, post-Castro."
19. Quiroga, *Cuban Palimpsests*, 31.

Bibliography

Acton, H. B. *The Illusion of the Epoch: Marxism-Leninism as a Philosophical Creed.* New York: Liberty Fund, 2003.

Alarcon de Quesada, Ricardo. *Helms-Burton Slavery Law.* Havana: Editorial José Martí, 1997.

Allison, Graham T. *Essence of Decision: Explaining the Cuban Missile Crisis.* Boston: Little, Brown, 1971.

Anderson, Jon Lee. "Castro's Last Battle." *New Yorker,* 31 July 2006, 44–55.

Anzaldúa, Gloria. *Borderlands/La Frontera: The New Mestiza.* San Francisco: Spinsters/ Aunt Lute, 1987.

Appadurai, Arjun. *Modernity at Large: Cultural Dimensions of Globalization.* Minneapolis: University of Minnesota Press, 1996.

———. "Disjuncture and Difference in the Global Cultural Economy." Appadurai 27–47.

———. "Here and Now." Appadurai 1–25.

———."The Production of Locality." Appadurai 178–200.

Arenas, Reinaldo. *Traidor. Persecución (Cinco piezas de teatro experimental).* Miami: Ediciones Universal, 1986.

Arrufat, Anton. *Los siete contra Tebas.* Havana: Ediciones Alarcos, 2001.

Artaud, Antonin. *The Theater and Its Double.* New York: Grove, 1958.

Auslander, Philip. *Liveness.* London and New York: Routledge, 1999.

Azicri, Max. *Cuba Today and Tomorrow: Reinventing Socialism.* Gainesville: University Press of Florida, 2000.

Báez, Antonio Carmona. *State Resistance to Globalisation in Cuba.* London and Virginia: Pluto, 2004.

Bakhtin, Mikhail. *Rabelais and His World.* Trans. Helene Iswolsky. Bloomington: Indiana University Press, 1984.

Beard, John R. *The Life of Toussaint L'Ouverture: The Negro Patriot of Hayti (Haiti).* New York: Inkling Books, 2002.

Behar, Ruth, ed. *Bridges to Cuba/Puentes a Cuba.* Ann Arbor: University of Michigan Press, 1995.

Bejel, Emilio. *Gay Cuban Nation.* Chicago: University of Chicago Press, 2001.

Benitez-Rojo, Antonio. *The Repeating Island: The Caribbean and the Postmodern Perspective (Post-Contemporary Interventions).* Durham: Duke University Press, 1996.

Benjamin, Walter. *Illuminations.* New York: Harcourt, Brace and World, 1968.

Bhabha, Homi K. *The Location of Culture.* London and New York: Routledge, 1994.

Bonefeld, Werner, and Sergio Tischler, eds. *What Is to Be Done? Leninism, Anti-Leninist Marxism, and the Question of Revolution Today.* Hampshire and Burlington: Ashgate, 2002.

Boudet, Rosa Ileana. *En tercera persona, crónicas teatrales cubanas: 1969–2002.* Irvine: Gestos, 2004.

———. *Este unico reino.* Havana: Editorial Letras Cubanas, 1988.
Brenner, Philip. "Cuba after Fidel." *NACLA Report on the Americas* 21, no. 2 (March/April 1988): 4–5.
Brundenius, Claes, and John Weeks, eds. *Globalization and Third World Socialism: Cuba and Vietnam.* New York: Palgrave, 2001.
Cano, Osvaldo. "A escena 'Charenton': El vértigo de lo auténtico." *Cubarte*, 16 July 2005. <www.cubarte.cuit.cu>. Accessed 10 Apr. 2007.
———. "El teatro cubano salda una antigua deuda." *Juventud Rebelde*, 31 Oct. 2007. <http://www.juventudrebelde.cu>. Accessed 6 Nov. 2012.
"Capitalizing on Cuba." *Los Angeles Times*, <http:www.latimes.com/news/opinion/editorials/>, 15 Sept. 2010. Accessed 24 Sept. 2010.
Carrió, Raquel, and Flora Lauten. *Charenton.* Havana: La Jiribilla, Año V, 13–19 May 2006. Accessed 3 Aug. 2006.
———. *Otra tempestad.* Havana: Ediciones Alarcos, 2000.
Castro, Fidel. *Capitalism in Crisis.* Melbourne and New York: Ocean, 2000.
———. *Palabras a los intelectuales.* Havana: National Cultural Council, 1961.
Centeno, Miguel Angel, and Mauricio Font, eds. *Toward a New Cuba? Legacies of a Revolution.* Boulder: Lynne Rienner, 1997.
Chanady, Amaryll. "Identity, Politics and *Mestizaje.*" *Contemporary Latin American Studies*, ed. Stephan Hart and Richard Young. New York and London: Arnold, 2003. 192–202.
Chaudhuri, Una. "*Marat/Sade* and the Politics of Interpretation." *Reading Plays: Interpretation and Reception*, ed. Hannah Scolnicov and Peter Holland. Cambridge and New York: Cambridge University Press, 1991. 216–26.
———. *Staging Place: The Geography of Modern Drama.* Ann Arbor: University of Michigan Press, 1995.
Chávez, Lydia, ed. *Capitalism, God, and a Good Cigar.* Durham and London: Duke University Press, 2005.
Cliff, Tony. *Marxism at the Millennium.* London, Chicago, and Sydney: Bookmarks, 2000.
Conde, Yvonne M. *Operation Pedro Pan: The Untold Exodus of 14,048 Cuban Children.* London and New York: Routledge, 1999.
Conner, Clifford D. *Jean Paul Marat: Scientist and Revolutionary.* Amherst: Humanity Books, 1998.
Corazzo, Nina, and Catherine R. Montfort. "Charlotte Corday: *Femme-homme.*" *Literate Women and the French Revolution of 1789*, ed. Catherine R. Montfort. Birmingham: Summa Publications, 1994. 33–54.
Corbett, Ben. *This Is Cuba: An Outlaw Culture Survives.* Cambridge: Westview, 2004.
Cortina, Rodolpho J. *Cuban American Theater.* Houston: Arte Publico, 1991.
Cruz, Nilo. *Anna in the Tropics.* New York: Theatre Communications Group, 2003.
———. *A Bicycle Country.* New York: Dramatists Play Service, 2004.
———. *Hortensia and the Museum of Dreams.* New York: Dramatists Play Service, 2004.
———. *Two Sisters and Piano.* New York: Dramatists Play Service, 2004.
Cruz-Malavé, Arnaldo. "Lecciones de cubanía: Identidad nacional y errancia sexual en Senal Paz, Martí y Lezama Lima." *Cuban Studies* no. 29 (1998): 129–54.
De Certeau, Michel. *The Practice of Everyday Life.* Trans. Steven Randall. Berkeley, Los Angeles, and London: University of California Press, 1984.
De la Campa, Román. *Cuba on My Mind: Journeys to a Severed Nation.* London and New York: Verso, 2000.

———. *Latin Americanism*. Minneapolis and London: University of Minnesota Press, 1999.
De la Fuente, Alejandro. *A Nation for All: Race, Inequality, and Politics in Twentieth-Century Cuba*. Chapel Hill: University of North Carolina Press, 2001.
Del Pino, Amado. "Buendía, virtuosismo a los veinte." *Actualidad Escénica Cubana*. 7 Apr. 2005. April 2007 <http://www.cniae.cult.cu/Charenton_porAPino.htm>.
Diamond, Elin. *Unmaking Mimesis*. London and New York: Routledge, 1997.
Dolan, Jill. "Gender Impersonation Onstage: Destroying or Maintaining the Mirror of Gender Roles." *Women and Performance* 2.2 (1985): 5–11.
———. "Performance, Utopia, and the 'Utopian Performative.'" *Theatre Journal* 53.3 (2001): 455–79.
Dominguez, Carlos Espinosa. "*Cuba teatro*: A Century of Theatre in Cuba." *Repertorio Español Study Guide*, <http://rep138.tempdomainname.com/education/>. Accessed 12 Jan. 2005.
Dufrenne, Mikel. "The World of the Aesthetic Object." *The Continental Aesthetics Reader*, ed. Clive Cazeaux. London and New York: Routledge, 2000. 129–50.
Eckstein, Susan. *Back from the Future: Cuba under Castro*. New York: Routledge, 2003.
Edwards, Susan. "Cuban Missive." *Weekly Planet: This Week in News*, 29 Nov. 2003. <http://www.weeklyplanet.com/current/news3.html>.
Elinson, Hannah. "Cuba *Jineteros*: Youth Culture and Revolutionary Ideology." Cuba Briefing Series Papers No. 20. Washington: Center for Latin American Studies, Georgetown University, 1999.
Erickson, Daniel P. *The Cuba Wars: Fidel Castro, the United States, and the Next Revolution*. New York: Bloomsbury, 2008.
Erickson, Jon. *The Fate of the Object*. Ann Arbor: University of Michigan Press, 1995.
Estorino, Abelardo. *El baile*. Havana: Ediciones Alarcos, 2000.
———. *Teatro escogido*. Havana: Editorial Letras Cubanas, 2004.
Fernandes, Sujatha. *Cuba Represent! Cuban Arts, State Power, and the Making of New Revolutionary Cultures*. Durham and London: Duke University Press, 2006.
Fernandez, Damián. "Cuba: Talking Big, Acting Bigger." *Latin American and Caribbean Foreign Policy*, ed. Frank Mora and Jeanne A. K. Hey, Oxford: Rowman and Littlefield, 2003. 84–103.
Fernandez, Damián, and Madeline Cámara Betancourt, eds. *Cuba, the Elusive Nation: Interpretations of National Identity*. Gainesville: University Press of Florida, 2000.
Foran, John, ed. *The Future of Revolutions: Rethinking Radical Change in the Age of Globalization*. New York: Zed Books, 2003.
Forrest, Alan. *The French Revolution*. Oxford and Cambridge: Blackwell, 1995.
Foucault, Michel. "Body/Power." *Power/Knowledge: Selected Interviews and Other Writings, 1972–1977*, ed. Colin Gordon. New York: Pantheon Books, 1980. 55–62.
———. *Discipline and Punish: The Birth of the Prison*. Trans. Alan Sheridan. New York: Vintage Books, 1977.
Freire, Natividad Gonzalez. *Teatro cubano (1927–1961)*. Havana: Ministerio de relaciones exteriores, 1961.
García Barrientos, José-Luis. *Análisis de la dramaturgia cubana actual*. Havana: Ediciones Alarcos, 2011.
García Canclini, Néstor. "Cultural Studies and Revolving Doors." *Contemporary Latin American Studies*, ed. Stephen Hart and Richard Young. New York and London: Arnold, 2003. 12–23.
———. *Hybrid Cultures: Strategies for Entering and Leaving Modernity*. Minneapolis and London: University of Minnesota Press, 1995.

García Luis, Julio. *Cuban Revolution Reader.* Melbourne: Ocean, 2001.

Godinez, Henry. "Toward a Revolution? A Reflection on Buendia." *American Theatre* 27.5 (May 2010): 32.

Goldberg, Jeffrey. "Fidel: 'Cuban Model Doesn't Even Work for Us Anymore.'" *Atlantic*, Sept. 2010. <http://www.theatlantic.com/ international/archive/2010/09/fidel-cuban-model-doesnt-even-work-for-us-anymore/62602/>.

———. "Fidel to Ahmadinejad: 'Stop Slandering the Jews.'" *Atlantic*, Sept. 2010. <http://www.theatlantic.com> Accessed 4 Oct. 2010.

———. "Fidel Tries to Wiggle Out of One." *Atlantic*, Sept. 2010. <http://www.theatlantic.com>.

Gomez-Peña, Guillermo. *Warrior of Gringostroika.* St. Paul: Graywolf, 1993.

Gonzalez, Edward, and Kevin F. McCarthy. "A Legacy of Dysfunction: Cuba after Fidel." Rand Corporation Research Brief. *Cuba after Castro: Legacies, Challenges, and Impediments.* <http://www.rand.org/publications/MG/MG111>. Accessed 6 Nov. 2006.

González-Cruz, Luis F., and Ann Waggoner Aken, eds. *Three Masterpieces of Cuban Drama.* Copenhagen and Los Angeles: Green Integer, 2000.

González-Cruz, Luis F., and Francesca M. Colecchia, eds. *Cuban Theater in the United States: A Critical Anthology.* Tempe: Bilingual Press/Editorial Bilingue, 1992.

Gott, Richard. *Cuba: A New History.* New Haven and London: Yale University Press, 2004.

Gramsci, Antonio. *Selections from the Prison Notebooks.* New York: International, 1971.

Guevara, Che. *Guerilla Warfare.* 1960. Lincoln: University of Nebraska Press, 1985.

Gunn, Gillian. *Cuba in Transition: Options for U.S. Policy.* New York: Twentieth Century Fund, 1993.

Hall, Stuart. "Encoding, Decoding." *Culture, Media and Language.* London: Unwin Hyman, 1990.

Hanson, Stephen E. *Time and Revolution: Marxism and the Design of Soviet Institutions.* Chapel Hill: University of North Carolina Press, 1997.

Harding, Neil. *Leninism.* Durham: Duke University Press, 1996.

Hardt, Michael, and Antonio Negri. *Empire.* Cambridge: Harvard University Press, 2000.

Hart, Stephen, and Richard Young, eds. Introduction. *Contemporary Latin American Cultural Studies.* New York and London: Arnold, 2003. 1–11.

Henderson, Mae G., ed. *Borders, Boundaries and Frames.* New York and London: Routledge, 1995.

Henken, Ted. *Cuba: A Global Studies Handbook.* Santa Barbara: ABC-CLIO, 2008.

Howe, Linda S. *Transgression and Conformity: Cuban Writers and Artists after the Revolution.* Madison: University of Wisconsin Press, 2004.

Hughes, John. "Future of Cuba Uncertain after Castro." *Deseret News*, 25 Apr. 2007. 30 Apr. 2007. <http://deseretnews.com/>.

Hurwitt, Sam. "He Keeps Returning to Cuba Onstage." Rev. of Rogelio Martinez's *Displaced,* Marin Theatre Company. *SFGate* <www.sfgate> 21 May 2006.

Jenks, Chris. *Transgression.* New York: Routledge, 2003.

Joseph, May. "Diaspora, New Hybrid Identities, and the Performance of Citizenship." *Women and Performance* 7:2 (1995): 3–13.

Karon, Tony. "Cuba Contemplates Life without Castro." *Time.* 14 Aug. 2001. 29 Nov. 2005. <http://www.time.com/>.

Kempadoo, Kamala, ed. *Sun, Sex, and Gold: Tourism and Sex Work in the Caribbean.* Lanham: Rowman and Littlefield, 1999.

Kuhn, Thomas. *The Structure of Scientific Revolutions*. Chicago: University of Chicago Press, 1962.

Kutzinski, Vera. *Sugar's Secrets: Race and the Erotics of Cuban Nationalism*. Charlottesville: University of Virginia Press, 1994.

Laffita, Graciela Chailloux, et al. *Globalization and Cuba-U.S. Conflict*. Havana: Editorial José Martí, 1999.

Lane, Jill. *Blackface Cuba, 1840–1895 (Rethinking the Americas)*. Philadelphia: University of Pennsylvania Press, 2005.

Leal, Rine. *Breve historia del teatro cubano*. Havana: Editorial Letras Cubanas, 1980.

Leffler, Melvyn P. *The Specter of Communism: The United States and the Origins of the Cold War, 1917–1953*. New York: Hill and Wang, 1994.

Leonard, Candyce. "*La Cubanía*: The Soul of Cuban Theatre in the Mid-1990s." *Latin American Theatre Review* 30.2 (Spring 1997): 139–52.

Levinson, Sandra. "Talking about Cuban Culture: A Reporter's Notebook." *The Cuba Reader: The Making of a Revolutionary Society*, ed. Phillip Brenner et al. New York: Grove, 1989.

Lievesley, Geraldine. *The Cuban Revolution: Past, Present, and Future Perspectives*. New York: Palgrave Macmillan, 2004.

Lightfoot, Claudia. *Havana: A Cultural and Literary Companion*. Oxford: Signal Books, 2002.

Limia, Miguel. "Sociedad civil en los 90: El debate cubano." *Temas* 16–17 (1999): 155–75.

Lindner, Burkhardt. "Hallucinatory Realism: Peter Weiss' Aesthetics of Resistance, Notebooks, and the Death Zones of Art." *New German Critique* 30 (Autumn 1983): 127–56.

Madan, Nora, ed. *Batalla por la liberación de Elián González*. Havana: Editora Política, 2000.

Mansur, Nara. *Charlotte Corday*. Trans. Rosa Ileana Boudet and Felipe Herba. 2001. Unpublished playscript in the author's possession.

———. *Charlotte Corday (Poema dramático). I Premio Casa de América festival escena contemporánea de dramaturgia innovadora*. Madrid: Casa de América, 2002. 222–42.

———. *Ignacio y Maria. Teatro cubano actual*. Havana: Ediciones Alarcos, 2003. 45–73.

———. *Ignacio and Maria*. Trans. Paul Verdier. 2003. Unpublished playscript in the author's possession.

Manwaring, Dr. Max G. "Uncomfortable Questions regarding the Inevitable Succession of Power in Cuba." Strategic Studies Institute of U.S. Army War College. Sept. 2004. <http://www.strategicstudiesinstitute.army.mil/pdffiles/pub669.pdf>.

Martí, José. *Selected Writings, 1853–1895*. New York: Penguin Classics, 2002.

Martinez, Rogelio. *Illuminating Veronica*. New York: Broadway Play Publishing, 2000.

Marx, Gary. "Castro Is Recovering, Official Says." *Chicago Tribune*, 6 Aug. 2006, 19.

Marx, Karl, and Friedrich Engels. *Capital: A Critique of Political Economy*, vol. 3. 1894. New York: Penguin Classics, 1993.

———. *The Communist Manifesto*. 1888. Trans. Samuel Moore. New York: Penguin Classics, 2002.

———. *The Marx-Engels Reader*. 2nd ed. Ed. Robert C. Tucker. New York: Norton, 1978.

McAuliffe, Jody. "Interview with Nilo Cruz." *South Atlantic Quarterly* 99.2/3 (Spring/Summer 2000). 461–70.

McKibben, Bill. "The Cuba Diet: What Will You Be Eating When the Revolution Comes?" *Harpers Magazine*, Apr. 2005. <http://www.harpers.org/archive/2005/04/0080501>.

Melo, Abel González. "Festín de los patíbulos (primera visita a *Charenton*)." *Actualidad Escénica Cubana*, 5 Jun. 2005. 10 Apr. 2007. <http://www.cniae.cult.cu/Charenton_porAGMelo.htm>.

Mesa-Lago, Carmelo, et al. *Market, Socialist, and Mixed Economies: Comparative Policy and Performance: Chile, Cuba and Costa Rica.* Baltimore: Johns Hopkins University Press, 2000.

Mignolo, Walter D. *Local Histories/Global Designs.* Princeton: Princeton University Press, 2000.

Miller, Warren. *Ninety Miles from Home.* New York: Crest Books, 1961.

Miyoshi, Masao. "A Borderless World? From Colonialism to Transnationalism and the Decline of the Nation-State." *Global/Local Cultural Production and the Transnational Imaginary*, ed. Rob Wilson and Wimal Dissanayake. Durham: Duke University Press, 1998. 78–106.

Mlinar, Zdravko ed. *Globalization and Territorial Identities.* Burlington: Ashgate, 1992.

Moore, Robin. *Nationalizing Blackness: Afrocubanismo and Artistic Revolution in Havana, 1920–1940.* Pittsburgh: University of Pittsburgh Press, 1997.

Morales, Ed. *Living in Spanglish: The Search for Latino Identity in America.* New York: St. Martin's Griffin, 2002.

Moreiras, Alberto. *The Exhaustion of Difference: The Politics of Latin American Cultural Studies.* Durham and London: Duke University Press, 2001.

Morley, Morris, and Chris McGillion. *Unfinished Business: America and Cuba after the Cold War, 1989–2001.* Cambridge: Cambridge University Press, 2002.

Moses, Catherine. *Real Life in Castro's Cuba.* Wilmington: Scholarly Resources, 2000.

Moya, Paula M. L., and Michael R. Hames-Garcia, eds. *Reclaiming Identity: Realist Theory and the Predicament of Postmodernism.* Berkeley and Los Angeles: University of California Press, 2000.

Muñoz, José Esteban. *Dissidentifications: Queers of Color and the Performance of Politics.* Minneapolis: University of Minnesota Press, 1999.

———. "The Onus of Seeing Cuba: Nilo Cruz's *Cubania*." *South Atlantic Quarterly* 99.2/3 (Spring/Summer 2000): 455–59.

———. "Performing Greater Cuba: Tania Bruguera and the Burden of Guilt." *Holy Terrors: Latin American Women Perform*, ed. Diana Taylor and Roselyn Costantino. Durham: Duke University Press, 2003. 399–416.

Navarro, Lygia. "Cuba: Island of Dreams and Isolation." *Christian Science Monitor* 15 Jul. 2005, 12.

Negri, Antonio. *Time for Revolution.* London and New York: Continuum Books, 2003.

Nieto, Clara. *Masters of War: Latin America and U.S. Aggression from the Cuban Revolution through the Clinton Years.* New York: Seven Stories Press, 2003.

Ortiz, Fernando. *Cuban Counterpoint: Tobacco and Sugar.* Trans. Reinaldo Jimenez. Durham: Duke University Press, 1995.

Ortiz, Ricardo L. *Cultural Erotics in Cuban America.* Minneapolis: University of Minnesota Press, 2007.

Osborne, John. *Look Back in Anger.* 1957. New York: Penguin Books, 1982.

Palls, Terry L. "A New Language for Today's Cuban Theatre." *Latin American Theatre Review* 31.2 (Spring 1998): 125–28.

Parham, Sidney F. "*Marat/Sade*: The Politics of Experience, or the Experience of Politics?" *Modern Drama* 20.3 (Sept. 1977): 235–50.

Parker, Andrew, and Eve Kosofsky Sedgwick. *Performativity and Performance.* New York and London: Routledge, 1995.

Paterson, Thomas G. *Contesting Castro.* New York and Oxford: Oxford University Press, 1994.
Pedraza, Sylvia. *Political Dissaffection in Cuba's Revolution and Exodus.* Cambridge: Cambridge University Press, 2007.
Pelligrini, Ann. *Performance Anxieties: Staging Psychoanalysis, Staging Race.* London and New York: Routledge, 1997.
Pérez, Dinorah Valdés, and Félix de la Paz, eds. *Guía de estudio: Historia y apreciación de la música y el teatro.* Havana: Ministerio de la cultura, 1980.
Pérez, Louis A., Jr. *Cuba: Between Reform and Revolution.* New York: Oxford University Press, 1995.
———. *On Becoming Cuban.* Chapel Hill: University of North Carolina Press, 1999.
Pérez-Firmat, Gustavo. *Life on the Hyphen: The Cuban American Way.* Austin: University of Texas Press, 1994.
Pérez-Stable, Marifeli, ed. *Looking Forward: Comparative Perspectives on Cuba's Transition.* Notre Dame: University of Notre Dame Press, 2007.
Petrey, Sandy, ed. *The French Revolution, 1789–1989: Two Hundred Years of Rethinking.* Lubbock: Texas Tech University Press, 1989.
Phelan, Peggy. *Unmarked: The Politics of Performance.* London and New York: Routledge, 2003.
Piñera, Virgilio. *Teatro completo.* Havana: Editorial Letras Cubanas, 2002.
Pipes, Richard. *Communism: A History.* New York: Modern Library Chronicles, 2003.
Price, S. L. *Pitching around Fidel: A Journey into the Heart of Cuban Sports.* New York: Harper Collins, 2000.
Quiroga, José. *Cuban Palimpsests.* Minneapolis and London: University of Minnesota Press, 2005.
Ramirez, Julio César. Email interview, 4 Jan 2012.
"Revolución." LaRousse diccionario de la lengua española esencial. 2002.
"Revolution." *Dictionary of the History of Ideas: Studies of Selected Pivotal Ideas*, ed. Philip P. Weiner. New York: Charles Scribner's Sons, 1973. 4:152–66.
"Revolution." *Webster's Encyclopedic Unabridged Dictionary of the English Language.* Indexed Edition. San Diego: Thunder Bay Press, 2001.
Ritter, Archibald. "Shifting Realities in Special Period Cuba." *Latin American Research Review* 45.3 (2010): 229–38.
Rivera-Servera, Ramón, and Harvey Young, eds. *Performance in the Borderlands.* New York and London: Palgrave Macmillan, 2011.
Rizk, Beatriz J. "Miami: Meca del exilio cubano y escenario medido aunque efervescente." *Latin American Theatre Review* 34.1 (Fall 2000): 229–46.
Roach, Joseph. *Cities of the Dead.* New York: Columbia University Press, 1996.
Rockmore, Tom. *Marx after Marxism: The Philosophy of Karl Marx.* Oxford and Malden: Blackwell, 2002.
Rosaldo, Renato. Introduction. *Hybrid Cultures: Strategies for Entering and Leaving Modernity,* by Néstor García Canclini. Minneapolis and London: University of Minnesota Press, 1995.
Rosendahl, Mona. *Inside the Revolution: Everyday Life in Socialist Cuba.* New York: Cornell University Press, 1998.
Ross, Oakland. "Rallying Cuba, post-Castro." *Toronto Star,* 15 Mar 2006, <http://www.thestar.com>. Accessed 6 June 2013.
Roy, Joaquin. *Cuba, the United States, and the Helms-Burton Doctrine.* Gainesville: University Press of Florida, 2000.

Saade, Carmen Lira. "Soy el responsible de la persecución a homosexuals que hubo en Cuba: Fidel Castro." *Periódico La Jornada*. 31 Aug. 2010, 26.

Sade, Marquis De. *120 Days of Sodom and Other Writings*. Ed. Richard Seaver and Austryn Wainhouse. New York: Grove, 1987.

Said, Edward. *Orientalism*. New York: Pantheon Books, 1978.

Saldaña-Portillo, María Josefina. *The Revolutionary Imagination in the Americas and the Age of Development*. Durham: Duke University Press, 2003.

Sarlo, Beatriz. *Scenes from Postmodern Life*. Minneapolis: University of Minnesota Press, 2001.

Sarraín, Alberto, and Lillian Manzor, eds. *Teatro cubano actual*. Havana: Ediciones Alarcos, 2005.

Sassen, Saskia, ed. *Globalization and Its Discontents*. New York: New Press, 1998.

Schama, Simon. *Citizens: A Chronicle of the French Revolution*. New York: Alfred A. Knopf, 1989.

Schumacher-Matos, Edward. "We Must Staunch Cuba's Coming Crisis." *Washington Post*, 18 Sept. 2010, <http://www.washingtonpost.com>. Accessed 20 Sept. 2010.

Scott, James C. *Domination and the Arts of Resistance: Hidden Transcripts*. New Haven and London: Yale University Press, 1990.

Shimakawa, Karen. *National Abjection: Asian American Body Onstage*. New York: Routledge, 2003.

Silverman, Kaja. "The Subject." *The Subject of Semiotics*. New York: Oxford University Press, 1983. 126–93.

Skocpol, Theda. *States and Social Revolutions: A Comparative Analysis of France, Russia, and China*. New York: Cambridge University Press, 1979.

Smith, Paul. *Discerning the Subject*. Minneapolis: University of Minnesota Press, 1988.

Snow, Anita. "Cuba's Castro Dismisses Illness Reports." *Associated Press*. 18 Nov. 2005. Accessed 5 May 2006.

Sofer, Andrew. *The Stage Life of Props*. Ann Arbor: University of Michigan Press, 2003.

Soja, Edward. *Postmodern Geographies: The Reassertion of Space in Critical Social Theory*. New York: Verso, 1989.

Soto, Francisco. "Reinaldo Arenas's *Persecución*: Extra- and Intertextual Links to Virgilio Piñera." *Latin American Theatre Review* 34.2 (Spring 2001): 39–51.

Stallybrass, Peter, and Allon White. *The Politics and Poetics of Transgression*. London: Methuen, 1986.

Stavans, Ilan. *The Hispanic Condition: The Power of a People*. New York: Harper Collins, 1995.

Stock, Ann Marie. *On Location in Cuba: Street Filmmaking during Times of Transition*. Chapel Hill: University of North Carolina Press, 2009.

Stokes, Bruce. "Cuba Samples Globalization." *Council on Foreign Relations*. 18 Jan. 2003. 5 May 2006. <http://www.cfr.org/publication/5467/cuba_samples_globalization.html>.

Suvin, Darko. "Weiss's *Marat/Sade* and Its Three Main Performance Versions." *Modern Drama* 31.3 (Sept. 1988): 395–419.

Svich, Cardidad. "A Flower in Havana." *American Theatre* 27.5 (May 2010): 30–32.

Taylor, Diana. *The Archive and the Repertoire: Performing Cultural Memory in the Americas*. Durham and London: Duke University Press, 2003.

———. "Framing the Revolution: Triana's *La noche de los asesinos* and *Ceremonial de guerra*." *Latin American Theatre Review* 24.1 (Fall 1990): 81–92.

Taylor, Diana, and Juan Villegas. *Negotiating Performance: Gender Sexuality and Theatricality in Latin/o America*. Durham and London: Duke University Press, 1994.

Terry, Miguel, and Raúl Alfonso. *Laberinto de lobos y El grito*. Havana: Editorial Letras Cubanas, 1994.

Torrance, Isabelle. "Brothers at War: Aeschylus in Cuba." *Alma Parens Originalis? The Receptions of Classical Thought in Africa, Europe, the United States and Cuba*, ed. John Hilton and Anne Gosling. Bern: Lang International Academic Publishers, 2007. 291–315.

Torres, Maria de los Angeles. "Cuba limbo." *Chicago Tribune*, 6 Aug. 2006. 2:1.

Trento, Angelo. *Castro and Cuba: From the Revolution to the Present*. New York: Interlink Books, 2000.

Verdery, Katherine. *What Is Socialism and What Comes Next?* Princeton: Princeton University Press, 1996.

Weinreb, Amelia Rosenberg. *Cuba in the Shadow of Change: Daily Life in the Twilight of the Revolution*. Gainesville: University Press of Florida, 2009.

Weiss, Judith, et al. *Latin American Popular Theatre*. Albuquerque: University of New Mexico Press, 1993.

Weiss, Peter. *The Persecution and Assassination of Jean-Paul Marat as Performed by the Inmates of the Asylum of Charenton under the Direction of the Marquis de Sade*. New York: John Calder, 1965.

Whitfield, Esther. *Cuban Currency: The Dollar and "Special Period" Fiction*. Minneapolis: University of Minnesota Press, 2008.

Wright, Thomas C. *Latin America in the Era of the Cuban Revolution*. Westport: Praeger, 1991.

Yan, Haiping. "Staging Modern Vagrancy: Female Figures of Border Crossing in Ama Ata Aidoo and Caryl Churchill." *Theatre Journal* 53 (2002): 245–62.

Ybarra, Patricia. "Havana Isn't Waiting: Staging Travel during Cuba's Special Period." Rivera-Servera and Young 58–81.

Index

In this index, created by Denise E. Carlson, photographs in the gallery are indicated by italic numbers preceded by the letter *g*.

Yael Prizant is a translator and an assistant professor in the Department of Film, Television, and Theatre and the Department of American Studies at the University of Notre Dame. She teaches dramaturgy and contemporary dramatic literature, with a focus on Latin American and multicultural theatre.

Theater in the Americas

The goal of the series is to publish a wide range of scholarship on theater and performance, defining theater in its broadest terms and including subjects that encompass all of the Americas.

The series focuses on the performance and production of theater and theater artists and practitioners but welcomes studies of dramatic literature as well. Meant to be inclusive, the series invites studies of traditional, experimental, and ethnic forms of theater; celebrations, festivals, and rituals that perform culture; and acts of civil disobedience that are performative in nature. We publish studies of theater and performance activities of all cultural groups within the Americas, including biographies of individuals, histories of theater companies, studies of cultural traditions, and collections of plays.

Other Books in the Theater in the Americas Series

Shadowed Cocktails: The Plays of Philip Barry from "Paris Bound" to "The Philadelphia Story"
Donald R. Anderson

A Gambler's Instinct: The Story of Broadway Producer Cheryl Crawford
Milly S. Barranger

Unfriendly Witnesses: Gender, Theater, and Film in the McCarthy Era
Milly S. Barranger

The Theatre of Sabina Berman: "The Agony of Ecstasy" and Other Plays
Translated by Adam Versényi
With an Essay by
Jacqueline E. Bixler

Staging Social Justice: Collaborating to Create Activist Theatre
Edited by Norma Bowles and Daniel-Raymond Nadon

Messiah of the New Technique: John Howard Lawson, Communism, and American Theatre, 1923–1937
Jonathan L. Chambers

Composing Ourselves: The Little Theatre Movement and the American Audience
Dorothy Chansky

Ghost Light: An Introductory Handbook for Dramaturgy
Michael Mark Chemers

The Hanlon Brothers: From Daredevil Acrobatics to Spectacle Pantomime, 1833–1931
Mark Cosdon

Richard Barr: The Playwright's Producer
David A. Crespy

Women in Turmoil: Six Plays by Mercedes de Acosta
Edited and with an Introduction by
Robert A. Schanke

Rediscovering Mordecai Gorelik: Scene Design and the American Theatre
Anne Fletcher

A Spectacle of Suffering: Clara Morris on the American Stage
Barbara Wallace Grossman

American Political Plays after 9/11
Edited by Allan Havis

Performing Loss: Rebuilding Community through Theater and Writing
Jodi Kanter

Unfinished Show Business: Broadway Musicals as Works-in-Process
Bruce Kirle

Staging America: Cornerstone and Community-Based Theater
Sonja Kuftinec

Words at Play: Creative Writing and Dramaturgy
Felicia Hardison Londré

Entertaining the Nation: American Drama in the Eighteenth and Nineteenth Centuries
Tice L. Miller

Documentary Trial Plays in Contemporary American Theater
Jacqueline O'Connor

Stage, Page, Scandals, and Vandals: William E. Burton and Nineteenth-Century American Theatre
David L. Rinear

Contemporary Latina/o Theater: Wrighting Ethnicity
Jon D. Rossini

Angels in the American Theater: Patrons, Patronage, and Philanthropy
Edited and with an Introduction by Robert A. Schanke

"That Furious Lesbian": The Story of Mercedes de Acosta
Robert A. Schanke

Caffe Cino: The Birthplace of Off-Off-Broadway
Wendell C. Stone

Teaching Performance Studies
Edited by Nathan Stucky and Cynthia Wimmer
With a Foreword by Richard Schechner

Broadway's Bravest Woman: Selected Writings of Sophie Treadwell
Edited and with Introductions by Jerry Dickey and Miriam López-Rodríguez

The Humana Festival: The History of New Plays at Actors Theatre of Louisville
Jeffrey Ullom

Our Land Is Made of Courage and Glory: Nationalist Performance of Nicaragua and Guatemala
E. J. Westlake